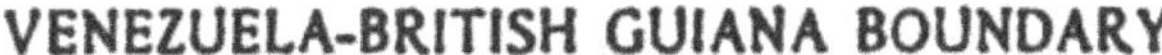
VENEZUELA-BRITISH GUIANA BOUNDARY

THE CASE

OF THE

UNITED STATES OF VENEZUELA

BEFORE THE

TRIBUNAL OF ARBITRATION

To Convene at Paris

UNDER THE

Provisions of the Treaty between the United-States of Venezuela and Her Britannic Majesty Signed at Washington February 2, 1897

VOLUME 1

NEW YORK

The Evening Post Job Printing House, 156 Fulton Street

1898

TRIBUNAL OF ARBITRATION

His Excellency F. de Martens, President

The Honorable Melville Weston Fuller

The Right Honorable Baron Herschell, G. C. B.

The Honorable Sir Richard Henn Collins, Kt.

The Honorable David Josiah Brewer

J. M. De Rojas
Agent of Venezuela

CONTENTS, VOLUME 1.

CASE OF THE UNITED STATES OF VENEZUELA.

I.—INTRODUCTION.

The Treaty of Arbitration signed at Washington on the second day of February, 1897, between the United States of Venezuela and Her Majesty, the Queen of the United Kingdom of Great Britain and Ireland, after making provision for the organization of the Tribunal of Arbitration, proceeds, in Article III, to define the questions which are to be investigated and determined. Treaty of Arbitration of 1897.

Article III is as follows:

"The Tribunal shall investigate and ascertain the extent of the territories belonging to, or that might lawfully be claimed by, the United Netherlands or by the Kingdom of Spain respectively at the time of the acquisition by Great Britain of the Colony of British Guiana, and shall determine the boundary line between the Colony of British Guiana and the United States of Venezuela." Questions submitted.

After laying down certain rules for the government of the Arbitrators in connection with the decision of the matters submitted, the Treaty then proceeds to specify the time and manner in which each party shall present its case.

Article VI, which provides for this, is as follows:

"The printed Case of each of the two parties, accompanied by the documents, the official correspondence, and other evidence on which each relies, shall be delivered in duplicate to each of the Arbitrators and to the Agent of the other Party as soon as may be after the appointment of the members of the tribunal, but within a period not exceeding eight months from the date of the exchange of the ratifications of this Treaty." Delivery of Case.

Submission of Case.

In compliance with this stipulation, the Agent of Venezuela before the Arbitral Tribunal has the honor to submit the present Case, accompanied by an Appendix printed in two volumes and an atlas. The Government of Venezuela reserves the right to hereafter present additional documents, correspondence and evidence pursuant to the provisions of Article VII of the Treaty.

The full text of the Treaty is as follows:

Treaty of Arbitration of 1897.

"Her Majesty the Queen of the United Kingdom of Great Britain and Ireland, and the United States of Venezuela, being desirous to provide for an amicable settlement of the question which has arisen between their respective Governments concerning the boundary between the Colony of British Guiana and the United States of Venezuela, have resolved to submit to arbitration the question involved, and to the end of concluding a Treaty for that purpose have appointed as their respective Plenipotentiaries:

Her Majesty the Queen of the United Kingdom of Great Britain and Ireland, the Right Honourable Sir Julian Pauncefote, a Member of Her Majesty's Most Honourable Privy Council, Knight Grand Cross of the Most Honourable Order of the Bath and of the Most Distinguished Order of St. Michael and St. George, and Her Majesty's Ambassador Extraordinary and Plenipotentiary to the United States;

"Los Estados Unidos de Venezuela y Su Majestad la Reina del Reino Unido de la Gran Bretaña é Irlanda, deseando estipular el arreglo amistoso de la cuestión que se ha suscitado entre sus respectivos Gobiernos acerca del límite de los Estados Unidos de Venezuela y la Colonia de la Guayana Británica, han resuelto someter dicha cuestión á arbitramento, y á fin de concluir con ese objeto un tratado, han elegido por sus respectivos Plenipotenciarios:

El Presidente de los Estados Unidos de Venezuela, al Señor José Andrade, Enviado Extraordinario y Ministro Plenipotenciario de Venezuela en los Estados Unidos de América;

Y Su Majestad la Reina del Reino Unido de la Gran Bretaña é Irlanda al Muy Honorable Sir Julian Pauncefote, Miembro del Muy Honorable Consejo Privado de Su Majestad, Caballero Gran Cruz de la Muy Honorable Orden del Baño y de la Muy Distinguida Orden

Treaty of Arbitration of 1897.

And the President of the United States of Venezuela, Señor José Andrade, Envoy Extraordinary and Minister Plenipotentiary of Venezuela to the United States of America;

Who, having communicated to each other their respective full powers, which were found to be in due and proper form, have agreed to and concluded the following Articles:—

de San Miguel y San Jorge, y Embajador Extraordinario y Plenipotenciario de Su Majestad en los Estados Unidos;

Quienes, habiéndose comunicado sus respectivos plenos poderes que fueron hallados en propria y debida forma, han acordado y concluido los artículos siguientes:—

Arbitral Tribunal.

ARTICLE I.

An Arbitral Tribunal shall be immediately appointed to determine the boundary-line between the Colony of British Guiana and the United States of Venezuela.

ARTÍCULO I.

Se nombrará inmediatamente un Tribunal arbitral para determinar la línea divisoria entre los Estados Unidos de Venezuela y la Colonia de la Guayana Británica.

Tribunal appointed.

ARTICLE II.

The Tribunal shall consist of five jurists: two on the part of Great Britain, nominated by the Members of the Judicial Committee of Her Majesty's Privy Council, namely, the Right Honourable Baron Herschell, Knight Grand Cross of the Most Honourable Order of the Bath; and the Honourable Sir Richard Henn Collins, Knight, one of the Justices of her Britannic Majesty's Supreme Court of Judicature; two on the part of Venezuela, nominated, one by the President of the United States of Venezuela, namely, the Honourable

ARTÍCULO II.

El Tribunal se compondrá de cinco Juristas; dos de parte de Venezuela, nombrados, uno por el Presidente de los Estados Unidos de Venezuela, á saber, el Honorable Melville Weston Fuller, Justicia Mayor de los Estados Unidos de América, y uno por los Justicias de la Corte Suprema de los Estados Unidos de América, á saber, el Honorable David Josiah Brewer, Justicia de la Corte Suprema de los Estados Unidos de América; dos de parte de la Gran Bretaña nombrados por los miembros de la Comisión Judicial del Consejo Privado de

Tribunal appointed.

Melville Weston Fuller, Chief Justice of the United States of America, and one nominated by the Justices of the Supreme Court of the United States of America, namely, the Honorable David Josiah Brewer, a Justice of the Supreme Court of the United States of America; and of a fifth Jurist to be selected by the four persons so nominated, or in the event of their failure to agree within three months from the date of the exchange of ratifications of the present Treaty, to be selected by His Majesty the King of Sweden and Norway. The Jurist so selected shall be President of the Tribunal.

In case of the death, absence, or incapacity to serve of any of the four Arbitrators above named, or in the event of any such Arbitrator omitting or declining or ceasing to act as such, another Jurist of repute shall be forthwith substituted in his place. If such vacancy shall occur among those nominated on the part of Great Britain the substitute shall be appointed by the members for the time being of the Judicial Committee of Her Majesty's Privy Council, acting by a majority, and if among those nominated on the part of Venezuela, he shall be appointed by the Justices of the Supreme Court of

Su Majestad, á saber, el Muy Honorable Barón Herschell, Caballero Gran Cruz de la Muy Honorable Orden del Baño, y el Honorable Sir Richard Henn Collins, Caballero, uno de los Justicias de la Corte Suprema de Judicatura de Su Majestad; y de un quinto Jurista, que será elegido por las cuatro personas así nombradas, ó, en el evento de no lograr ellas acordarse en la designación dentro de los tres meses contados desde la fecha del canje de las ratificaciones del presente Tratado, por Su Majestad el Rey de Suecia y Noruega. El Jurista á quien así se elija será Presidente del Tribunal.

En caso de muerte, ausencia ó incapacidad para servir de cualquiera de los cuatro Arbitros arriba mencionados, ó en el evento de que alguno de ellos no llegue á ejercer las funciones de tal por omisión, renuncia ó cesación, se sustituirá inmediatamente por otro Jurista de reputación. Si tal vacante ocurre entre los nombrados por parte de Venezuela, el sustituto será elegido por los Justicias de la Corte Suprema de los Estados Unidos de América por mayoría; y si ocurriere entre los nombrados por parte de la Gran Bretaña, elegirán al sustituto, por mayoría, los que fueren entonces miembros de la

the United States, acting by a majority. If such vacancy shall occur in the case of the fifth Arbitrator, a substitute shall be selected in the manner herein provided for with regard to the original appointment.

Comisión Judicial del Consejo Privado de Su Majestad. Si vacare el puésso de quinto Arbitro, se le elegirá sustituto del modo aqui estipulado en cuanto al nombramiento primitivo.

Tribunal appointed.

ARTICLE III.

The Tribunal shall investigate and ascertain the extent of the territories belonging to, or that might lawfully be claimed by the United Netherlands or by the Kingdom of Spain respectively at the time of the acquisition by Great Britain of the Colony of British Guiana, and shall determine the boundary line between the Colony of British Guiana and the United States of Venezuela.

ARTÍCULO III.

El Tribunal investigará y se cerciorará de la extensión de los territorios pertenecientes á las Provincias Unidas de los Países Bajos ó al Reino de España respectivamente, ó que pudieran ser legítimamente reclamados por aquéllas ó éste, al tiempo de la adquisición de la Colonia de la Guayana Británica por la Gran Bretaña, y determinará la línea divisoria entre los Estados Unidos de Venezuela y la Colonia de la Guayana Británica.

Questions submitted.

ARTICLE IV.

In deciding the matters submitted, the Arbitrators shall ascertain all facts which they deem necessary to a decision of the controversy, and shall be governed by the following Rules, which are agreed upon by the High Contracting Parties as Rules to be taken as applicable to the case, and by such principles of international law not inconsistent therewith as the Arbitrators shall determine to be applicable to the case:—

ARTÍCULO IV.

Al decidir los asuntos sometidos á los Arbitros, estos se cerciorarán de todos los hechos que estimen necesarios para la decisión de la controversia, y se gobernarán por las siguientes reglas en que están convenidas las Altas Partes contratantes como reglas que han de considerarse aplicables al caso, y por los principios de derecho internacional no incompatibles con ellas, que los Arbitros juzgaren aplicables al mismo.

Rules adopted.

	Rules.	*Reglas.*
Rules adopted.	(*a*) Adverse holding or prescription during a period of fifty years shall make a good title. The Arbitrators may deem exclusive political control of a district, as well as actual settlement thereof, sufficient to constitute adverse holding or to make title by prescription.	(*a*) Una posesión adversa ó prescripción por el término de cincuenta años constituirá un buen título. Los Arbitros podrán estimar que la dominación política exclusiva de un distrito, asi como la efectiva colonización de él, son suficientes para constituir una posesión adversa ó crear título de prescripción.
	(*b*) The Arbitrators may recognize and give effect to rights and claims resting on any other ground whatever valid according to international law, and on any principles of international law which the Arbitrators may deem to be applicable to the case, and which are not in contravention of the foregoing rule.	(*b*) Los Arbitros podrán reconocer y hacer efectivos derechos y reivindicaciones que se apoyen en cualquier otro fundamento válido conforme al derecho internacional, y en cualesquiera principios de derecho internacional que los Arbitros estimen aplicables al caso y que no contravengan á la regla precedente.
	(*c*) In determining the boundary-line, if territory of one Party be found by the Tribunal to have been at the date of this Treaty in the occupation of the subjects or citizens of the other Party, such effect shall be given to such occupation as reason, justice, the principles of international law, and the equities of the case shall, in the opinion of the Tribunal, require.	(*c*) Al determinar la línea divisoria, si el Tribunal hallare que territorio de una parte ha estado en la fecha de este Tratado ocupado por los ciudadanos ó súbditos de la otra parte, se dará á tal ocupación el fecto que, en opinión del Tribunal, requieran la razón, la justicia, los principios del derecho internacional, y la equidad del caso.
	ARTICLE V.	ARTÍCULO V.
Meeting of Tribunal.	The Arbitrators shall meet at Paris, within sixty days after the delivery of the printed arguments mentioned	Los Arbitros se reunirán en Paris dentro de los sesenta días después de la entrega de los argumentos impresos mencio-

Meeting of Tribunal.

in Article VIII, and shall proceed impartially and carefully to examine and decide the questions that have been, or shall be, laid before them, as herein provided, on the part of the Governments of Her Britannic Majesty and the United States of Venezuela respectively.

Provided always that the Arbitrators may, if they shall think fit, hold their meetings, or any of them, at any other place which they may determine.

All questions considered by the Tribunal, including the final decision, shall be determined by a majority of all the Arbitrators.

Each of the High Contracting Parties shall name one person as its agent to attend the Tribunal, and to represent it generally in all matters connected with the Tribunal.

nados en el Artículo VIII, y procederán á examinar y decidir imparcial y cuidadosamente las cuestiones que se les hayan sometido ó se les presentaren, según aquí se estipula, por parte de los Gobiernos de los Estados Unidos de Venezuela y de Su Majestad Británica respectivamente.

Pero queda siempre entendido que los Arbitros, si lo juzgan conveniente, podrán celebrar sus reuniones, ó algunas de ellas, en cualquier otro lugar que determinen.

Todas las cuestiones consideradas por el Tribunal, inclusive la decisión definitiva, serán resueltas por mayoría de todos los Arbitros.

Cada una de las Altas Partes Contratantes nombrará como su Agente una persona que asista al Tribunal y la represente generalmente en todos los asuntos conexos con el Tribunal.

Article VI.

Delivery of Case.

The printed Case of each of the two Parties, accompanied by the documents, the official correspondence, and other evidence on which each relies, shall be delivered in duplicate to each of the Arbitrators and to the Agent of the other Party as soon as may be after the appointment of the members of the Tribunal, but within a peri-

Artículo VI.

Tan pronto como sea posible después de nombrados los miembros del Tribunal, pero dentro de un plazo que no excederá de ocho meses contados desde la fecha del canje de las ratificaciones de este Tratado, se entregará por duplicado á cada uno de los Arbitros y al Agente de la otra parte, el Alegato impreso de

Delivery of Case.

od not exceeding eight months from the date of the exchange of the ratifications of this Treaty.

cada una de las dos partes, acompañado de los documentos, la correspondencia oficial y las demás pruebas, en que cada una se apoye.

ARTICLE VII.

Delivery of Counter-Case.

Within four months after the delivery on both sides of the printed Case, either Party may in like manner deliver in duplicate to each of the said Arbitrators, and to the Agent of the other Party, a Counter-Case, and additional documents, correspondence, and evidence, in reply to the Case, documents, correspondence, and evidence so presented by the other Party.

If in the Case submitted to the Arbitrators either Party shall have specified or alluded to any report or document in its own exclusive possession, without annexing a copy, such Party shall be bound, if the other Party thinks proper to apply for it, to furnish that Party with a copy thereof, and either Party may call upon the other, through the Arbitrators, to produce the originals or certified copies of any papers adduced as evidence, giving in each instance notice thereof within thirty days after delivery of the Case, and the original or copy so requested shall be delivered as soon as may be, and within a period not

ARTÍCULO VII.

Dentro de los cuatro meses siguientes á la entrega por ambas partes del Alegato impreso, una ú otra podrá del mismo modo entregar por duplicado á cada uno de dichos Arbitros, y al Agente de la otra parte, un contra-Alegato y nuevos documentos, correspondencia y pruebas, para contestar al Alegato, documentos, correspondencia y pruebas presentados por la otra parte.

Si en el Alegato sometido á los Arbitros una ú otra parte hubiere especificado ó citado algún informe ó documento que esté en su exclusiva posesión, sin agregar copia, tal parte quedará obligada, si la otra cree conveniente pedirla, á suministrarle copia de él; y una ú otra parte podra excitar á la otra, por medio de los Arbitros, á producir los originales ó copias certificadas de los papeles aducidos como pruebas, dando en cada caso aviso de esto dentro de los treinta días después de la presentación del Alegato; y el original ó la copia pedidos se entregarán tan pronto como sea posible y dentro de un plazo

exceeding forty days after receipt of notice.

que no exceda de cuarenta días después del recibo del aviso.

Delivery of Counter-case.

ARTICLE VIII.

It shall be the duty of the Agent of each Party, within three months after the expiration of the time limited for the delivery of the Counter-Case on both sides, to deliver in duplicate to each of the said Arbitrators, and to the Agent of the other Party, a printed argument showing the points, and referring to the evidence upon which his Government relies, and either Party may also support the same before the Arbitrators by oral argument of counsel; and the Arbitrators may, if they desire further elucidation with regard to any point, require a written or printed statement or argument, or oral argument by counsel upon it; but in such case the other party shall be entitled to reply either orally or in writing, as the case may be.

ARTÍCULO VIII.

El Agente de cada parte, dentro de los tres meses después de la expiración del tiempo señalado para la entrega del contra-Alegato por ambas partes, deberá entregar por duplicado á cada uno de dichos Arbitros y al Agente de la otra parte un argumento impreso que señale los puntos y cite las pruebas en que se funda su Gobierno, y cualquiera de las dos partes podrá también apoyarlo ante los Arbitros con argumentos orales de su Abogado; y los Arbitros podrán, si desean mayor esclarecimiento con respecto á algún punto, requerir sobre él una exposición ó argumento escritos ó impresos, ó argumentos orales del Abogado; pero en tal caso la otra parte tendrá derecho á contestar oralmente ó por escrito, según fuere el caso.

Delivery of Printed Argument.

ARTICLE IX.

The Arbitrators may, for any cause deemed by them sufficient, enlarge either of the periods fixed by Articles VI, VII and VIII by the allowance of thirty days additional.

ARTÍCULO IX.

Los Arbitros por cualquier causa que juzguen suficiente podrán prorrogar uno ú otro de los plazos fijados en los Artículos VI, VII y VIII, concediendo treinta días adicionales.

Extensions.

ARTICLE X.

The decision of the Tribunal shall, if possible, be made

ARTÍCULO X.

Si fuere posible, el Tribunal dará su decisión dentro de tres

Decision.

Decision.

within three months from the close of the argument on both sides.

It shall be made in writing and dated, and shall be signed by the Arbitrators who may assent to it.

The decision shall be in duplicate, one copy whereof shall be delivered to the Agent of Great Britain for his Government, and the other copy shall be delivered to the Agent of the United States of Venezuela for his Government.

meses contados desde que termine la argumentación por ambos lados.

La decisión se dará por escrito, llevará fecha y se firmará por los Arbitros que asientan á ella.

La decisión se extenderá por duplicado; de ella se entregará un ejemplar al Agente de los Estados Unidos de Venezuela para su Gobierno, y el otro se entregará al Agente de la Gran Bretaña para su Gobierno.

ARTICLE XI.

Record of Proceedings.

The Arbitrators shall keep an accurate record of their proceedings, and may appoint and employ the necessary officers to assist them.

ARTÍCULO XI.

Los Arbitros llevarán un registro exacto de sus procedimientos y podrán eligir y emplear las personas que necesiten para su ayuda.

ARTICLE XII.

Agents and Counsel.

Each Government shall pay its own Agent and provide for the proper remuneration of the counsel employed by it, and of the Arbitrators appointed by it or in its behalf, and for the expense of preparing and submitting its Case to the Tribunal. All other expenses connected with the Arbitration shall be defrayed by the two Governments in equal moieties.

ARTÍCULO XII.

Cada Gobierno pagará á su propio Agente y proveerá la remuneración conveniente para el Abogado que emplee y para los Arbitros elegidos por él ó en su nombre, y costeará los gastos de la preparación y sometimiento de su causa al Tribunal. Los dos Gobiernos satisfarán por partes iguales todos los demás gastos relativos al arbitramento.

ARTICLE XIII.

Result to be Final.

The High Contracting Parties engage to consider the result of the proceedings of the Tribunal of Arbitration as a full,

ARTÍCULO XIII.

Las altas Partes Contratantes se obligan á considerar el resultado de los procedimientos del Tribunal de Arbitramento

perfect, and final settlement of all the questions referred to the Arbitrators.

como arreglo pleno, perfecto y definitivo de todas las cuestiones sometidas á los árbitros.

Result to be Final.

Article XIV.

The present Treaty shall be duly ratified by Her Britannic Majesty and by the President of the United States of Venezuela, by and with the approval of the Congress thereof, and the ratifications shall be exchanged in London or in Washington within six months from the date hereof.

In faith whereof we, the respective Plenipotentiaries, have signed this Treaty and have hereunto affixed our seals.

Done in duplicate, at Washington, the second day of February, one thousand eight hundred and ninety-seven.

Julian Pauncefote. [seal.]
José Andrade. [seal.]

Artículo XIV.

Ratification of Treaty.

El presente Tratado será debidamente ratificado por el Presidente de los Estados Unidos de Venezuela con la aprobación del Congreso de ellos, y por Su Majestad Británica: y las ratificaciones se canjearán en Washington ó en Londres dentro de los seis meses contados desde la fecha del presente tratado.

En fé de lo cual los respectivos Plenipotenciarios hemos firmado este tratado y le hemos puesto nuestros sellos.

Hecho por duplicado en Washington, a dos de Febrero, de mil ochocientos noventa y siete.

José Andrade. [sello.]
Julian Pauncefote. [sello.]

II.—GEOGRAPHICAL SKETCH OF THE DISPUTED TERRITORY.

Location and Extent of Disputed Territory.

The disputed territory lies on the north-eastern border of South America, between the Essequibo and Orinoco rivers. It extends from the coast southward as far as the boundary with Brazil. Venezuela claims the entire region as far east as the western bank of the Essequibo: Her Majesty's Government has, at various times, made mention of an "extreme British claim" from the Essequibo west as far as the main mouth of the Orinoco, on the coast, and, in the interior, as far as the divide which separates the drainage basin of the Cuyuni from the drainage basin of the Orinoco. *

Division of Territory into four tracts.

The relations of the various parts of this territory to the question in controversy will be best appreciated if the entire region be considered as divisible into four great tracts:

First.—That which drains directly into the Orinoco below the junction of that river with the Caroni.

Second.—That which, lying between the Essequibo on the east, the Moruca on the northwest, and the Imataca mountains on the southwest, drains directly into the Atlantic Ocean.

Third.—That which, constitutes the great interior Cuyuni-Mazaruni basin.

Fourth.—That which, stretching from the junction of the Cuyuni, Mazaruni and Essequibo towards the south, constitutes the upper drainage basin of the Essequibo.

These four tracts will be considered in the order named.

---

* In British Blue Book, Venezuela, No. 1 (1896), map 9, however, it is stated that this "extreme British claim * * * is not pressed."

1.—ORINOCO DELTA REGION.

Orinoco Delta Region.

The first of these tracts, which for convenience may be called the *Orinoco Delta Region*, includes a portion of the lower drainage basin of the Orinoco, and a great part of its delta. It is bounded on the north and west by the Orinoco itself; on the south by a range of hills or mountains, to different parts of which have been applied the designations "Piacoa mountains" and "Imataca mountains"; on the east it is separated from the second of the four tracts above mentioned; first, by a wet savanna difficult to traverse; and, further inland, by a tract of white sand, miles in length, white almost as the driven snow, hot and dazzling to the eyes, difficult and even painful to travel over.

Points of special importance.

The points to be especially noted in connection with this tract are: 1st, its essential unity or indivisibility, geographically speaking; and 2d, the importance of Barima as a point from which the entire Orinoco system may be controlled.

1st. Geographic Unity of the Orinoco Delta Region.

Geographic Unity of Orinoco Delta Region.

A glance at the nature and extent of the Orinoco river and of its delta will make this apparent.

The Orinoco, except for the Amazon the greatest river of South America, and one of the world's great rivers, after flowing for miles 1,500 through a region of large precipitation, discharges its waters through a mighty, forest-clad delta. The area of this delta is about 12,000 square miles; and its coast line is fully 250 miles long. Through this delta the Orinoco discharges its waters by an uncounted number of channels, estimated at 150; of which three or four may be navigated by craft of considerable size. The main or "Ship's Mouth," that which alone is available for large steamers, and that which to-

Orinoco River.

day serves as the main channel of commerce, is the one which empties into the Atlantic Ocean between Crab island and Barima point.

Into the Orinoco, at and above Barima point, flow various streams: the Barima, Amacura, Arature, Aguire and Imataca.

Barima River and Mora passage.

The Barima, between Mora passage and Barima point, can hardly be called an independent stream; it is rather one of those many channels through which the Orinoco empties its waters into the ocean. At certain states of the tide the waters of the Barima flow westward and are discharged into the Orinoco; at other states the current is in the opposite direction, the water from the Orinoco flowing eastward through this same Barima channel, and discharging through the Mora passage into the sea. This set of conditions, which converts the lower Barima and the Mora passage into a veritable Orinoco mouth, gives rise to unusual conditions in the Mora passage itself; conditions which serve to emphasize the intimate connection between the Mora passage and the main mouth of the Orinoco.

Description of Mora passage by Perkins.

H. I. Perkins, F. R. G. S., government surveyor, in an article published in *Timehri*,* in June, 1889, thus describes these conditions:

"A peculiar feature of this (Mora) passage is the remarkable swiftness of its current, both at ebb and flow, and the presence of large trees which have been washed down and anchored by their roots, and have become fixed in the centre of the channel, where they sway, bend, creak and groan, as the water swirls past them at the rate of five or six miles an hour. As the distance from the sea of the Barima and Waini ends of the passage, is respectively fifty-one and eight miles, there is considerable difficulty in comprehending the state of the water in the passage, for sometimes it is falling at one end and rising at the other, and *vice versa*, or

**Timehri* is the journal of the Royal Agricultural and Commercial Society of British Guiana, published at Demerara.

Description of Mora passage by Perkins.

rising or falling at both ends, according to the state of the tide in the sea at the time."*

Waini River.

Also intimately connected with the Lower Orinoco, as will appear from the passage just quoted, is the Waini, a river which empties into the ocean, in part through its own mouth, but in part also, through this same Mora passage and the Barima river. The Waini, with the region through which it flows, constitutes a part of the great Orinoco delta.

Connection of Barima, etc., with Orinoco.

The intimate connection, with each other and with the Orinoco, of these various streams, the Waini, the Barima, the Amacura, the Arature, and the rest, is evidenced by the physical features of the region, proved by the history of settlement and trade (to be examined later), and explicitly recognized by British explorers and British writers.

Description of the Coast Region by im Thurn

Mr. Everard F. im Thurn, in a paper read before the Royal Geographical Society, and published in its *Proceedings* for 1892, thus describes the coast region:

"Its coast region, which consists mainly of a series of river deltas, is almost everywhere very low,—indeed, almost invariably below the level of the sea. It is everywhere, except where the hand of man has worked a change, covered by a dense growth of trees, of which so large a proportion are the semi-aquatic, stilt-raised mangroves (*Rhizophora mangle*), or the somewhat similar courida (*Avicennia nitida*), that it requires a careful eye to distinguish the presence of any other species amid the scenery to which these two trees give a very distinctive character. From this low-lying mangrove belt, which may be said to be yet only half land, half sea, there is a gradual, at first scarcely perceptible, rise; but, further inland, the alluvial tract ending at varying distance from the sea, the land rises far more rapidly, in a series of terraces, till it culminates in the comparatively high, dry table-land

* Timehri, 12°, Demerara, 1889, June, vol. 3, p. 55. For further information regarding the Mora passage, see U. S. Commission, Report, iii., pp. 249–253.

which, in Guiana, is called savannah, and which forms so much of the interior of the continent of South America."*

Description of Coast Region by Im Thurn.

Further on he adds:

"The network of rivers is in itself a natural wonder; the Waini, with its sister, or tributary, the Barama, and the Barima, and the Amakuru, all of which, though they have long appeared on our maps, have virtually remained unknown until the last few years, and have remained completely outside the limits of civilization and settlement. The Waini system and the Barima are wide and deep rivers, affording water-passage for vessels up to 15 or 16 feet draught, for 80 or more miles inland from the sea; the Morawhanna, navigable for equally large vessels, forms a link between these two main rivers. Thus we have one splendid water-way, and many small water-ways affording passage to small boats between all the rivers of the district, and between these and the Orinoco on the one hand, and the old civilised portion of the colony on the other."†

Schomburgk, in a letter to Governor Light, dated June 22, 1841, says:

Description of Delta Rivers by Schomburgk.

"We reached in the afternoon, at 3 o'clock, the Coyuni [this is elsewhere more correctly called by him Brazo, *i. e.*, Coyoni Pass, a stream connecting the Amacura with the Arature, and not to be confounded with the great Cuyuni river in the interior] which, like the Mora from the Waini to the Barima, and *vice versa*, forms an uninterrupted passage in canoes from the Amacura to the Araturi. The Coyuni connects the Amacura with the Waicaicaru or Bassama, which falls into the Araturi. This river flows opposite the island Imataca into the Orinoco, and is another instance of a remarkable connection between the tidal rivers of this coast."‡

2D.—The Political, Military and Commercial Importance of Barima Point.

Importance of Barima Point.

The importance of Barima point, and of the land and rivers immediately surrounding it, is due to its

---

* Royal Geog. Soc. Proceedings, London, 1892, October, vol. XIV, pp. 666–667.

† Same, p. 668.

‡ Appendix to Case, iii, 89.

Importance of Barima Point.

commanding position with reference to the "Ship's Mouth" or main channel of the Orinoco. As a result of this, the essential unity of the Orinoco Delta Region from a *geographical* standpoint is emphasized, while its indivisibility from a *political* standpoint is made apparent. This importance of Barima, political and otherwise, has been forcibly set forth by explorers and writers, and has been recognized and acted upon by British statesmen.

Humboldt's testimony as to its importance.

Humboldt, in his *Personal Narrative of Travels to the Equinoctial Regions of the New Continent during the years 1799–1804*, after some description of the Orinoco, says of the facts he mentions:

"They will I think suffice to show, how intimately the political security of the United Provinces of Caraccas and New-Grenada is connected with the defence of the mouths of the Oroonoko; and how Spanish Guyana, though scarcely cleared, and desitute of population, acquires a high importance in the struggle between the colonies and the mother country. This military importance was foreseen more than two centuries ago by the celebrated Raleigh."*

McCreagh's testimony as to its importance.

Another authority to be quoted in this connection is Major McCreagh, a British officer who was sent, in 1802, to make a military survey of the Orinoco. He reported where the Spanish forts and military posts were, and pointed out the military and commercial importance of holding the Orinoco. He said:

"Except the conversion of the aboriginal natives (which is certainly not the primary motive), the Spanish Government has obviously no other object in occupying the Oronoque than the very important one of excluding other Powers from a river which runs along the rear of the Provinces of Popayan, Venezuela, Carraccas, Cumana, and Paria; which, therefore, in the hands of a commercial nation would carry away from them the productions,

* Humboldt (A. von), "Personal narrative of travels, etc., 1799–1804," London, 1821, Vol. V, p. 714.

and monopolize the traffic of those rich territories, and which, if possessed by a warlike Power, might immediately paralyze the authority and gradually destroy the tenure by which Spain holds her vast Empire in South America."*

McCreagh's testimony as to importance of Barima Point.

Schomburgk, on various occasions, gave his testimony to the same effect. Referring to Colonel Moody's survey of the Orinoco in the early part of this century, he says:

Schomburgk's testimony as to importance of Barima Point.

"This point (Barima point) in the possession of Great Britain is of great value in a military respect. The peculiar configuration of the only channel (Boca de Navios), which admits vessels of some draught to the Orinoco, passes near Point Barima, so that if hereafter it became of advantage to command the entrance to the Orinoco, this might be easily effected from that point. This assertion is supported by Colonel Moody's evidence, who visited this spot in his military capacity in the commencement of this century."†

Expressing his own opinion Schomburgk, on another occasion, says:

"Of equal importance is the determination of the western boundary, the limits of which have never been completely settled, and it merits the greatest attention on account of the political importance of the mouth of the Orinoco."‡

Again, speaking of the importance of the Amacura and Arature, he mentions an inland waterway or pass which there exists; and adds that it

"offers an uninterrupted passage in canoes from the Amacura to the Araturi. . . . This river flows opposite the island Imataca into the Orinoco, and is another instance of a remarkable connection between the tidal rivers of this coast. A short distance above the mouth of the River Araturi is the Venezuelan post Coriabo. The importance of this natural canal in a military or a commercial point of view is undeniable, but its importance to Venezuela (if a denser population should make it such) is ren-

* Appendix to Case, iii, 58.

† Appendix to Case, iii, 82.

‡ Parliamentary Papers, 1840, Vol. 34, p. 327.

Schomburgk's testimony as to importance of Barima Point.

dered abortive in a military aspect if Great Britain possesses the right or eastern bank of the Amacura."*

In his work on British Guiana, he says:

"Between the Essequibo and Orinoco are the rivers Pomeroon, Marocco, and Wa-ina or Guayma; and although these outlets are comparatively of small size, they are so closely connected by branches and tributaries, that they afford an inland navigation from the Marocco to the Orinoco. Their importance in a political and commercial respect becomes therefore evident."†

In a note in his edition of Raleigh's Guiana, published in 1848, Schomburgk also says:

"A strong battery established at Punta Barima, where the Dutch had as early as 1660 a fortified outpost, would prevent any vessel from entering the Orinoco drawing more than eight feet of water. Punta Barima, or Point Breme, as it was called by the Dutch, commands entirely the entrance of the Orinoco by the Boca de Navios; and when on a late occasion the right of possession to this point was the subject of discussion between the British Government and the Republic of Venezuela, Punta Barima was appropriately and emphatically styled 'the Dardanelles of the Orinoco.'"‡

A *confidential* letter of Schomburgk to Governor Light, dated October 23, 1841, deserves to be quoted in full in this connection. He says:

Sir, *Demerara, October* 23, 1841.

In my letter of this day's date, I informed your Excellency upon what grounds I founded the right of possession of Her Majesty to the Barima, and I have now to point out the importance which is attached to this position, should the British Government establish the Amacura as the boundary between British Guiana and Venezuela.

The River Orinoco may be termed the high-road to the interior of the territories of Venezuela and New Granada. It has at its

* Appendix to Case, iii, 89.

† Schomburgk (R. H.) Description of British Guiana, etc., London, 1840, p. 17.

‡ Schomburgk (R. H.) Discovery of Guiana, by Sir W. Raleigh, London, 1848, p. 115, note.

Schomburgk's testimony as to importance of Barima Point.

mouth the appearance of an ocean, and articles of commerce may be transported on this stream for 400 or 500 leagues. Nearly three hundred tributary streams, of more or less importance, flow into it, which may serve as additional canals and facilitate the commerce of the interior. Santa Fé de Bogota may be reached within a distance of eight miles by one of its tributary streams, the Meta, and operations of commerce or war, combined with others from the Pacific, could be carried on by means of the vast plains or llanos. A small fleet may go up the Orinoco and the Meta within fifteen or twenty leagues of Santa Fé, and the flour of New Grenada may be conveyed down the same way.

And the only access to this vast inland communication for sailing vessels of more than ten feet draft of water is by means of the Boca de Navios, which is *commanded from Point Barima.*

The River Barima falls into the south side of the Orinoco near the most eastern point of its mouth and in a direction almost parallel to the coast. Point Barima is, therefore, bounded to the west by the river of that name, to the north by the Orinoco, to the east by the Atlantic, and to the south by impenetrable forests. Colonel Moody considers this position "susceptable [*sic*] of being fortified so as to resist almost any attack on the sea-side—the small depth of water, the nature of the tides, and its muddy shores, defend it. The Barima, and the uncultivated forests on marshy ground, present an impenetrable barrier against the interior, and debarkation from the Orinoco might be put under the fire of any number of guns—and the land-reproaches [*sic*] on that soil could be easily rendered inaccessible to an invading force."

This is the importance which Colonel Moody in a military respect has attached to this point, and which, so far as my knowledge goes in this matter, is fully borne out by personal inspection during my late survey of the entrance to the Barima.

The Venezuelan Government, as at present organised, tottering in their interior relations, and embarassed by a number of slaves who would hail the opportunity to shake off their fetters, hated and despised by the aborigines, whom maltreatment and cruelties have alienated, would be an insignificant enemy—but in the hands of any of the maritime European powers, matters would assume another aspect.

France has attempted to establish a fortified position at the mouth of the Amazon near Macapa, which she claims as the eastern

Schomburgk's testimony as to importance of Barima Point.

boundary of Cayenne. A settlement at this spot commands the commerce of the Amazon, and this, no doubt, is the reason why this Power puts such importance upon its possession. Supposing that unforeseen circumstances should put France in occupation of Point Barima at the Orinoco, and that Macapa at the Amazon is ceded to her, she will then command the commerce of the two first rivers of South America and hold the military keys of the northern provinces of Brazil and of the former Spanish provinces of South America, north of the equator, which territories will be always at the mercy of that power which commands the channels to their commerce.

Finally, trusting to the prospects of prosperity and a continued emigration to British Guiana, there could not be a more favourable position for a commercial settlement than Point Barima. The capital of Spanish Guayana is Angostura, situated a distance of 85 leagues from the mouth of the Orinoco, and the intricate navigation of that river presents numerous difficulties to foreign vessels going up the Orinoco as far as Angostura.

A commercial settlement established at the extreme point of Barima, where one part of the town would front the River Barima, and the other the Orinoco, would soon induce foreign vessels to dispose of their cargoes at the new settlement, and leave the further transport to the interior to smaller craft; naturally this premises the supposition that amicable relations and commercial treaties exist between Great Britain and Venezuela. The bar at the Barima admits vessels of sixteen feet draft of water, which if once entered, may safely anchor in from four to five fathoms water. The peculiar formation of the fluvial system of the coastland between the Barima and the Essequibo admits an inland navigation, in punts and barges, to Richmond Estate, on the Arabisi Coast of the Essequibo, which with a few improvements might vie with any of the interior canals of England.*

Importance of Barima Point admitted by Great Britain.

The recognition of what is here so forcibly set forth in the preceding extracts is by no means confined either to foreign writers or to minor British officials. It has, *in words*, been admitted by no less than three of Great Britain's Prime Ministers, and it has been *acted upon*

* Appendix to Case, iii, 125–127.

by at least four of them. On March 30, 1844, Lord Aberdeen wrote as follows to the Venezuelan Government:

Importance of Barima Point admitted by Lord Aberdeen.

"Believing, then, that the undivided possession of the Orinoco is the object most important for the interests of Venezuela, Her Majesty's Government are prepared to cede to the Republic a portion of the coast amply sufficient to insure Venezuela against the mouth of this her principal river being at the command of any foreign power. With this view, and regarding it as a most valuable concession to Venezuela, Her Majesty's Government are willing to waive their claim to the Amacura as the western boundary of the British territory, and to consider the mouth of the Moroco River as the limit of Her Majesty's possessions on the sea-coast." *

On September 15, 1881, Lord Granville wrote as follows:

Importance of Barima Point admitted by Lord Granville.

"8. They [Her Majesty's Government] are disposed, therefore, to submit the following as a line of boundary, which they consider will yield to Venezuela every reasonable requirement while securing the interests of British Guaina:—

"The initial point to be fixed at a spot on the sea-shore 29 miles of longitude due east from the right bank of the River Barima, and to be carried thence south," etc.

"9. This boundary will surrender to Veneznela what has been called The Dardanelles of the Orinoco. It will give to Venezuela the entire command of the mouth of that river, and it yields about one-half of the disputed territory, while it secures to British Guiana a well-defined natural boundary along almost its whole course, except for about the first 50 miles inland from the sea, where it is necessary to lay down an arbitrary boundary in order to secure to Venezuela the undisturbed possession of the mouths of the Orinoco.†

On June 7, 1886, Lord Rosebery wrote:

Importance of Barima Point admitted by Lord Rosebery.

"The line which they [Her Majesty's Government] intend to trace will run as follows:—

"The initial point to be fixed at a spot on the sea-shore 29 miles

* Appendix to Case, iii, 210.

† Appendix to Case, iii, 156.

Importance of Barima Point admitted by Lord Rosebery.

of longitude due east from the right bank of the River Barima, and to be carried thence south," etc.

"This line is identical with that which was suggested in Lord Granville's note to Señor de Rojas of the 15th September, 1881, a copy of which accompanied his Lordship's despatch to your predecessor of the 30th of that month.

"Her Majesty's Government, however, still reserve their right to insist on a more westerly boundary hereafter, although, partly for the purpose of establishing a more convenient natural boundary, and partly from their willingness to gratify the wish of the Venezuelan Government to possess the right bank of the Orinoco from its mouth, they are ready to come to an understanding with the Venezuelan Government, and are prepared to concede to Venezuela a portion of the disputed territory beyond the line now to be marked out, provided," etc.*

Points of special importance.

The facts so set forth, in the opinion of the Venezuelan Government, clearly establish the two points first mentioned with regard to the Orinoco Delta Region. These are:

1st. That *geographically* it is a unit, knit together by its net-work of connecting rivers and streams; and,

2nd. That *politically* it is likewise a unit; the commercial, political and military control of the entire Orinoco being necessarily dependent upon the exclusive possession and control of all its mouths, especially of its principal mouth.

2.—MORUCA-POMEROON REGION.

Moruca-Pomeroon Region.

The second tract into which the disputed territory may be divided, and which, for convenience, will here be designated as the *Moruca-Pomeroon Region*, has the Essequibo and the ocean for its eastern boundary; is separated on the west from the rest of the coast region by the water parting which divides the Orinoco delta from the region watered by the Moruca, Wacupo and Pome-

* Appendix to Case, iii, 160.

roon; and extends inland as far as the junction of the Essequibo with the Cuyuni and Mazaruni rivers.

Moruca-Pomeroon Region.

Its general character near the coast is like the Orinoco Delta Region above described. There is a fringe of alluvial mud from one to four or five miles wide; back of that are the sand reefs, and yet farther back the lowest slopes of the Imatacas and the Blue mountains.

Its separation from the Orinoco.

The point of special importance regarding this tract is its entire separation from the Orinoco, by natural barriers.

To make this clear, it is needful to understand the formation of the coast region in general, and in particular the conditions which divide the coast at the Moruca into two distinct parts.

The present coast is alluvial: it constitutes the delta or river-made land. An enquiry as to what preceded this made land reveals the fact that there was formerly a sand beach from which the ocean has gradually receded, but which, by reason of its still existing peculiar shape, has exercised an appreciable influence upon subsequent events.

The Sand Reefs.

Rodway, in his "*Hand-Book of British Guiana, 1893,*" says:

"*The Sand-Reefs.* Behind the fringe of plantations, which rarely extend beyond three miles from the sea-shore, lie swamps choked with tall sedges, the soil being a kind of disintegrated peat, called pegass. Here and there an island of sand crops up, on which a few trees and bushes manage to exist, with grand clumps of the Eta palm (*Mauritia flexuosa*) scattered here and there, or perhaps surrounding what looks like an extensive meadow. Wherever the land begins to rise these magnificent palms rear their heads in the foreground, while behind, the wall of interminable forest closes the view. Here comes the white sand beach of long ages ago. Miles and miles of pure sand, washed as clean as driven snow, throw up a glare under the noonday sun which is dazzling to the eyes and sometimes quite pain-

The Sand Reefs. ful. The barefooted Indian cuts two pieces of bark, and makes himself a pair of slippers when crossing the 'Mourie,' as it is called, and even the well-shod European feels it hot to the soles of his feet. But even here, where there is hardly a trace of mould, some hardy bushes manage to exist, their roots penetrating far below the surface where it is always cool and moist."*

Schomburgk, in his "*Description of British Guiana,*" p. 3, says:

"This alluvial flat extends from ten to twenty, and in some instances (as between the rivers Berbice and Corentyn) even to forty miles inland, and is terminated by a range of sand-hills, from about 30 to 120 feet high, which approach the sea within two miles of the Arabisi coast of the Essequibo."†

Line of Old Beach. The geological survey, made between 1867 and 1873, on behalf of the British Government by Messrs. Brown and Sawkins, has traced approximately the line of this old beach; that is to say, the line which divides the *firm* land from the *filled delta*; and where this line has not actually been followed out, it may nevertheless be traced by the places where the water-courses change from true flowing streams to interlacing bayous.

To map 4 of the Atlas accompanying this Case, the results of the survey by Brown and Sawkins have been transferred.

By reference to this map it will be seen that the old beach line, which in the Orinoco delta is now well inland, makes its nearest approach to the present seaboard near the mouth of the Moruca: it is now elevated land, according to the quotation from Schomburgk above given, and approaches the sea within about two miles.

A result of this is that the alluvial deposit at this point is, comparatively speaking, a mere strip which

* Rodway (J.) Hand-Book of British Guiana. 12°, Georgetown, 1893, p. 10.

† Schomburgk (R. H.) Description of British Guiana, etc. 12°, London, 1840, p. 3.

contains no natural waterways; and as a consequence there is no natural inland water communication between the Orinoco delta, on the west, and the Moruca, on the east.

Line of Old Beach.

The *practical* effect of this lack of natural water communication is that *actual* communication between the two regions has been very slight. The difficulty of crossing from the Moruca to the region west has been so great as to constitute an *actual* barrier between them, a barrier which, in the history of settlement has in fact served to keep the two regions apart.

Communication between Moruca and Orinoco Delta Region, difficult and limited.

Mr. im Thurn, in a paper read before the Royal Geographical Society and published in its *Proceedings* for October, 1892, gives the following account of a journey from the Moruca to the Waini:

Difficulty of this communication, according to im Thurn.

"After five hours' boat journey up the Moruka, the country on each side of the river becoming gradually more and more open—the river at last winding through open savannahs, and broadening out here and there into pools so thickly set with water-lilies that it was difficult to force the boat through them—we reached the point where the waterway leaves the river and passes along a narrow itabbo, or artificial water-path, which connects the Moruka with the Waini River. This connecting passage is in all about 30 miles in length; but only about the first 10 miles of this is actually semi-artificial itabbo, made by the constant passage of the canoes of the Redmen through the swampy savannah. After that it runs into the Barabara and then into the Biara River, which latter runs into the Baramanni River, and that again into the Waini, at a point about 80 miles from its outflow into the sea.

We found the itabbo section of this passage very difficult to get through. Generally, it was hardly wider than the boat, and its many abrupt windings added to our difficulties. Again, the trees hang down so low over the water, that even after we had taken the tent off the boat, we had either to force the boat under the low-lying branches or make a passage by cutting them away. On either side of the channel the ground is so swampy as hardly anywhere to allow foothold of even a few inches in extent. The

Difficulty of communication between Moruca and Orinoco Delta Region, according to Im Thurn.

light hardly penetrates through the dense roof of leaves; and in the gloom under the roof only a few aroids, ferns, lilies, orchids, and great masses of a palm which had at the time of my journey not been described, * * * grew among the fantastically twisted tree-roots which rose from the bare mud. Only close to the channel itself, where just a little more light penetrated, did these same plants grow a little more densely.

This itabbo is quite dry in the longer dry seasons, and is then, of course, impassable; for walking along its banks is out of the question—a circumstance which has had a good deal to do with the fact that the parts beyond had up till then been almost completely shut off from the rest of the colony. Even now, though the overhanging trees have been cleared from this part of the waterway, it presents no slight obstacle to the swarm of gold boats which would press through it to the goldfields beyond." *

Physical Barrier between the two.

The above facts would seem to place beyond question the point of special importance regarding this *Moruca-Pomeroon Region;* viz., that a natural and effective physical barrier separates it from the *Orinoco Delta Region.*

3.—CUYUNI-MAZARUNI BASIN.

Cuyuni-Mazaruni Basin.

The third of the tracts to be considered is the great interior Cuyuni-Mazaruni basin. The two rivers from which this basin derives its name unite and flow into the Essequibo—*this fact constitutes the sole connection between this and the Essequibo.* Except for this connection, a connection which in this instance is without *practical* importance, the interior basin, watered by the two streams, is a region quite separate and distinct from the Essequibo.

Its connection with the Orinoco.

The Cuyuni-Mazaruni basin is connected, geographically and historically with the *Orinoco*—not with the Essequibo: the approach to it is from the *west*—not from the east: its fluvial connection with the Essequibo, as will in a moment be made apparent, serves rather

* Royal Geog. Soc. Proc., London, 1892, Oct., vol. 14, p. 674.

to emphasize than to lessen their real separation. Nature has forced these two regions apart; and the fact that the waters of the one flow through the territory of the other has been entirely insufficient either to unite them, or to divorce the Cuyuni-Mazaruni basin from the western regions upon which, geographically and politically, it naturally depends.

Cuyuni-Mazaruni basin distinct and separate from the Essequibo.

Hilhouse, the first Englishman to attempt the ascent of the Cuyuni, found the falls so perilous and insuperable a barrier that he declared it to be "evident that colonization could never be attempted on this river."*

Hilhouse's testimony.

This interior basin is bounded on the north by the same range of hills which, under the name of Piacoa, Imataca, and Blue mountains, forms the southern boundary of the coast region; on the south it is shut in by a range of mountains sufficiently high and rugged to make their crossing difficult at most places and impossible at others; on the east a spur of this same rugged range, under the name of the Ayangcanna mountains (at places nearly 5,000 feet high) runs north until it meets the Blue mountains, which, as a spur of the Imatacas, run south; these two ranges effectively separate the Cuyuni-Mazaruni basin from the Essequibo. Near the point of junction of the Cuyuni and Mazaruni there is a break in these mountains, and through this break, over rapids and falls, the Cuyuni and the Mazaruni rivers pour their united waters into the Essequibo.

Boundaries of Basin.

* "When, in 1837, an Englishman (Hilhouse) first went up the Cuyuni, he wrote: 'I can find no traces of any one having preceded me in the survey of the lower part of this river.' And, having described in his journal the first day's ascent, to the head of the Camaria Falls—'we ascended this day,' he thinks, 'fully seventy-seven feet'—he declares that 'it is evident that colonization can never be attempted on this river: the first day's journal determines that.' 'Beyond all other rivers,' he avers, 'the Cuyuni is the most difficult and dangerous of ascent.'—*Journal of the Royal Geographical Society of London*, 1837, pp. 446-454). Yet Hilhouse was no 'tenderfoot:' he had long been colonial surveyor and protector of the Indians. [Note by Prof. Burr, U. S. Commission, Report, i, 306].

Barriers separating interior basins from Essequibo.

These rapids and falls effectively bar the only eastern entrance to the interior basin; and thus, with the mountains on the north and south, constitute a natural physical barrier between the Essequibo and this inland region.

Schomburgk's testimony.

Of these rapids and falls Schomburgk thus speaks:

"The difficulties which the Cuyuni presents to navigation, and those tremendous falls which impede the river in the first day's ascent, will, I fear, prove a great obstacle to making the fertility of its banks available to the colony."*

Barriers separating basin from Essequibo.

The *Local Guide* of 1843, published at Demerara, says:

"A short distance above their junction, these rivers [the Mazaruni, Cuyuni and Essequibo] become impeded by rapids, above which they are frequented only by a few wandering Indians."†

Perkins' testimony.

Mr. H. I. Perkins says of the Cuyuni:

"It has long been known as amongst the most dangerous, if not *the* most dangerous, of all the larger rivers of British Guiana, and there are times when the height of its waters, either above or below a certain point, gives it every right to claim this unenviable notoriety. My first experience of it was a highly unpleasant one in 1877, when, with a brother surveyor, I spent about four weeks journeying up and down a portion of it, and surveying placer claims on its right bank. On this memorable occasion we lost two boat-hands from dysentery, a third dying on his return to Georgetown from the same disorder, and last but not least, in coming down stream our boat capsized at the Accaio—the lowest fall in the river—where one man was drowned and everything was lost." ‡

Rodway's testimony.

Rodway, speaking of English efforts, since 1884, to establish armed stations in the disputed district, says:

"Another move in the same direction was made in 1892, by establishing a boundary post up the Cuyuni near its junction with Yuruan. Except for its bearing upon the boundary this post is quite useless and might be abandoned if the question

* Appendix to Case, III, 119-120.

† Local Guide to British Guiana. Demerara, 1843.

‡ Timehri. 12°, Demerara, 1893, June, vol. 7, p. 75.

were settled; under present circumstances however it is highly desirable that it be kept up notwithstanding the fact that the police who reside there have to perform a very hazardous and long journey of forty or fifty days to reach it and then are cut off from all communication until relieved."* Rodway's testimony.

Mr. Geo. G. Dixon, who visited the recent British station on the Yuruan in 1894, thus contrasts the difficulty of reaching the center of the Cuyuni basin from the English settlements, and the ease with which the same point is reached from the Spanish Orinoco. He says: Dixon's testimony. Barriers separating interior basin from Essequibo.

"This made me, as an Englishman, feel considerably mortified to think that it takes our Government from five to six weeks to reach their frontier station, whereas the Venezuelan outpost was then being put, and by this time probably is, in direct communication with their capital by road and wire. Also, whereas it costs our Government an immense annual sum to maintain their small number of police at Yuruan on salt and tinned provisions (sent all the way from Bartica Grove, on the Essequibo, in paddled boats); within 200 yards on the other bank of Kuyuni is the Venezuelan outpost, supplied with all kinds of fresh food from their cattle farms and plantations." †

In further explanation of the difficulty of access to this region, it should be stated that its eastern part is covered with a dense forest which renders access to it, overland, well nigh impossible. A few paths or trails have been at times chopped out by the Indians, but these, under the stimulus of a tropical sun and abundant moisture, are speedily overgrown. Dense forests as additional barriers on the east.

In striking contrast with this difficulty of access from the *east* is the natural and easy entrance from the Orinoco on the *west*, by gentle slopes and over delightful pasture land. Easy entrance from the Orinoco.

This region, which forms the real and only entrance to the Cuyuni-Mazaruni basin, is usually spoken of as the Mission Savanna country. Every traveller has Mission Savannas.

* Appendix to Case, iii, 349.
† Appendix to Case, iii, 358.

Mission Savannas.

admired these savannas, and has noted the ease of travel over this open parklike country. The following is an extract from *Venezuela; a Visit to the Gold Mines of Guayana, etc., during 1886, by William Barry, C. E., London, 1886*, p. 128.*

"In the district of Upata, which forms a part of this great belt, the fertility of the land is said to be inferior to no part of South America, while the climate is deliciously temperate, at a height of 1,400 feet above the level of the sea. The traveller through this delightful region is perpetually meeting new beauties each time he passes through a belt of forest, where he is sheltered by overhanging trees, full of color; and, regaled with a hundred various perfumes of flowers, he emerges on open tracts of moderate extent not bare, but diversified by clumps of trees dotted about, while the rolling ground reminds him of the most beautiful parts of English country scenery. Park, as it were, succeeds park, till he is at last fairly puzzled where to select to encamp, among so much contended and rival loveliness, and here, at a nominal rent, the cattle breeder may come and establish himself, with the certainty of realizing thirty per cent. per annum on his outlay, and the possibility of very much more. Always on horseback, in a most lovely climate, and with pure air and clear blue skies, is it a wonder if I felt tempted to leave civilization, and remain in such a spot forever?"

* * * * *

"Upata is a considerable town standing in a plain surrounded by hills, and is 1,000 feet above the level of the sea.

"Here the climate is delicious, the air pure and cool, and the temperature perfectly endurable to Europeans (p. 98).

"Leaving Upata, on Saturday at five a. m., we rode through a delicious country, always ascending, until we reached the highest point of the range, 1,400 feet above sea level. On crossing this, a magnificent view burst upon us. Away below, as far as the eye could reach, stretched vast undulating plains of waving grass, dotted at intervals with clumps of splendid trees—some in bloom,

---

* Mr. Barry was an engineer sent out by Englishmen interested in the mines. He went in by the usual route from Las Tablas on the Orinoco. He rode back on horseback from the Callao mine south of Guacipati to Las Tablas in three days of ten hours each. This is the usual length of the journey.

others in leaf, and of every tint of flower or leaf, from deepest crimson to palest yellow. Occasionally a thin belt of forest marked the course of a stream, or a denser mass of trees showed where lay a lagoon, while in the extreme distance, grey against the crimson dawn, rose the peaks of the distant mountains. This does not open by degrees, but, on turning a corner of the road, the whole panorama suddenly lies spread before you in all its impressive beauty. I can never forget it." Mission Savannas.

"It is at this point the watershed changes. On the Upata side, all the streams and rivers run to the north, and empty into the Orinoco; on the other side all the mountain streams run to the southward, emptying into the Yuruari, and eventually into the Essequibo" (pp. 99–100).

The general character of the basin further inland toward the Cuyuni may be stated in a word.

The upper parts of the various water courses probably run nearly or quite dry during the dry season, and the banks are usually free from trees. Further down stream a fringe of trees begins to appear, scattered at first, then continuous, and gradually increasing until these widening borders of woodland along the adjacent streams meet, and the savannas give place to forests, broken here and there by other savannas. The dividing line between the savannas and forrests is irregular, and not always sharply defined.

From the foregoing statements the following facts appear:

Cuyuni-Mazaruni basin a natural dependency of the Orinoco.

The Cuyuni-Mazaruni basin is an interior region, the eastern part of which is covered by dense tropical forests and is made inaccessible from that side by these forests, by mountains, and by falls and rapids. Toward the west its connection with the Orinoco is so intimate as to render the dividing line between the two scarcely perceptible. The open savannas of the Orinoco extend over the divide, and down *across* the great bend of the Cuyuni to the very center of the great basin *and even*

Cuyuni-Mazaruni Basin.

beyond, thus making the entire valley a natural dependency of the Orinoco.

4.—UPPER ESSEQUIBO BASIN.

Upper Essequibo Basin.

The fourth and last of the tracts, which together constitute the territory in dispute, is what may be called the *Upper Essequibo Basin*. It comprises the region lying south of the Pacaraima mountains, and west of the Essequibo. It is a mountainous district of broken table-land; and is quite shut off, both from the Cuyuni-Mazaruni basin and from the lower Essequibo. The falls and rapids which impede the Cuyuni and the Mazaruni are repeated in the case of the Upper Essequibo; and, beginning as these do, but a short distance above the confluence of the three rivers, they too serve as a barrier to separate this interior region from the coast.

III.—HISTORICAL SKETCH SHOWING BASIS OF SPAIN'S ORIGINAL TITLE TO GUIANA AND OF VENEZUELA'S TITLE TO THE DISPUTED TERRITORY.

Spain first discovered the New World, first explored its continents; first discovered, explored, possessed and settled Guiana; and first firmly established herself in that province as its sole and lawful owner.

1.—DISCOVERY AND EXPLORATION.

Early discoveries and explorations.

The discovery of the New World by Spain, and her admitted right to be regarded as the first explorer of its continents, rests upon the following facts:

Columbus on his third voyage, coasting the southern shore of Trinidad, saw to the southward, on August 1, 1498, the main land which formed part of the delta of the Orinoco. The volume of fresh water was such that he wrote it must come from a land of "infinite" extent. In 1499 his lieutenants coasted the entire line from Surinam to Panama, sailing up the estuaries of the Essequibo and the Orinoco; and on this voyage the name of *Venezuela*, or "Little Venice," was given to the mainland, in consequence of the Indian dwellings, which they found constructed over the water and swampy lands. In 1500 Pinzon discovered the Amazon, and coasted the shore to the Orinoco, where he took in a cargo of Brazil wood. Other discoverers, Spanish and Portuguese, pushed south along the Brazilian coast. In 1519-1520, Magellan, a Portuguese in the service of Spain, sent by Charles V, touched at or near the Bay of Rio de Janeiro, followed down the coast, passed through the strait which now bears his name, went up the west

Early discoveries and explorations.

coast a considerable distance, and then crossed the Pacific to the Moluccas.

Meantime in 1513, Balboa, crossing the Isthmus of Darien, discovered the Pacific: this was followed by many Spanish expeditions to the Pacific coast, touching from Chili to upper California, so that, by 1535 or 1540, the west shore of America was known from upper California to Cape Horn, and its outlines were shown with respectable accuracy on maps.*

This was the work of Spain, by innumerable expeditions helped out at a few points by Portuguese navigators; and thus, within forty or fifty years from Columbus' first voyage, the nation which sent him had not only discovered the existence of the two Americas, but had explored and made known their entire coast line from Labrador, round Cape Horn, at least to upper California.†

2.—SETTLEMENT AND POSSESSION.

Spain followed exploration by settlement and effective possession.

The work of Spain did not stop with the discovery and exploration of America. This was at once followed by settlement; and, with regard to nearly all of South America, it was followed also by the formal taking and effective keeping of possession. The following facts will serve to support this statement:

Early charters.

Ferdinand granted colonizing charters before his death in 1516. Charles V followed with a considerable number of them from 1520 onward. Settlements were made at Cumaná by Ojèda and by the missionaries of Las Casas in 1520; these settlements were often devastated by the Indians; nevertheless they were renewed, and Cumaná is one of the most ancient cities on the continent.

Cumaná settled.

In 1528 the Emperor made a large colonization con-

* Winsor (J.) Narrative and Critical History. Boston, ii, 177, vii, 389.
† Same, ii, 242.
‡ Fiske, ii, 459.

Early grants.

tract with the Velsers, rich merchants of Augsburg, granting them a right to the coast from Cabo de la Vela (near the western end of Venezuela) to Maracapana (close to Cumaná)—that is, over nearly the whole Carribean sea-coast of Venezuela; while in 1530–31 a colonization grant was made to Diego de Ordaz, covering the shore from the Velsers' grant to the Amazon—that is, including the entire Guiana coast. The Velsers had a royal governor; and a Bull of July 21, 1531, made Venezuela a bishopric, for which a cathedral was erected at Coro.*

Expeditions inland.

Each of these grants also covered the interior as far inland as the grantees might go, and this led to a series of expeditions into the interior. In 1530 Pedro de Acosta founded a settlement at the mouth of the Orinoco, but was not long afterwards driven off by the Caribs. In 1531 Cornejo sailed up the Orinoco. In 1530–31 Ordaz, exploring under a grant, ascended the Orinoco to the Meta, near six hundred miles; and in 1537 another expedition commanded by Herrera, under the Ordaz grant, ascended both the Orinoco and its affluent the Meta, to its headwaters close to Bogotá, and marched to that city.

The account of Keymis, Raleigh's lieutenant, written in 1596, enumerates twenty expeditions down to 1560, all Spanish, taken from "*Primera Parte de las Elegias de Varones Illustres de Indias*," by Castellanos; and Raleigh's "*Discoverie of Guiana*" adds more. These expeditions were often of great size, The accounts of them mention 200 men; 400 men; 600 men.†

* Documentos para la Historia del Libertador, i, 35–37; also Bollaert (Wm.) Expedition of Pedro de Ursua, etc., with introduction by C. R. Markham. London, 1861, pp. iv–v.

† Hakluyt (R.) Principal navigations, etc.; edited by E. Goldsmid, Edinburgh, 1890, vol. xv, pp. 93–96; *see* also Rodway (J.) and Watt (T.) Annals of Guiana, 1888, vol. i, p. 12; also Raleigh (W.) Discovery of Guiana, edited by R. H. Schomburgk. London, 1848, p. 16 *et seq.*

Expeditions inland.

Spain continued her efforts. Not to speak of others, Berreo in 1582 started from New Grenada with 700 horsemen, 1,000 head of cattle, and a horde of Indian slaves; reached the Orinoco; went down to its mouth; and subdued or received the peaceful homage of the Indians of that region.*

Early settlements.

The confluence of the Caroni and the Orinoco was pointed out, by the nature of the land and by its position, as a place especially fitted for settlement; for both the river and the easy, open savannas which stretch far back from it mark it as the natural entrance to the interior of Guiana. In 1531-32 Ordaz had here found a settlement of Indians;† and about 1591 the Spanish town of Santo Thomé, and opposite, on an island, the Spanish fort or citadel of Faxardo, were regularly established.‡

Santo Thomé founded.

Before the end of the 16th century, the Spaniards were seriously occupying themselves with the interior of Guiana.

Formal possession of Guiana taken by Spain.

In the year 1594 Captain George Popham captured, at sea, certain letters on their way to Spain. These letters have preserved to us an account of the formal act by which in 1593 Domingo de Vera, on behalf of Antonio de Berreo, "Governor and Captain-General for our Lord the King betwixt the rivers Orinoco and Amazon," took possession of the Province of Guiana for Spain.

One of these letters deserves to be quoted in full. It is as follows:

"Part of the Coppy that was sent to his Maiesty of the discovery of Nueuo Dorado.

In the riuer of *Pato* otherwise called *Orenoque*, the principall

---

* Raleigh's Guiana, Schomburgk, ed., pp. 26, 39.

† Raleigh's Guiana, Schomburgk ed., p. 79, note 2.

‡ Simon (*Fray* Pedro). Noticias Historiales de las Conquistas de Tierra Firme en las Indias Occidentales. Cuenca, 1627; see also U. S. Commission, Report, i, 39.

Formal Possession of Guiana taken by Spain.

part thereof called *Warismero*, the 23 of Aprill 1593. *Domingo de vera*, Master of the Campe and Generall for Anth. de Bereo Gouernour and Captaine generall for our Lorde the King, betwixt the riuers of *Pato* and *Papamene* alias *Orenoque*, and *Marannon*, and of the Iland of *Trinedado*, in presence of me *Rodrigo de Caranca* register for the sea, commanded all the soldiers to be drawne together and put in order of battaile, the Captaines and soldiers, and master of the campo standing in the middest of them, said vnto them ; Sirs, Soldiers, and Captaines, you vnderstand long since that our Generall *Antho. de Berreo*, with the trauell of 11 yeares, and expence of more than 10000 pesoes of Gold, discouered the noble prouinces of *Guiana* and *Dorado*: Of the which hee tooke possession to gouerne the same, but through want of his peoples health, and necessary munition, he issued at the Iland of *Marguarita*, and from thence peopled the *Trinedado*. But now they had sente me to learne out and discouer the ways most easily to enter, and to people the saide prouinces, and where the Campos and Armies may best enter the same. By reason whereof I entend so to do in the name of his Maiesty, and the said gouernour *Antho: de Berreo*, and in token thereof I require you *Fran. Carillo* that you aide me to aduance this crosse that lieth here on the ground, which they set on end towardes the east, and the said Master of the Campe, the Captains and soldiers kneeled down and did due reuerence vnto the said crosse, and thereupon the Master of the Campe tooke a bole of water and dranke it of, and tooke more and threw abroad on the ground: he also drew out his sword and cut the grasse of the ground, and the boughs of the trees saying I take this possession in the name of the king *Don Phillip* our master, and of his gouernour *Antho: de Berreo*: and because some make question of this possession, to them I answere that in these our actions was present the *Casique* or principal *Don Antho.* otherwise called *Morequito*, whose land this was who yeelded consent to the said possession, was glad there of, and gaue his obedience to our Lord the King, and in his name to the said gouernour *Antho: de Berreo*. And the said Master of the Campe kneeled downe being in his libertie, and all the Captaines and soldiers saide that the possession was wel taken, and that they would defend it with their liues, vpon whosoeuer would say to the contrary. And the saide master of the Camp hauing his sword drawen in his hand

Formal Possession of Guiana taken by Spain.

said vnto me, register that art here present, giue me an instrument or testimoniall to confirme me in this possession, which I haue taken of this land, for the gouernour *Antho. de Berreo* and if it be needfull I wil take it a new. And I require you all that are present to witnes the same, and do further declare that I will goe on, taking the possession of all these laudes wheresoeuer I shall enter. Signed thus.

Domingo de vera *and vnderneath, Before me* Rodrigo de Caranca, *Register of the Army.*

And in prosecution of the said possession, and discouery of the way and prouinces, the 27 of April of the said yere, the Master of the Camp entred by little and little with all the Campe and men of warre, more than two leagues into the Inland, and came to a towne of a principall, and conferring with him did let him vnderstand by meanes of *Antho: Bisante* the Interpretor that his Maiesty and *Antho: de Berreo* had sent him to take the said possession. And the said fryer *Francis Carillo* by the Interpretor, deliuered him certain thinges of our holy Catholique faith, to al which he answered, that they vnderstood him well and would becom Christians, and that with a very good wil they should aduance the crosse, in what part or place of the towne it pleased them, for he was for the gouernour *Antho: de Berreo,* who was his Master. Thereupon the said master of the Campe tooke a great crosse, and set it on ende toward the east, and requested the whole Campe to witnesse it and *Domingo de vera* firmed it thus.

It is well and firmly done, and vnderneath, before me Rodrigo Caranca, *Register of the Army.*

The first of May they prosecuted the saide possession and discouery to the towne of *Carapana.* From thence the said Master of the Camp passed to the towne of *Toroco* whose principall is called *Topiawary* beeing fiue leagues farther within the land then the first nation, and well inhabited. And to this principall by meane of the interpretor they gaue to vnderstand that his Maiesty and the said *Corrigidor* commanded them to take the possession of that land, and that they should yeeld their obedience to his Maiesty, and to his Corrigidor, and to the Master of the Campe in his name, and that in token thereof he would place a crosse in the middle of his towne. Whereunto the said *Cassique* answered they should aduance it with a very good will, and that he remained in the obedience of our Lorde the King, and of the saide Gouernour *Antho: de Berreo* whose vassale he would be."*

Formal Possession of Guiana taken by Spain.

This act of possession was no mere fiction. In 1595 Berreo followed it up by a colonizing expedition which started from Spain with 2,000 colonists.

In 1598 a Dutch visitor reported that the Spaniards "have begun, about six days journey to the south of the river Orinoco, at the mountains of Guiana, to make a road through the rocks and hills about 1,600 stadia (200 miles) long and wide enough for five horses to march abreast, and by these means they hope to conquer it."†

Mission work began very early.

Mission work began with the beginning of Spanish settlement. When Domingo de Vera, in 1595, returned from Spain with re-enforcements for Berreo, he brought with him ten clergymen and twelve Franciscan friars. Seven of these went to Santo Thomé and found there *already established* a convent in charge of friars of their own order.‡ In 1617 this convent was transferred from the jurisdiction of the province of Santa Fé to that of the province of Caracas; and on April 25, 1618, the transfer was effected at Santo Thomé.§ Shortly after, in 1618 or 1619, another convent was founded there by the Dominicans.‖

Spread of Spanish occupation.

But it must not be supposed that the occupation of the Spaniards was limited to the Orinoco river, or to the interior, so rich in gold.

In 1618, King James could say:

"It is confessed by all, that the parts of Guiana, where St. Thome was scituate, were planted by Spaniards, who had divers Townes in the same tract, with some Indians intermixed, that are their Vassals."¶

* Raleigh (*sir* W.) Discovery of Guiana; edited by R. H. Schomburgk. London, 1848, pp. 123–126.

† Appendix to Case, ii, 9.

‡ Simon (*fray* P.) Noticias historiales, etc., Cuenca, 1627, pp. 599, 606.

§ Caulin (*friar* A.) Historia corographica, etc., fol. Madrid, 1779, p. 180.

‖ U. S. Commission, Report, i, 54, and authorities there cited.

¶ "A declaration of the Demeanor and Cariage of Sir Walter Raleigh, Knight, as well in his Voyage, as in, and sithence his Returne," p. 30.

Early Spanish exploration and occupation of the Essequibo.

The Essequibo was early explored and occupied by Spain.

Early Spanish exploration and occupation of the Essequibo.

As early as 1553 a Spanish explorer went up the Essequibo with four canoes, pushed up into the interior and crossing the divide, descended by the other slope into another river and so into the Amazon.*

1553. The map which records this expedition, the date of which cannot be much later, gives the courses not only of the Essequibo but of the Cuyuni and Mazaruni as well.* It also marks on the Pomeroon, the Amacura, the Waini and the Barima the name of the Indian Cacique there ruling.†

1591. De Laet, in his "Beschryvinghe van West Indien" says:

> "The Spaniards had here (*i. e.*, in the Essequibo) some people in the year 1591."‡

1596. In 1596, Keymis, Sir Walter Raleigh's lieutenant, while asserting that "further to the eastward than Dessekebe (Essequibo) no Spaniard ever travelled," reports that "in this river, which wee now call Devoritia, the Spaniards doe intend to build them a towne."§

1597. In 1597 the Spaniards were found in the Essequibo by the expedition sent out by Raleigh under the command of Captain Leonard Berrie. Thomas Masham, who accompanied him and wrote the account of the voyage, says, that he there learned from an Indian that in the Essequibo "there were some 300 Spaniards, which for the most part now are destroyed and dead."

He also adds:

> "It was reported that the Spaniardes were gonne out of Desekebe, which was not so. . . . The next night wee had newes brought . . . that there were tenne canoas of Spaniardes in the mouth of Coritine . . . who went along the coast to buy

* U. S. Commission, Report, i, 175, 190.

† Appendix to Case, atlas, map 76.

‡ Laet (Jan de). Beschijvinghe van West Indien. Leyden, 1625, p. 474.

§ Keymis (L.) Relation, etc., London, 1596, fol. B 4 verso.

bread and other victuals for them in Orenoque, Marowgo and Desekebe." *

Early Spanish exploration and occupation of the Essequibo.

Unpublished Spanish documents tell of another expedition in 1597, led by Ibarguen, the camp master of Domingo de Vera.† 1597.

In 1608, Unton Fisher, an Englishman whom Harcourt had left in the Marowyn for exploration, reports that the Spaniards have "cleare left Dissikeebe, and not a Spaniard there."‡ 1608.

In 1615, however, the Duke of Lerma, writing to the Council of the Indies, speaks of the Essequibo *as a place peopled by Spaniards;* and mentions that they are settled there and *engaged in cultivating the soil.*§ 1615.

In 1617 Raleigh, speaking of the Essequibo, referred to it thus: 1617.

> "I also gave them order to send into Desseckebe for I assured them that they could not want Pilotts ther for Orenoke, being the next great river adioyning vnto it, and to which the Spaniards of Orenoke had dayly recourse."‖

As a monument to the early Spanish occupation of the Essequibo, there still exist on the Island of Kykoveral the remains of an ancient fort, attributed formerly to the Portuguese, but which recent investigations clearly show to have been Spanish.¶

Disputed territory was discovered, explored, settled, and possessed by Spain.

The facts which have thus been cited attest the discovery, possession, exploration and settlement of Guiana by Spain: more especially do they show the exploration and settlement of the western part of Guiana, that

---

* Hakluyt (R.) Principal navigations, etc., 1811, iv, 193-194.

† Rodway; *in* Temehri, 1895, Dec., p. 325; *see* also U. S. Commission, Report, iii, 189, foot note.

‡ "Relation of the habitations and other observations of the river of Marwin and the adjoining regions," in Purchas, *Pilgrimes* (London, 1625), iv, 1285.

§ Appendix to Case, ii, 263-4.

‖ Raleigh (*sir* W.) Discovery of Guiana, Schomburgk edition, 1848, pp. 202, 203.

¶ U. S. Commission, Report, i, 185-187; and iii, 190-191.

Disputed Territory was discovered, explored, settled and possessed by Spain.

which comprises the Orinoco and Essequibo rivers and the region lying between.

3.—SPAIN'S EFFECTIVE CONTROL OF GUIANA.

Spain effectually controlled it.

While the above facts might safely be allowed to stand by themselves, the completeness and *effectiveness* of Spanish control in Guiana cannot fail to be emphasized if the ineffectual attempts of other nations to dispossess her be considered. At times these attempts were open, and were attended with bloodshed and loss of life; at other times they were surreptitious, those engaged in them limiting themselves to trading with the Indians and to the quiet occupation of a bit of coast or river bank. All these attempts were unavailing.

Foreign armies, foreign traders, and foreign settlers were all driven from Guiana, and though at times the Spaniards suffered defeat at the hands of these invaders, and though Santo Thomé was more than once taken pillaged and destroyed, yet, in the end, the invaders were invariably repulsed, and Spain remained mistress of the province.

She successfully repelled all invaders.

The strength of Spain in Guiana, her exercise of dominion there by the exclusion of other nations, and her subjugation of the native inhabitants, were facts—facts which in those days England attempted to dispute, but to the truth of which the strongest witnesses are the very Englishmen whom she put forward in that attempt, and who, at that time, represented the strength, the chivalry and the enterprise of that great nation.

Raleigh's expeditions.

Of all foreign adventurers, Raleigh was the most famous. His expeditions were the best planned and the best manned. His ambition, ability and resources were greater than those of any other foreigner who ever attempted to penetrate into the interior of Guiana, and his failure to accomplish this was the most signal of which any record remains. Raleigh's expeditions.

His expedition of 1595 was somewhat in the nature of a preliminary survey. He went quietly up the Orinoco as far as the Caroni, avoiding the Spaniards and intent merely upon reaching the fabled "Manoa del Dorado." In his enterprise he endeavored to enlist the Indians of that region, but he found that they had been so subdued by the Spaniards that they would not lift hand against them except by secret murder. A chief was found ready to guide him to the mines of Guiana, *provided Raleigh would leave in his town men enough to protect it against the Spaniards,* but this Raleigh was unable to do, as it would have required more than his entire force.* 1595.

Of another Indian town he says that ten Spaniards dwelt there; and that the Chief was, therefore, afraid to have anything to do with the English. Finally Raleigh was obliged to abandon his project of getting into the interior, because, having only fifty soldiers, "the rest being labourers and rowers," he could not leave a sufficient guard with proper equipment on the river; for that "without those thinges necessarie for their defence, they shoulde be in daunger of the Spaniardes in my absence."†

In 1596 Keymis visited this region, and talked with the Indian chiefs. From them he heard how they hated the Spaniards, but the Indians refused further intercourse than a little secret talk "least perhaps some Spie might inform the Spaniards thereof, whereby danger would grow to Carapana." Keymis 1596.

Commenting upon this Keymis adds:

---

* Raleigh (*sir* W.) Discovery of Guiana. Schomburgk edition, London, 1848, pp. 92, 93, 98.

† Same, pp. 92, 149.

"By this I perceiued that to stay longer for him . . . . . would be purposelesse." *

Raleigh's expeditions.

Raleigh was never able to get assistance from the natives. In his last expedition he did not even try. Two Englishmen whom he left in Guiana in 1595 to foment friendship for England and hatred towards Spain, came to an untimely end: as soon as the Spaniards heard of them, an order was issued for their arrest; one of them was at once seized, and the other would doubtless have shared his fate had he not already been destroyed by a tiger.

Down on the coast Keymis found further proof of Spanish power over the Indians. Speaking of his experiences with the natives in that quarter he says:

"It was long time before wee could procure them [the Indians] to come neere vs, for they doubted least wee were Spanish."

And he adds that the Indian chief informed him that the Arwacas

"doe for the most part serue and follow the Spanyards."†

From Keymis, also, we have a statement showing the strength of Santo Thomé in 1597, and the character of the fortifications on the island of Faxardo.

Keymis states that on the approach of the Englishmen the Spaniards stationed themselves at the mouth of the Caroni

"to defend the passage to those mines from whence your Oare and white stones were taken the last yeere: Wee all not without griefe see ourselues thus defeated, and our hungry hopes thus made voyde."

Keymis concludes his account thus:

"Sorie I am, that where I sought no excuse, by the Spaniardes being there I found my defeat remedilesse."‡

* Hakluyt (R.) Principal navigations, etc., edited by E. Goldsmid. Edinburgh, 1890, vol. xv, p. 77.

† Same, xv, p. 60.

‡ Same, xv, pp. 69, 70, 80.

Immediately on his first return from Guiana, and planning for a second expedition, Raleigh wrote: Raleigh's expedition.

"For wee are not to goe as Cortez, Pisarro, or the other conquerors against a naked vnarmed people (whose warrs are resembled by some to the childrens play called Iogo di Canne [Juego de Cañas]). *Butt we are to encounter with the Spaniards*, armed in all respectes, and as well practised as ourselves".*

In 1611 he was engaged in preparing another expedition, and in his "Proposals" of that year he undertook to send Keymis with such men 1611.

"as should be able to defend him against the Spaniards inhabiting vpon Orenoke if they offered to assaile him (not that itt is meant to offend the Spaniards there or to beginne any quarrell with them except themselves shall beginne warre).

To knowe what number of men shall be sufficient may itt please your Lordshipps to informe your selves by Captaine More, a servant of Sir John Watts, who came from Orenoke this last spring, and was oftentimes ashore att St. Thome, where the Spaniards inhabite."†

This expedition, however, never took place. It was merged in the final one of 1617.‡ 1617.

This last expedition of 1617 carried 121 pieces of ordnance in one squadron of seven vessels, joined presently by seven more vessels; and 400 men were sent up the Orinoco to Santo Thomé.§

Raleigh noted that no small part of the Spanish strength was due to the ease with which the Commandant of Guiana could obtain reinforcements from Cumaná and the other provinces.‖

The expedition started up the river. Santo Thomé and a stronghold twenty-five miles below it, marked on

---

* Raleigh (*sir* W.) Discovery of Guiana. Schomburgk edition, London, 1848, p. 149.

† Same, pp. 165, 166; Rodway (J.) and Watt (T.) Annals of Guiana. Georgetown, 1888, vol. i, p. 57.

‡ Same, pp. 167 *et seq.*

§ Same, pp. 172–4.

‖ Same, pp. 93, 149, 211-216.

Raleigh's expeditions.

the maps as "old Guayana," were the keys to the whole interior. The Santo Thomé which made Keymis retreat in 1596 was of itself a sufficient protection to the interior. Raleigh in 1595 had pointed out that two small forts on and near the bluff twenty-five miles below, at the place where old Guayana Castle still stands, would close both the river and the country to all commerce, no matter how strong.*

1617.

When he started on his final expedition in 1617, Raleigh believed that the Spaniards had not occupied the latter place. His plan was to land at the lowest and nearest available point on the river, and thence push for the mines, thus avoiding Santo Thomé; but his forces found there a town of 140 houses, a church and two convents, defended by 57 men, well armed and with some ordnance, commanded by the Governor of the Province assisted by a valiant officer, Captain Geronimo de Grados. The English had 400 men. They took the place at the cost of young Raleigh's life; held it twenty-six days; heard that Spanish re-inforcements were approaching; plundered it; burned it, and retreated.†

Raleigh's defeat.

The expedition was ruined. Keymis, who commanded for Raleigh, committed suicide; and Raleigh went back to England, and to the block.‡

The most brilliant commander of England had tried for twenty years to penetrate Guiana. He had failed because the Spaniards held it, and held it too strongly for him.

Dutch witnesses of Spain's control of Guiana.

But witnesses to the strength of the Spaniards in Guiana and to their effective occupation of that province are not confined to Englishmen alone.

Cabeliau, clerk of the Dutch Expedition to the coast

---

* Raleigh (*Sir* W.) Discovery of Guiana. Schomburgk edition, London, 1848, p. 115.

† Same, pp. 210-216.

‡ Same, pp. 217, 222.

of Guayana in 1597–98, describes the strength of the Spaniards at that time as follows:

Dutch testimony as to Spanish control.

"We travelled . . . . up to the place or settlement where the Spaniards are, which is named St. Thomé, whereof Don Fernando de Berreo is Governor and also Marquis of Guiana. . . . . Their strength consists of abont 60 horsemen and 100 musketeers, who daily seek to conquer the gold-land of Guiana."*

Further on Cabeliau says:

"To sum up briefly, there is up that river in the kingdom of Guiana certainly much gold, as we were told by the Indians from there as well as by our Indians here present, and the Spaniards themselves say so; but for people busied with trade it is not feasible to expect any good therefrom unless to that end considerable expeditions were equipped to attack the Spaniards. This is the only means of learning the whereabouts of any gold mines from the Indians; for whosoever are enemies, and bear enmity to the Spaniards, are friends with the Indians, and they hope steadily that they shall be delivered from the Spaniards by the Dutch and English, as they told us." †

Dutch trade to Orinoco prevented by Spain, 1602–3.

Cabeliau's statement with regard to the strength of the Spanish was put to a practical test by the Dutch in 1602–3 when Dutch vessels authorized by the States General attempted to penetrate up that river. But this was "prevented by the multitude of the Spaniards who were found there."‡

Santo Thomé in 1629.

In 1629 a Dutch fleet of a dozen ships, fitted out for a raid, attacked, sacked and burned Santo Thomé, but at once retired, attempting no permanent occupation. At that time Santo Thomé consisted of 130 or 140 houses, a church and a convent.§

Dutch unable to hold Santo Thomé in 1637.

In 1637 the Dutch once again attacked and plundered Santo Thomé, but they were not strong enough to hold

* Appendix to Case, ii, 9.

† Appendix to Case, ii, 10.

‡ U. S. Commission Report, ii, 25, 26.

§ Laet (Jan de) Bechrijvinghe van West Indien. Leyden, 1630, p. 593; *also* his Historie ofte Jaerlyck Verhael, p. 166.

Dutch unable to hold Santo Thomé in 1637.

the city; and the Spanish chronicler of this event states that,

"In their retreat we pursued them to the port, where they embarked, suffering the loss of a great number of their party, as also Flemish and Indians. The small force at our command is well known, but it pleased God to help us, and prevent them establishing themselves here, and so it happened that they retreated, with the loss of life referred to."*

The Spanish Colossus remained firm and unshaken.

A writer of seventy years ago, after pointing out the many defects in Spanish rule and Spanish administration, has, in a word, summed up the situation. He says:

"But notwithstanding all these defects, the Spanish colossus was firm and unshaken; its coasts were ravaged; its seaport towns burned, and its fortresses besieged, but its territory was still intact."†

What has been above set forth relates, in the main, to that region of Guiana which includes the present disputed territory; but it was not there alone that the Spaniards made their presence felt in those early days. In a remonstance, addressed in 1633 by the Dutch West India Company to the States-General, there is a description of *New Spain*, and of Guiana. That description concludes with the following words:

"The country is bounded by the great river of the Amazons, which also is not free from Spanish settlements, as our people have experienced to their damage."‡

Early Dutch attempts to gain foothold ended in failure.

The early attempts of the Dutch to gain a foothold at various points on the coast of Guiana ended invariably in failure.

In 1614 Juan Tostado, Acting Governor of Trinidad, hanged several Flemish seeking to reconnoitre that port; and in company with Antonio de Muxica Buitron, Lieutenant of Guiana, proceeded to the Corentine and there

* Blue Book, 3, 213.

† Mollien (G. T.), Travels in Colombia, 1822–23. London, 1824, p. 124.

‡ "Documents relative to the Colonial History of New York," Vol. I, p. 66; U. S. Commission Report, i, 356.

destroyed the fort and tobacco plantations which the Dutch had established there.*

Early Dutch attempts to gain foothold ended in failure.

Of an attempt in 1615 to found a Dutch settlement on the Cayenne, Major John Scott thus wrote:

"The fifth colony consisted of about 280 Zealanders, with two small ships, landed their men at Cayan, anno 1615, but could not bring the natives to a trade, were often gauled by the Indians, and were at length forced to quit their post. Returned to Zealand the same year.†

In this same year of 1615, the King of Spain issued a general order, directing that the coast of Guiana be cleared of any foreign settlements which might there be found.‡

Speaking of these early attempts at Dutch settlement in Guiana, Professor Burr, in his report to the United States Commission, writes as follows:

"This silence of the English explorers as to Dutch settlement in Guiana cannot weaken the force of the positive Spanish testimony, which makes it certain that as early as 1613, and at the least until 1615, the Dutch were settled on this coast. But, in view of it, it is very unlikely that, save in the Amazon, they were there much earlier, and both the English and the Spanish evidence, as well as the Dutch, suggest that these earliest Dutch settlements may have perished in their infancy, and in part or wholly at Spanish hands."§

Speaking in another place of other Dutch attempts at settlement, Professor Burr writes:

"Their duration, however, was probably but transient. When in 1621 there was created a Dutch West India Company, with monopoly of Dutch commercial and colonial interests on the coasts of America, the only claim for reimbursement mentioned anywhere in the records is that made by the Zeelanders for their 'tobacco plantation on the River Amazon.'"‖

* Appendix to Case, ii, 261, 262.

† U. S. Commission Report, i, 165.

‡ Appendix to Case, ii, 264.

§ U. S. Commission Report, i, 164-165.

‖ U. S. Commission Report, i, 159.

English view of Spanish rights in 1623.

The English view of Spanish rights in Guiana during this period is well illustrated by the consideration given to the protests of the Spanish Ambassador in England against any English settlements in that province. In a document addressed to King James, ascribed conjecturally to 1623, and intended to set forth "Briefe motives" to maintain the right of the English "vnto the river of Amazones and the coast of Guiana," certain English subjects petitioned the King as follows:

"Your Majesty's subjects, with the faire leave and good liking of the native inhabitants, have theis 13 or 14 yeares continuallie remayned in the said River and also in the River of Wiapoco, being upon the same Coaste." "Your Matie hath bine pleased to graunte severall Commissions for these parts, and (wth good advice of your Councell) hath granted two severall letters Pattents the one in the 11th of your Raigne of England, the other, the 17th." "The Count of Gondomer did bouldlie and most confidentlie affirme that his Master had the actuall and present possession of theis parts; whereupon he obtained from your Matie a suspence and stay of all our proceedings for a tyme. And two yeares and a halfe afterward the said Embassadour caused about 300 men to be sent into the River of Amazones, then to beginn the foresaid possession and to destroy the English and Dutch there abideinge."*

Summary of foregoing.

What has been set forth will amply support the statement first made to the effect that Spain was the first discoverer, explorer, possessor and settler of Guiana; and that she held the entire Province effectively against the attempted encroachments of other nations.

It is upon these facts that Venezuela relies to establish the original right of Spain—and of herself as Spain's successor—to the territory now in dispute.

* Calendar of State Papers, Colonial Series, 1574-1660, pp. 36, 37.

IV.—HISTORICAL SKETCH SHOWING DERIVATION OF THE DUTCH-BRITISH TITLE TO ESSEQUIBO.

In 1581 the Dutch renounced their allegiance to the King of Spain, and entered upon a war which finally resulted in their independence in 1648. Dutch revolt against Spain.

Prior to the latter date they had obtained a certain foot-hold on the coast of Guiana, the extent and nature of which will be later considered. By the Treaty of Munster of January 30, 1648,* the right to such possessions as they at that time held was confirmed to them by Spain. Their possessions in Guiana confirmed by Treaty of Munster.

The Dutch West India Company† had, on June 3d Dutch West India Company charter, 1621.

*Appendix to Case, iii, pp. 4-21.

†The Dutch West India Company, modeled after the older Dutch East India Company and after the government of the Netherlands, was made up of five local Chambers—Amsterdam, Zeeland, the Maas (Meuse), Friesland and Groningen, and "the Northern Quarter." In each of these the Chief-Shareholders (*Hoofdparticipanten*) chose a body of Directors (*Bewindhebberen*), who managed the affairs of the Chamber, and who were currently known as the Chamber itself. The policy of the Company as a whole was shaped by a Board, or Committee of Conference, made up of nineteen deputies from these local Chambers, and known as "the Nineteen." Of these the Amsterdam Directors chose eight; Zeeland, four; Maas, Friesland and Groningen, and the Northern Quarter each two; the nineteenth being named by the States-General. The Nineteen, however, was not a body of permanent membership or of stated meetings. It was convened at the will of the Chambers, though with a growing regularity. The Deputies were chosen afresh for its every session; and it dealt only with the topics for deliberation (*Poincten van Beschrijving*) drawn up for it by the Chambers. Its sessions were held alternately at Amsterdam and at the Zeeland capital, Middelburg (six years at the one, then two at the other); and the Chambers of Amsterdam and Zeeland hence bore the honorary designation of "presidial" chambers. Besides the meetings of the Nineteen and of the local boards of Directors of each Chamber, the Chief-Shareholders of each Chamber came together at intervals, mainly for the election of Directors or the consideration of purely financial concerns; and there was also a commission of the Nineteen which sat in The Hague for the conduct of the Company's business at the seat of government. All these bodies have left more or less of record; but the only ones which have proved fruitful for the present research are those of the Nineteen and of the directors of the Zeeland Chamber. Those of the Zeeland Chamber, long in exclusive charge of the Guiana colonies, have been much the most prolific source.—(Note by Professor Burr, U. S. Commission Report, Vol. 2, pp. 38-39).

Dutch West India Company charter, 1621.

1621, been chartered by the States-General of the United Netherlands.*

The nature of the charter, and the extent of territory assigned to the operations of the Company, will appear from the following extract taken from the charter:

"We, therefore, being moved by many different and pregnant considerations, have, after mature deliberation of the Council and for very pressing causes, decided that the navigation, trade, and

*"[The United Provinces] were republics, they were the freest lands in the world, but they were anything but democracies. The governing body was, indeed, differently constituted in the different provinces. In Friesland and Groningen the provincial States were chosen by something closely approaching popular election. In some of the other provinces the nobility, and in one the clergy, enjoyed a greater or less degree of representation. But for the most part the provincial Estates consisted of deputies who represented the magistracies of the cities.

"The municipal councils were, then, in most cases the ultimate authority; and these were, under some limitations, self-electing. Friesland and Groningen excepted, nowhere, virtually, was there any provision for popular representation. The city council chose all the officers of the city, and sent, to represent it in the provincial States, most commonly one or two burgomasters, several councillors, and the pensionary or the secretary. .. The number of persons deputed might be greater or smaller, for in any case each city had but one vote. The States of the province of Holland may best be selected as an illustration. . . . That body consisted of nineteen members; the nobility of the province formed one and were represented by one of their number; and the others were the eighteen chief towns, each represented in the manner already mentioned. The pensionary or advocate of the province presided over their deliberations and arranged their business. Their meetings took place at the Hague. Through this assembly the sovereign powers of the province were exercised, but it should not be forgotten that the sovereignty itself resided in the nineteen members, and not in their deputies; and many of the most important matters of deliberation were subjected, as we shall see, to enormous delays, because the deputies in the provincial States must refer them to their principals, the city councils.

"The seven provinces were independent and sovereign States, but the loose union in which they were joined had as its organ an assembly long familiar in the affairs of Europe under the title of 'The High and Mighty Lords the Lords States General of the United Netherlands.' This assembly was not a sovereign legislative and executive body; rather was it a permanent congress of ambassadors, deputed by the provincial States to represent them in deliberations at the Hague upon common affairs, but with little power of concluding, save with the unanimous consent of the assemblies which deputed them, and of the city magistracies and other ultimate repositories of sovereignty which deputed those

commerce in the West Indies, Africa, and other countries hereafter enumerated, shall henceforth not be carried on otherwise than with the common united strength of the merchants and inhabitants of these lands, and that to this end there shall be established a General Company which, on account of our great love for the common welfare, and in order to preserve the inhabitants of these lands in full prosperity, we shall maintain and strengthen with our assistance, favour and help, so far as the present state and condition of this country will in any way allow, and which we shall furnish with a proper Charter, and endow with the privileges and exemptions hereafter enumerated, to wit :

Dutch West India Company charter, 1621.

I.

That for a period of twenty-four years no native or inhabitant of this country shall be permitted, except in the name of this United Company, either from the United Netherlands or from any place outside them, to sail upon or to trade with the coasts and lands of Africa, from the Tropic of Cancer to the Cape of Good Hope, nor with the countries of America and the West Indies, beginning from the southern extremity of Newfoundland through the Straits of Magellan, Le Maire, and other straits and channels lying thereabouts, to the Strait of Anjan, neither on the North nor on the South Seas, nor with any of the islands situated either on the one side or the other, or between them both ; nor with the Australian and southern lands extending and lying between the two meridians, reaching in the east to the Cape of Good Hope, and in the west to the east end of New Guinea, inclusive."*

Pursuant to the terms of this charter, the Company became at once vested with whatever rights the States-General may have had in Guiana. The trade to that

Company vested with all Dutch rights to Guiana.

assemblies. Each province fixed the form of its representation to suit itself, since the voting was by provinces. A general council of State also existed." (Jameson (J. F.) Willem Usselinx; *in* Amer. Hist. Assn. Papers. New York, 1887, vol. 2, No. 3, pp. 23–25.)

This was meant as an outline of the condition of things at the beginning of the seventeenth century, when the Stadhouderate was temporarily in eclipse. With the addition of that dignity, whose functions, though less important, were not wholly unlike those of the American Presidency, it is substantially correct for the whole history of the republic. (Note by Professor Burr; U. S. Commission Report, ii, 4.)

*Appendix to Case, ii, pp. 1–3.

Company vested all Dutch rights to Guiana.

country, so far as the Dutch were concerned, was thereafter for a long time exclusively in the hands of the Company; and such occupation of Guiana as the Dutch may have had in 1648 was limited to the possessions of the Company itself at that time.

Renewal of Charter, 1647.

The charter of 1621 expired in 1645. On March 22, 1647, the States-General renewed it for another quarter of a century.* The limits remained unchanged and were not restated.†

New Company chartered, 1674.

Towards the close of 1674 this Company, after three further brief renewals of its charter, expired; and a new Company, created by fresh charter in 1674, entered on the inheritance of the old at the beginning of 1675. The territorial limits of the old had included the entire coast of both North and South America; those of the new included, on the mainland of those continents, nothing but "the places of Isekepe [Essequibo] and Bauwmerona [Pomeroon]." The following is taken from the new charter:

Limits: Essequibo and Pomeroon.

Charter, 1674.

"We, therefore, having taken into due consideration that naught can be done, protected, and upheld in the districts hereafter mentioned without the usual aid, assistance, and resources of a General Company . . . . have determined that navigation, trade, and commerce in the districts of West India and Africa and other places hereafter mentioned, shall henceforth be carried on only by the common and united strength of the former shareholders and depositors of the aforesaid Company who are willing and shall be encouraged to do so . . . . and to this end a new General West India Company shall be established which we, out of particular affection for the common weal . . . . shall strengthen with our help, favour and assistance . . . . and provide with a proper Charter and with the following privileges and exemptions:

"To wit, that within the present century and to the year 1700

* Appendix to Case, ii, p. 4.

† U. S. Commission, Report, i, 102.

inclusive, none of the natives or inhabitants of this or any other country, shall be permitted other than in the name of this United Company to sail or trade upon the coasts and lands of Africa, reckoning from the Tropic of Cancer to the latitude of 30 degrees south of the Equator, with all the islands in that district lying off the aforesaid coasts, and particularly the Islands of St. Thomé, Annebon, Isle of Principe, and Fernando Polo, together with the places of Isekepe and Bauwmerona, situated on the continent of America, as well as the Islands of Curaçao, Aruba, and Buonaire. The former limits of the previous grant are to be open to all the inhabitants of our State without distinction, so that they may navigate and trade there as best they like."* Charter, 1674.

This charter had been long in process of creation. As early as June 7, 1669, it was under discussion in the provincial estates of Holland, the limits then suggested being precisely those later adopted. On April 2, 1674, this provincial body submitted to the States-General another draft, in which to Essequibo and Pomeroon was added New Netherland, and also a provision that the new West India Company might retain "such further places and districts on the American mainland as it should take actual possession of by the creation of forts, warehouses, or established trade." In the new draft, however, submitted by the estates of Holland on August 13, 1674, this supplementary clause was omitted.†

The charter of 1674 was renewed at various times; first on November 30, 1700;‡ again on August 8, 1730;§ once more in 1760; and finally on January 1, 1762. Each time the renewal was without change of limits. The Company was dissolved at the close of the year 1791.‖ Charter renewed in 1700, 1730, 1760 and 1762. Company dissolved, 1791.

On the 1st of January, 1792, the States-General as- States-General assume control, 1792.

* Appendix to Case, iii, 22-23.

† U. S. Commission, Report, i, 103, note.

‡ Groot Placaat-Boek, iv, pp. 1338, 1334.

§ Groot Placaat-Boek, vi, pp. 1401-1407.

‖ U. S. Commission, Report, i, 104.

States-General assume control 1792.

sumed control of Demerara and Essequibo. These colonies continued under State control until after the establishment of the Batavian Republic, which in 1795 replaced the government of the States-General.

British occupation 1796–1802.

In April, 1796, Great Britain and the Batavian Republic being at war, an English fleet appeared at Demerara and took possession of that river and of Essequibo. The British occupation continued from 1796 until 1802. In the latter year peace was restored in Europe; and by the Treaty of Amiens Great Britain returned to the Batavian Republic "all the possessions and colonies which belonged to" it, and which had "been occupied or conquered by British forces during the course of the war." *

Treaty of Amiens.

British occupation 1803–1814.

The peace of Amiens proved short-lived; and in June, 1803, war once more broke out in Europe. In September of that year the British again took possession of Essequibo; and this time they remained in occupation, until, by the Treaty of London, of August 13, 1814, the Netherlands finally ceded to Great Britain "the establishments of Demerara, Essequibo and Berbice."

The following is taken from the treaty of cession:

Treaty of London.

"In consideration of the engagements above mentioned, the Prince Sovereign of the Netherlands consents to cede in all sovereignty to His Britannic Majesty the Cape of Good Hope and the establishments of Demerara, Essequibo and Berbice, on condition, however, that the subjects of H. R. H. the Prince Sovereign, who own property in said colonies or establishments, shall be at liberty (saving the regulations which shall be agreed upon in a supplementary convention) to navigate and trade between said establishments and the territories of said Prince Sovereign in Europe." †

Great Britain the successor of the Dutch.

Such rights as Great Britain has to-day in Guiana, she has acquired by virtue of the Treaty of London, and

* From this restoration were excepted the island of Trinidad and the Dutch possessions in the island of Ceylon.

† For treaty in full, see Appendix to Case, iii, 43–48.

as the successor of the Dutch. It is the province of the Tribunal to determine the extent of those rights so far as they relate to the territory between the Orinoco and the Essequibo rivers.

Great Britain the successor of the Dutch.

Having set forth thus broadly: first, the basis of Venezuela's title to the entire disputed territory, and second the derivation of British title to that portion of Guiana which admittedly is hers, it becomes necessary to set forth in more detail the special facts upon which Venezuela relies for the substantiation of her claims.

Purpose of succeeding chapter.

This is the purpose of the succeeding chapter.

V.—EARLY DUTCH RELATIONS WITH GUIANA. 1597-1648.

It is proposed to consider first the early relations of the Dutch with Guiana; and then to define the extent of Dutch possessions in the Essequibo on January 30, 1648, on which date in the shape of the Treaty of Munster, the Netherlands received from Spain a quit-claim deed for what they then held.

Early relations of Dutch with Guiana, and extent of their possessions on January 30, 1648.

It would be difficult to formulate a clearer or more concise statement of these early relations than that contained in Professor Burr's report to the United States Commission.

The following is an extract from that report:

Prof. Burr's statement.

"The national existence of the Dutch began with the year 1579. In 1581 they formally renounced their allegiance to the King of Spain. Till then, however rebellious, they had been his subjects. Such title as their exploration or commerce could give was the King of Spain's title. Even the assertion of their independence brought with it no claim to lands outside the Netherlands; nor is there reason to suppose that the Dutch yet dreamed of such a claim. The King of Spain, indeed, was now their foe; and they knew well that he was not King of Spain alone. That realm but gave him his most familiar title. He was lord of Portugal as well, lord of the fairest lands of Italy, lord of the Mediterranean isles, lord still of half the Netherlands; but his proudest title was that of lord of the Indies. Thence he drew the treasures with which he dazzled and bullied the world. America was but a Spanish island. No other European State, save Portugal, had yet planted a colony on its shores; and Portugal was now one of the dominions of the King of Spain. Whatever cloud might rest on the exclusiveness of his right by discovery to the northern half of the continent, none now obscured his title to the southern. That this title had, further, the explicit approval of the Pope of Rome was hardly likely to give it added sanctity in the eyes of Protestant powers; but as yet that title, however its basis might

Prof. Burr's statement.

be questioned, was not attacked from any quarter. If Drake, the Englishman, and his fellow-freebooters made the Caribbean seas their own and took tribute of the treasures of Peru, it was confessedly but a raid into an enemy's territory; land they neither sought nor claimed.

Yet if the English, though in name at peace with the King of Spain, might thus singe his beard on these far shores, so with double warrant might the Dutch. And such, not conquest or settlement, was, so far as the records show, the aim of the first Dutch project for a visit to these coasts.(pp. 134–135.)

* * * * * * * * * *

In March of 1595, the Estates of Zeeland granted freedom of convoy to one Balthazar de Moucheron for a cargo of goods to the Spanish Indies. This was, of course, for peaceful traffic, and his objective point would seem to have been the island of Margarita, long the leading Spanish entrepôt for these parts. It was just at this time that by a Zeeland ship, not impossibly this one, was discovered just south of that island of Margarita, on the Spanish mainland of South America, the remarkable deposit of salt which for years made Punta de Araya (or Punta del Rey, as the Dutch more often called it) one of the leading destinations of Dutch commerce; and the established route thither led along the whole length of the Guiana coast. In the same year there is record of a venture to Santo Domingo by a union of Holland and Zeeland merchants. In the following year we hear of another Zeeland expedition to the Spanish Indies, and there were not improbably many similar enterprises not mentioned in the records, for it was only when freedom from convoy dues was sought that legislative action was needed, and even after the establishment of the admiralties no ship need seek a commission unless it chose.

It was in 1591 or 1592, according to his own statement, that William Usselinx, the inspirer above all others of the West India trade, returning from the Spanish islands, began his agitation in the Netherlands in behalf of Dutch trade with South America. I have already spoken of Jan de Laet's statement as to Dutch trade with the Spaniards on the Orinoco even before Raleigh's expedition of 1595. Yet it is improbable that this trade to the West Indies antedates 1594; for to that year is ascribed the beginning of direct trade with Brazil, and all tradition and probability make Brazil the earliest, as it was the nearest, destination of Dutch trade in America. Prof. Burr's statement.

It will be noted that as yet, so far as the records show, the trade is with recognized Spanish settlements, and therefore not of a sort to create a territorial title. Of Guiana or of direct trade with the Indians, there is thus far no mention.

But in 1596 there was published in England a book which set the imagination of all Europe on fire—Sir Walter Raleigh's *Discoverie of Guiana*. It called universal attention to the wealth of these coasts and to the advantages of trade with the natives. The Netherlands were not the last to feel its influence. Already before the end of 1596 one begins to hear in the records of the States-General of the trade with the West Indies; and on March 24, 1597, the merchant-banker Hans van der Veken, of Rotterdam, was granted a commission for two vessels, "manned with Germans and other foreigners, to go to the coast of Guinea [in Africa], Peru and the West Indies, and there to trade and bargain with the savages," this commission "containing also request to all princes and potentates to let these ships and their crews pass freely and in peace thither and return again to these provinces." Guiana is not yet mentioned; but, in the children's phrase, we are growing warm. On September 3 of this same year (1597) the States-General were requested by Gerrit Bicker and his associates, merchants of Amsterdam, "who have it in mind to equip two ships, so as to send them to a certain coast and haven of *America Peruana*, being a place where never any from these [Nether]lands have been, and which is also not held by the Spaniards or the Portuguese," to grant them freedom of convoy both going and coming, "and this for two full voyages, if so be that God Almighty should be pleased to bless their first voyage as they hope,—and this out of regard to the great sums they will lay out on this voyage and the risk therein lying." Whereupon it was resolved to grant them the desired convoy "to a certain coast and haven of *America Peruana*, provided that they shall lade in the aforesaid ships no forbidden goods, and that they shall further be bound, on their return, to bring satisfactory evidence that never anybody from these lands has traded to the aforesaid haven, and shall make true report in the meeting of the States-General of their experiences, with specification of the places where they have been and have carried on their trade." And "it is

Prof. Burr's statement.

the understanding," goes on the record, "that like freedom shall be granted to others who shall likewise desire to go to other unknown havens." "But this," ends this significant passage, "the deputies of Zeeland declared themselves uninstructed to grant."

The encouragement was not lost; for but three months later, on December 15, 1597, Jan Cornelisz. Leyn, of Enkhuisen, and his partners, having it in mind with two ships "to sail to the land of Guiana, situate in the realm of Peru," sought freedom of convoy for their first six voyages, both going and returning. Whereupon it was voted to grant their request, but only for the two voyages "which they have it in mind to make with their two ships to the unknown and unnavigated havens of America, to wit, to the land of Guiana, situate in the Kingdom of Peru, as herein specified;" and this upon precisely the same conditions as to lading and report as in the preceding case. And a week later, on December 23, the Estates of Holland voted aid toward the arming of this expedition "to Guiana, in the Kingdom of Peru."

"*Het Landt van Guiana gelegen in het Coninckryck van Peru:*" clearly we have in these expeditions the very earliest Dutch voyages to the Guiana coast. And luckily, to make the matter doubly sure, we have left us from one of these voyages, and that the first, the stipulated final report to the States-General. At least, there is no reason to doubt that the ship's clerk, Cabeliau, whose "report concerning the unknown and unsailed course [*voiage*] of America, from the river Amazon as far as the island of Trinidad," still rests in the archives of the States-General, and who sailed from Holland in a squadron of two ships on December 3, 1597, was the scribe of this expedition to "America Peruana."

* * * * *

They were able to report that "in this voyage we have discovered, found, and navigated more than twenty-four rivers, many islands in the rivers, and various havens besides, which have hitherto neither been known in these provinces nor sailed to therefrom; nay, more, were before our voyage unknown to any map or geographer." And to this statement, Cabeliau, "as clerk of this expedition," makes affidavit. It was the certificate demanded by the States-General, and its validity was conceded, for on October 19, 1599, the freedom of convoy conditioned upon it was without protest awarded by the States-General to Gerrit Bicker and Company, "having made the voyage to America Peruana," as already on August 11 it had been to their colleagues "returned from Guiana, in the Kingdom of Peru."

By these acts the supreme political authority of the Netherlands becomes a witness that the coast of Guiana was theretofore unvisited by the Dutch. An investigator of political titles may well be content with such evidence. Nor is there, so far as I can find, the slightest reason to question its truth.*

This admirable account of early Dutch relations with Guiana, with what else we know on the subject, makes it clear that the object of those early voyages to Guiana, was, in the first place to harass the Spaniards,† and, in the second place, to gain profit by trade and

Dutch sought only to trade and plunder.

* U. S. Commission, Report, i, 134, 135, 139-143, 144-145.

† Regarding the request of skipper Jan Corneliss. Leyen, citizen of Enkhuizen, both for himself and in the name and on behalf of his Company, that in furtherance of their projected voyage to Guiana in the Kingdom of Peru, they be granted assistance by the loan of eight bronze guns, to wit, four of a weight of thirteen or fourteen hundred, and the other four of about two thousand pounds apiece, with all ammunition belonging thereto, for the defence of the ships, on like conditions as have been graciously granted to other laudable sea-voyages, it was Resolved as hereinafter follows:

The Estates of Holland and Westfriesland, having considered the petition and request made in this matter, have resolved that, in furtherance of navigation, the merchants petitioners, for their projected voyage, to be made with two ships to the land of Guiana situate in the realm of Peru, shall be assisted by the credit of the State for two pieces of ordnance, to be borrowed by the petitioners from the cities, each not to exceed two thousand pounds in weight. [Appendix to Case, ii, 5-6.]

* * * * *

It should perhaps be remembered that it was in this year 1599 that there sailed forth from the Zeeland port of Flushing the Dutch armada under Pieter van der Does, which, after taking a town in the Canaries and avenging at the Isle de Principe that unsuccessful enterprise of Balthazar de Moucheron in 1598 which Berg van Dussen Muilkerk calls the "earliest attempt at colonization from out the Netherlands," sent seven or eight of its ships across the Atlantic to ravage the coast of Brazil. They returned, with great booty of sugar, in the following year. [*Note by Prof. Burr in U. S. Commission Report, Vol. 1, p. 147.*]

* * * * *

Having, off and on for more than twenty-five years, as set forth in an earlier memorial to Your Princely Highness, sailed the seas to various places, namely, to Guinea, to the West Indies, and lastly with Commandeur Spilbergen through the strait of Magellan along the coast of Chili and Peru and around the world, I think I have during that time observed the right way of attacking the Spaniards where they are weakest and feeblest, as follows. [*Extract from memorial of C. J. Vianen of Jan. 25, 1621, in Appendix to Case, ii, 17.*]

plunder. Settlement upon Spanish soil, or the acquisition of territorial rights was hardly thought of.*

Early Dutch trade.

The trade then begun continued with more or less regularity during the early years of the 17th century, during which time Dutch vessels sailed along the Guiana coast, and ascended some of its rivers. They were at times driven off by the Spaniards,† but at other times they were successful in capturing Spanish booty, or in

* In the matter of the request of the Burgomaster of Middelburg, Adriaen ten Haeft, setting forth how that in the preceding year, 1598, at heavy cost to himself, he caused to be investigated on the continent of America many different rivers and islands,—and how that in this voyage were discovered various coasts and lands where one could do notable damage to the King of Spain,—and how that he is well minded to send out again two ships, in order, in the country's behalf, to discover certain places, a thing which can not be done so effectively with seafaring folk alone. Wherefore, and in view of the fact that in Holland for the encouragement of exceptional enterprises of this sort great favor is shown to the promoters of such voyages, such as the providing them with cannon, powder, and soldiers, he doth petition that there be granted to his ships from sixteen to twenty experienced soldiers, among them a good Commandant, and doth engage that he will himself provide their rations. Whereupon the representative of the nobility gave verdict that commerce ought here to receive the same favor as in Holland, and that therefore it ought to be learned through the deputies there [*i. e.*, to the States-General] what is done in Holland in this behalf, in order to be able to do the same here; the deputies of Middelburg, however, grant soldiers to the number of 16; those of Zierikzee likewise, to the number of 12, on half wages, subject to the approval of their constituents; those of Goes, Tholen, Flushing and Vere promise that they will send in at once their report to their town-councils on this point and that the councils will find out what is done in Holland in such cases. [*Extract from proceedings of Zeeland Estates, Nov.* 20, 1599, in Appendix to Case, ii, 12–13.]

Sixthly, regarding the opinion sometimes advanced, that notable profits might be obtained through diverse products and fruits which might be found or raised on the mainland of America, between Brazil on the east and the river Orinoco on the west, in and about the river Amazon.

I answer, that several of our Netherlanders have as yet attained little by the aforesaid means, although up to now they engage there in peaceful trade; and if an attempt were made with superior force to gain the land there and by such cultivation introduce the products of Brazil and the West Indies, the Spaniards would beyond doubt seek forcibly to prevent this, the more so as thereby their navigation to Brazil and the West Indies would be impeded. It therefore is my opinion that, in view of the imminent danger of war, little can be achieved there. [*From memorial of C. J. Vianen, Jan.* 25, 1621, in Appendix to Case, ii, 17.]

† Dutch vessels attempting to pass up the Orinoco in 1602–3, were

quietly trading with the natives at places from which the Spaniards were at the moment absent. Early Dutch trade.

The earliest date at which Dutch settlement in Guiana is known is 1613.* In that year they were established in the Corentyn; possibly also in the Amazon, the Wia- Earliest Dutch Settlements.

"prevented by the multitude of Spaniards whom they found there." [U. S. Commission Report, ii, 26].

* * * * *

To all this evidence drawn from other sources should be added that, positive and negative, of the English colonizers, Leigh, Harcourt, and their fellows, whose ventures about the Wiapoco were in precisely the region where Dutch settlements are earliest vouched for by the Spanish papers. Yet, though we have from these undertakings several reports of one sort or another, and though evidence of rival Dutch enterprises would unquestionably have been of value in allaying the hesitation caused by the Spanish sympathies of King James, we find in them no mention of Dutch settlements outside the Amazon. Harcourt in 1608 made a careful exploration of the coast as far west as the Marowyn, and in his detailed *Relation* (printed in 1613, and reprinted in Purchas's Pilgrimes, 1625, vol. iv, pp. 1267-1283), he expressly says (p. 1278 of Purchas):

. . . I took possession of the Land, by Turfe and Twigge, in behalfe of our Sovereigne Lord King James: I took the said possession of a part, in name of the whole Continent of *Guiana*, lying betwixt the rivers of *Amazones*, and *Orenoque*, not being actually possessed, and inhabited by any other Christian Prince or State; wherewith the Indians seemed to be well content and pleased.

The territory granted him by the English King's charter stretched from the Amazon to the Essequibo. [U. S. Commission Report, i, 161.]

* This silence of the English explorers as to Dutch settlement in Guiana can not weaken the force of the positive Spanish testimony, which makes it certain that as early as 1613, and at least until 1615, the Dutch were settled on this coast. But, in view of it, it is very unlikely that, save in the Amazon, they were there much earlier; and both the English and the Spanish evidence, as well as the Dutch, suggest that these earliest Dutch settlements may have perished in their infancy, and in part or wholly at Spanish hands.

To these must be added the testimony of the later Englishman, Major John Scott, who, not far from 1670, in his account of the colonization of Guiana, wrote thus of what he thought the earliest Dutch settlement:

"The fifth colony consisted of about 280 Zealanders, with two small ships, landed their men at Cayan, anno 1615, but could not bring the natives to a trade; were often gauled by the Indians, and were at length forced to quit their post. Returned to Zealand the same year."—[U. S. Commission Report, i, 164-165.]

Teodoro Claessen, resident in Amsterdam outside the old "Haarlemmer Poort," at the sign of the town of Leyden, is establishing a settlement on the River Viapoco, and another on the River Caena (Cayenne), which have been started with a hundred men, divided between the two settlements, which are situated two degrees one from the other. Here the settlers collect a species of silk found on the tobacco plant, and "palo de litre," red with black spots. [Blue Book, Venezuela No. 3 (1896), p. 206.]

poco, the Cayenne, and in one or two of the neighboring rivers; but that on the Corentyn was the westernmost.*

Destroyed by the Spaniards.

As has already been shown, however, these settlements, whatever may have been their exact nature, number or location, were temporary. As soon as the Spaniards learned of them they attacked them, and drove them from Guiana.†

Truce of 1609.

In 1609 Spain and the Netherlands made a truce for twelve years. Article III of this provides that "Chacun demeurera saisi et jouira effectuellement des Pais, Villes, Places, Terres et Seigneuries qu'il tient et possède à present, sans y être troublé durant la dite tréve; en quoi on entend comprendre les Bourgs, Villages, Hameaux et plat Pais qui en dependent."‡

* From dispatches of the government of Trinidad and Spanish Guayana, reprinted by Great Britain from the Spanish archives of the Indies, we learn of a certainty that by June of 1613 the Dutch were established in the Corentyn, and, though they were driven from there the next year by the Spaniards, were alleged to have already three or four more settlements between the Amazon and the Orinoco—four from the Wiapoco to the Orinoco, says a later letter of the same year. Two of these, according to a letter of the year 1615, were on the Wiapoco and the Cayenne, having been established in 1614 (so the confused passage seems to mean) by Theodoor Claessen of Amsterdam—that on the Wiapoco, according to another letter, by two merchants of Flushing. It is probable that these others were on neighboring rivers, that on the Corentyn being the westernmost. [U. S. Commission, Report, i, 159–160.]

On the map of Jan de Laet, first published in 1625, and probably drafted in 1624 (De Laet's preface is dated November 15, 1624), there appear along the coast and rivers east and west of the Wiapoco and Cayenne, as well as on these streams themselves, a number of the tiny circles which elsewhere on this map indicate villages, European or native. To most of them no names are attached, and they indicate possibly Indian towns, possibly settlements; but it is noticeable that the westernmost are on the Corentyn. (They are oddly retained, with no additions, in the maps of Blaeuw.) Quite apart from this, the interpretation of which is doubtful, it is highly probable that it was the westernmost settlement which would most attract Spanish notice and Spanish hostility; and this seems from the Spanish documents to have been just the case with that on the Corentyn. After the colony on the Essequibo is known to be established, we find all Spanish aggression directed against that. [U. S. Commission, Report, i, 160, note.]

† Supra, pp. 50–51.

‡ Treaty of Antwerp, April 9, 1609; Dumont, *Traités*, vol. v. pt. ii, p. 99.

The Twelve Years' Truce with Spain, which in 1609 went into effect, embodied the provisions discussed by Usselinx. The Dutch might no

This truce stopped the formation of the Dutch West India Company, incipient steps towards which had been taken.*

Dutch West India Company chartered 1621.

In 1621, however, upon the expiration of the truce, the company was chartered;† and the trading theretofore carried on by the Dutch was thereafter controlled exclusively by the company.‡

First Dutch trade in Essequibo, 1626.

The year 1626 brings us to the first mention of Dutch trade with the Essequibo.§

As has already been shown, the Spaniards had had occupation of this river but a few years before. They

---

longer trade to the Spanish ports in the Indies, but were free to traffic, even there, with "all other princes, potentates, and peoples." To the Spaniards this can hardly have implied a permission to found colonies; but the Dutch, at least in private, were hardly likely to share this view, and in 1614 we find both the States-General and the provincial Estates of Holland seeking to encourage discovery and settlement by general provisions granting to the finders a temporary monopoly of trade. That such enterprises were, however, not wholly safe may be inferred from the fact that in 1618 the Zeelander Jan de Moor and his partners asked permission to arm their ships engaged in trade with the West Indies, and that the government was concerned to protect the truce is shown by its granting this only under pledge that they should not be used except in self-defense. [U. S. Commission, Report, i, 157-158.]

* Jameson (J. F.), Willem Usselinx. *In* American Hist. Assn. Papers. 8°, New York, 1887, vol. ii, p. 46.

† Appendix to Case, iii, 1-3.

‡ In June, 1621, the truce with Spain having now expired, there came at last into existence the long-projected Dutch West India Company. Its charter granted it monopoly of trade over all the coasts of America, both Atlantic and Pacific, not to mention West Africa, the islands, and the Antarctic continent, and this without a suggestion of frontier within these bounds. All existing Dutch colonies on these coasts passed, therefore, into its hands. The only claim for reimbursement which finds mention in the official records is one made by the Zeelanders for their "tobacco-plantation on the Amazon." Of other establishments on the South American coast nothing is heard. [U. S. Commission, Report, i, 177.]

§ And at last, on November 26, 1626, we find what I believe the earliest mention in extant records of any Dutch establishment on the Essequibo:

The committee on wares is authorized to make up a suitable cargo to the Amazons for the yacht *Arnemuyden*.

Resolved, To send with the aforesaid yacht *Arnemuyden* 20 ripening youths, in order to land them in the Amazon, the Wiapoco, or the Essequibo—wherever the folk of our Chamber may be found—for the purpose of being employed there. And each of them shall be granted 2, 3,

had erected a fort on the island subsequently known as Kykoveral; and a Spanish colony had, as late as 1615, been engaged here in the cultivation of the soil.*

First Dutch trade to Essequibo, 1626.

The river having been temporarily vacated by the Spaniards, the Dutch could enter there for trade with the natives; and towards the close of 1626 there is mention in the records of the Dutch West India Company of men sent "to lie in the river Essequibo."†

In 1632 Company decided to abandon Essequibo.

Trade, however, did not prosper here, and in 1632 the Nineteen [the governing body of the Company] decided to abandon it,‡ as they had already abandoned, in 1631, the settlement on the Cayenne.§

Jan Van der Goes, who had been in charge on the Essequibo, returned home with those who had accompanied him; and it looked as though Essequibo would be definitely given up. On April 8, 1632, however, the

---

or 4 guilders a month, according to their capacities. [U. S. Commission, Report, i, 179-180; see, also, *same*, ii, 42.]

Thereafter nothing more in 1627. But from these brief items out of the first year of its known existence I think it possible, if due weight be given to what is omitted as well as to what is said, to draw with safety two or three important inferences. First, that the establishment in the Essequibo antedates May, 1626. Second, that so late as 1627, it was still a trading post rather than a settlement, with not so much as a fort yet erected. Third, that its commander, as yet a mere agent without a title, had in August, 1627, not yet completed the third year of his service. It is of course possible to reconcile all these with a longer Dutch occupation; but, when taken in connection with the absence of all authentic evidence for their earlier presence in that river and with the purpose of the West India Company, so clearly implied in September, 1624, to plant new establishments on this coast, I think it not rash to conjecture that Jan van der Goes was at the head of the first Dutch occupation of the Essequibo, and that the beginning of that occupation was in or about the year 1625. [U. S. Commission, Report, i, 181.]

* Supra, p. 43.

† *December* 12, 1626. Johannes Beverlander is taken into the service of the Company for three years, to lie in the river of Essequibo along with Jan Adriaansz. van der Goes; and that for twenty-one guilders a month. [Appendix to Case, ii, 19; see *also* entries of Nov. 26 and Dec. 10 of that year.]

‡ Nederlandsche Jaerboeken, 1750, p. 1494.

§ Nederlandsche Jaerboeken, 1751, p. 1090.

Zeeland Chamber of the Company voted not to abandon it,* and the trade was therefore continued.

Unprofitableness of Essequibo and its demoralized condition.

Still the Essequibo did not pay; and on April 16, 1637, there was again discussion in the Zeeland Chamber as to its profitableness; and the matter was referred to the Committee on Commerce.†

On August 17, 1637, the Zeeland Chamber adopted the following resolution:

> Inasmuch as Jan van der Goes had written from Essequibo that he, with all the folk who were there with him, was minded to come home by the first ship, it was some time ago resolved to send thither in the place of the said Van der Goes, by the ship *de Jager*, Cornelis Pieterz. Hose; and on account of the great demoralization of the folk and their wish to come home, it is resolved that they shall be allowed to come home, and the colony provided anew with five-and-twenty other respectable persons, from whom the Company may receive more service and more edifying withal. And Confraters Lonissen and Van Pere are by a majority vote made a committee to engage the aforesaid persons, being requested to look for the discreetest persons, so far as shall be possible.‡

Thus did this Dutch trading post in the Essequibo continue oscillating between life and death during the few years which preceded the Treaty of Munster. During all of those years it was a trading post and nothing more; § its sole article of commerce was annato dye; ‖ and the Dutch occupation, such as it was, was limited exclusively to the Island of Kykoveral.¶

The Treaty of Munster of January 30, 1648, ended

* On the report of Messrs. de Moor and Eltsdyck, after speaking with Van der Goes, it was resolved not to abandon the colony at Essequibo. [Appendix to Case, ii, 19; *see*, also, note 2 on same page.]

† The Committee on Commerce and Finance was instructed to inspect and determine whether the trade to Essequibo is profitable to the Company or not, in order at an early day to make report, so as to know whether the wares for which they ask shall be ordered made or not. [Appendix to Case, ii, 20.]

‡ Appendix to Case, ii, 20.

§ Appendix to Case, ii, 27.

‖ U. S. Commission, Report, ii, 104–108, 110–112.

¶ That its center, if not its sole seat, was the island at the junction of Mazaruni and Cuyuni is, however, made nearly certain by several con

Treaty of Munster.

the war between Spain and the revolted Netherlands. By Article V of that Treaty the Netherlands obtained from Spain a title to what they at that time held upon the coasts of America. That treaty fixed the boundary of Dutch dominion at that time. British rights to-day, so far as the territory in dispute is concerned, are what Dutch rights were two hundred and fifty years ago—no more.

The following is a translation of Articles V and VI of the Treaty of Munster:

V.—The navigation and trade to the East and West Indies, shall be kept up according, and conformably to the grants made or to be made for that effect; for the security whereof the present treaty shall serve, and the Ratification thereof on both sides, which shall be obtained: and in the said treaty shall be comprehended all potentates, nations, and people, with whom the said Lords the States, or members of the East and West-India Companies in their name, within the limits of their said grants, or in friendship and alliance. And each one, that is to say, the said Lords the King and States respectively, shall remain in possession of and enjoy such lordships, towns, castles, fortresses, commerce and countries of the East and West Indies, as well as of Brazil, and on the coasts of Asia, Africa and America respectively, as the said Lords the King and States respectively hold and possess, in this being specially comprised the spots and places which the Portuguese since the year 1641, have taken from the said Lords the States and occupied; comprising also the spots and places which the said Lords the States hereafter without infraction of the present treaty shall come to conquer and possess. And the directors of the East and West India Companies of the United Provinces, as also the servants and officers high and low, the soldiers and seamen actually in the service of either of the said Companies, or such as have been in their service, as also such

siderations. In the first place, there is found nowhere in later records any tradition of another site or of a removal. In 1764 the Zeeland Chamber declared to the States-General that "from all old time" the fort had been at this place. Again, the island was the only natural stronghold of its sort. It was, moreover, probably suggested by a prior occupation—an occupation leaving a tangible inheritance in solid stone walls which to the end were utilized in the Dutch constructions here, and which in part remain to this day. [U. S. Commission, Report, I, 185.]

who in this country or within the district of the said two companies, continue yet out of the service, but who may be employed afterwards, shall be and remain to be free and unmolested in all the countries under the obedience of the said Lord the King in Europe; and may sail, traffic and resort, like all the other inhabitants of the countries of the said Lords and States. Moreover it has been agreed and stipulated, That the Spaniards shall keep their navigation to the East Indies, in the same manner they hold it at present, without being at liberty to go further; and the inhabitants of those Low Countries shall not frequent the places which the Castilians have in the East Indies. Treaty of Munster.

VI.—And as to the West Indies, the subjects and inhabitants of the kingdoms, provinces and lands of the said Lords, the King and States respectively, shall forbear sailing to, and trading in any of the harbours, places, forts, lodgments or castles, and all others possessed by the one or the other party, viz. the subjects of the said Lord the King shall not sail to, or trade in those held and possessed by the said Lords and States, nor the subjects of the said Lords and States sail to or trade in those held and possessed by the said Lord the King. And among the places held by the said Lords the States, shall be comprehended the places in Brazil, which the Portuguese took out of the hands of the States, and have been in possession of ever since the year 1641, as also all the other places which they possess at present, so long as they shall continue in the hands of the said Portuguese, anything contained in the preceding article notwithstanding.

Effect of Treaty.

The effect of this treaty was twofold: on the one hand it conferred upon the Dutch a title to territory which before belonged to Spain: on the other hand it constituted an engagement on the part of the Netherlands that, as against Spain, and at the cost of Spain, the Dutch would acquire nothing more than they then possessed.

It will serve to define and narrow the issues which subsequent events present, if, before proceeding to their consideration, the result of the examination thus far be repeated in a few words.

Situation at date of Treaty of Munster.

At the date of the Treaty of Munster the situation was briefly this:

Situation at date of Treaty of Munster.

Spain had discovered and explored America: she had discovered, explored, taken possession of, and settled Guiana: she held undisputed control of the Orinoco and of that coveted interior whose famed wealth had been the cause of so many foreign expeditions uselessly undertaken, and of so much blood uselessly spilt: the key to that interior was in her hands—alone: into the great interior Cuyuni Mazaruni basin she had pushed her roads and extended her conquests; and the entrance—the only entrance—to it, over the gentle rolling savannas of the Orinoco, was in her keeping: the Essequibo itself she had settled, cultivated, fortified: for the moment she had left its mouth unoccupied, thus permitting the Dutch to trade there: upon the restoration of peace she gave them a title to territory which up to that time they had held as mere trespassers.

The extent of the grant.

The extent of this grant cannot be difficult to define: the entire Dutch colony, if indeed it might be dignified by such a name, consisted of a body of two or three dozen unmarried employés of the West India Company, housed in a fort on a small island, and engaged in traffic with the Indians for the dyes of the forest: at the time when the treaty was signed, they were not cultivating an acre of land.* This and an establishment on the Berbice were the only Dutch settlements in Guiana in 1648. Neither then, nor at any time prior thereto, had the Dutch occupied or settled a foot of ground west of their Essequibo post.†

* *The only other avocation mentioned is that of fishing:* one Jan van Opstall, an employé of the Company in Essequibo, in 1644, complained of the loss of a finger while fishing for the Company, and asked compensation, but the Company could not find this in the contract. The fishing was probably for the food supply of the post—as often later. [U. S. Commission, Report, i, 192.]

† Such as it was, the post on the Essequibo remained in 1648, as it had always been, the westernmost establishment of the Dutch on this coast, and was now, with the exception of Berbice, their only Guiana colony. [U. S. Commission, Report, i, 193.]

VI.—HISTORY OF THE ESSEQUIBO DUTCH POST. 1648–1674.

Dutch West India Charter renewed 1647.

The charter of the Dutch West India Company having expired in 1645, was in 1647 renewed for 25 years more.*

Privateering, the Company's principal source of revenue.

But the West India Company was not founded for the sake of Guiana: that region always constituted its most insignificant field.† Its main business was privateering.‡ The peace with Spain therefore took from it its principal source of revenue; and the company, after the peace of Westphalia (Treaty of Munster), found itself in great danger of coming to an end.§

Discouragement of the Company.

The care of the Essequibo post was in the hands of the Zeeland Chamber of the Company, and for some years they struggled along hardly keeping their heads above water. The hope of recovering Brazil sustained them; but when that hope was gone, the company was driven to desperate expedients to keep the trade of Essequibo alive.

---

* In thinking the charter "reaffirmed in 1637" the English Blue Book is in error. Granted for 24 years, it did not expire till 1645. Even then it was not at once renewed, for its friends sought strenuously the consolidation of the West India Company with the East, whose charter had also just run out. It was not until July 4, 1647, that the States-General promulgated the intelligence that on March 20 preceding they had prolonged for another quarter-century the charter of the West India Company. The limits were unchanged, and are not restated. [U. S. Commission, Report, i, 102.]

† Note by Prof. Burr.—Even of their colonies it was by no means the chief. New Netherland by actual figures grew as much in five years as Essequibo in a hundred.

‡ Reprisals on Spanish commerce were the great object of the West India Company. . . . The Spanish prizes, taken by the chartered privateers, on a single occasion in 1628, were almost eighty-fold more valuable than the whole amount of exports from New Netherlands for the four preceding years.—[Bancroft (G.) History of the United States, 4th ed., Boston, 1889, ii, 277–278.]

§ With the conclusion of a lasting peace with Spain and with the renewal for another quarter century of the Dutch West India Company's charter, one might look for a rapid colonial development. But the company was now robbed of the privateering which had been its leading source of revenue, and bankrupted by the long and fruitless struggle for Brazil. [U. S. Commission, Report, i, 193.]

Coast thrown open to colonization.

In 1656 they determined to try the result of throwing the coast open to colonization. The preamble of the resolution by which this act was accomplished is, of course, merely formal; yet it records the disappointment of the company; and serves to show the little that had been accomplished toward developing the Essequibo. This preamble and the introductory resolution are as follows:

Whereas the directors of the Zeeland Chamber of the West India Company, for many years, by all conceivable means and ways, both by its, the Chamber's own means, and by contracting with private persons, have tried, not only to increase its trade and commerce from here to the coasts and islands situate under the charter, but also and especially have made it their aim to further the colonization and agriculture of the aforesaid lands, and yet without such success, results, and fruits as they could have hoped,

Therefore, inasmuch as they have found by careful observation and long experience, that not only the islands lying in their district but also the mainland coasts, and especially the Wild Coast, extending from the river Amazon to . . . degrees northward, are of such situation and soil that one can there cultivate, plant, raise, and gather everything which it has been possible to cultivate and gather in the famous regions of Brazil, yet that there are needed, for the greater increase of population and agriculture, not only persons of reasonable means, skill, and experience, but also all others of lesser condition and ability; they are disposed to offer, and do hereby offer, with the knowledge and approval of the States General of the United Netherlands and of the General Chartered West India Company, in order thereby to encourage each and everyone, these following conditions: *

New "liberties and exemptions" offered.

Then follow tempting conditions; which, however, were apparently not tempting enough; for the following year new "liberties and exemptions" had to be offered before colonists could be induced to embark upon the uncertain undertaking.†

* Appendix to Case, II, 28–29.
† Appendix to Case, II, 30–32.

As a result of all these efforts, on March 22, 1657, more than nine years after the treaty of Munster, the first free colonists, to the number of twelve persons, arrived in the Essequibo.* First free colonists 1657.

Whether it was that this small number of colonists was not sufficient to insure success, or that for other reasons the Zeeland Chamber felt discouraged at the prospects, the fact is that it shrank from assuming the management of the Colony, and on June 9, 1657, petitioned the provincial Estates of Zeeland to themselves assume its control.† Zeeland Chamber loath to continue direction of Colony.

The Estates of Zeeland did not regard the proposition with favor, and so it fell through.‡

Having been unable to get rid of its load in this direction, the Zeeland Chamber next turned to the Walcheren cities; and, towards the close of 1657, succeeded in inducing Middelburg, Flushing and Vere to assume the risks of the undertaking.§ Control assumed by Middelburg, Flushing and Vere.

The cities, however, recognizing the failure of the

---

* Nederlandsche Jaerboecken, 1751, p. 1093.

† Appendix to Case, ii, 33.

‡ U. S. Commission, Report, i, 195.

§ *From the Provisional Contract between the West India Company (Zeeland Chamber) and the Walcheren Cities, December 24, 1657.*

The West India Company shall approve and so far as in it lies make effective this agreement, basis, and ordinance whereby the aforesaid cities, together with a committee from the aforesaid directors, are to establish and plant colonies on the continental Wild Coast between the first and the tenth degrees, and that in conformity with the liberties and exemptions granted or to be granted by the Board of Nineteen.

To the aforesaid cities, as founders and colonizers of the aforesaid Coast, the States-General shall concede and grant high, middle and low jurisdiction, in order the better to maintain the necessary authority over their subordinates.

The sovereignty and supremacy, with all that thereto belongs, remaining nevertheless to the States-General, and to the Company, in so far as the latter is by the charter entitled thereto.

From proceedings of committee governing for the Walcheren cities the colony of Nova Zeelandia, Monday, Dec. 24, 1657.—The provisional contract between the cities of Middelburg, Flushing, and Vere, and the Directors, having been submitted for approval, it was approved without change and signed by the respective members of the committee, and is entered in these minutes under date of January 21, 1658, following hereafter. [Appendix to Case, ii, 33–34.]

Pomeroon settlement *planned*.

efforts theretofore made to establish any settlement on the Essequibo itself, looked around for a more promising location; and, disregarding Spanish rights, planned a settlement on the Pomeroon and Moruca rivers.

Cornelis Goliat, an engineer, was sent out to survey the region and lay out the new colony. Great things were promised. "There was to be a town which should bear the name of Nieuw Middelburg. Above this was to be built an imposing fortress called, after the colony, Nova Zeelandia. Below the town, on the same side of the river, was to stand the 'House of the Height.'"*

What was actually done.

These proved to be mere air-castles. What actually happened was this:

The buildings planned were begun, but never completed; probably nothing was done beyond laying some of the foundations.† A few Portuguese Jew sugar-planters, driven from Brazil for their religion, were induced to settle on the Pomeroon.‡ The enterprise was neglected and soon languished. In September, 1660, the Jews complained, asking "whether the Commissioners [directors] propose to attend to the colony, since, if otherwise, they intended to depart and abandon it."§ In this same year, Vere was unable to pay its stipulated share of the costs. Before the end of 1663 the Managing Council in Zeeland had become so embarrassed that it broke up altogether.‖

---

* U. S. Commission Report, i, 214–215.

† Netscher, taking the account from the Ryks Archief, says that they "at once began to fit up or build fort Nova Zeelandia, a few miles up the river, the village of New Middelburg and the Huis ter Hooge, which establishments, however, were probably never completed." [Geschiedenis van Essequebo, etc. 8°, 's Gravenhage, 1888, p. 73.]

‡ Netscher (P. M.) Geschiedenis van Essequebo, etc. 8°'s Gravenhage, 1888, pp. 74–75.

§ Rodway (J.) and Watt (T.) Annals of Guiana. Georgetown, 1888, i, 147.

‖ Appendix to Case, ii, 56; see *also* U. S. Commission Report, i, 215, note 3.

But this attempt at a colony was not permitted to die the natural death that awaited it. The events of 1665–66, which put an end to its existence, are best told in the words of Professor Burr: Colony attacked and destroyed in 1666.

"In the winter of 1665–66 the English from Barbados, led by Major John Scott, after taking possession of the Essequibo, swooped down also on the Pomeroon, and left the colony in ruins. What was left was devoured by the military occupation of the French, who followed the English in its possession. It was an entire year before the invaders were here dispossessed, and the settlers had meanwhile scattered to the four winds. But, though thus destroyed prematurely from the earth, Nova Zeelandia still lived on paper. Even before the colony's ruin the chart of Goliat fell into the hands of his enterprising townsman, the geographer Arend Roggeveen of Middelburg, and when a little later that map-maker brought out his fine atlas of these coasts—the 'Burning Fen, lighting up all West India'—Nieuw Middelburg, with its fortress Nova Zeelandia and its Huis der Hoogte, took a handsome place on the map, which it did not lose till almost our own day."*

Thus, at the hands, first of the English,† and then

---

* U. S. Commission, Report, i, 216.

† Scott himself says:

"Anno 1665, . . . in the month of October, the author having been commissionated Commander-in-chief of a small fleet and a regiment of soldiers, for the attack of the Island Tobago, and several other settlements in the hands of the Netherlanders in Guiana, as Moroco, Wacopow, Bowroome, and Disseckeeb, and having touched at Tobago, in less than six months had the good fortune to be in possession of those countries, and left them garrisoned for his majesty of Great Britain, and sailed thence for Barbados, where meeting with the news of the eruption of war between the two crowns of England and France, endeavoured to persuade Francis Lord Willoughby to reduce those several small garrisons into one stronghold, and offered that was the way to make good our post in those parts, having to do with two potent enemies, but his Lordship, that was his majesty's captain-general in those parts, was of another opinion, and before he embarked on the unfortunate voyage for the reducing of St. Christopher's, in which design he perished by a hurricane, the wages he had prescribed for supplies to the forementioned garrisons proved ineffectual; and they were lost the year following to the Dutch after they had endured great misery in a long siege by the French." [Appendix to Case, iii, 360-361.]

On the second page of his journal, Byam thus narrates the conquest and loss of the Dutch colonies:

Colony attacked and destroyed in 1666.

of the French,* did this proposed Pomeroon colony come to an end: it lasted hardly more than half a dozen years.

The result was tersely and graphically stated by the Zeeland Estates themselves: "Essequibo and Pome-

---

"In Novem[r] [1665] here arrived from his Exc[llce] his Serj[t]. Maj[r] Jn[o] Scott after his victory at Tobago wth a smal Fleet & a regim[t] of Foote und[r] the Carrect[r] of Maj[r] Gen[ll] of Guiana, Cheife Commission[r] and Command[r] in Cheife by Land & Sea in few months his great Fortune and gallantry prudent and Industrious Conduct made him master of all the great province new Zealand & Desseceub settled a peace wth the Arrowayes [*sic*] left both Collonys in a Flourishing Condition and well garrison'd for the King of England New Zealand und[r] the Conduct of one Captaine Boxlson [*sic*] and Dessecube undr the Comand of one Cap[t] Kenn, both old Soldiers and sober Gent.

"About two months after his arrivall at Barbados the Indians understanding he was not to returne withdrew all Commerce wth the English in the Forts. Many the Dutch French and Jews were soone upon y[e] Wing to the French Islands Martinico & St. Christophers &c. and those that remained grew discontent . . . and onely for want of supplies . . . after many brave defences [our men] were forced to submit themselves many to the merciless French and in April following the whole Colony to the Dutch." [Appendix to Case, iii, 363.]

A little further on in his narrative Byam goes into more detail as to this disaster:

"Nor was Cap[t] Rendar unsuccessful at leeward, having stormed two warehouses of the Arwacas and had other bickerings wth them wherin he slew about 30 men and took 70 captives. But for the releife of o[r] men at Dissekebe he came too late, who about 3 weeks before through want of ammunicion and iresistable hungar were forced to surrender themselves and 12 hundred slaves w[ch] they had taken to Burgunas a Dutch Gener[ll] who beseiged them, But on good articles, w[ch] those Complaine hee afterwards broke, And as for o[r] poore men at Bawrooma they were also for want of timely supplies destroyed by the French who most unhumanly (after they were starved out of the fort [)] delivered them to the cruelty of the Arwacasto at the mouth of that River to be massacred. This was informed me by one of that fort who was absent when it was taken, who learned it from the Indians: But since I understood the maine fort was not taken untill the coming of the Fleet from Zealand 1667." [Appendix to Case, iii, 363-364.]

* "During the war that followed, France employed her pirates and filibusters against the Dutch colonies. These were authorised to attack the Spanish possessions as well, war having been also declared with Spain. The West India colonies of all nations were now in a most critical state, England and France being pitted against Spain and Holland, with 1,200 French pirates let loose to burn and plunder." [Rodway (J.) and Watt (T.) Annals of Guiana, Georgetown, 1888, ii, 15.]

roon, first taken by the English, then plundered by the French," and now "by the whole world abandoned."*

Essequibo and Pomeroon abandoned.

The Zeeland Estates took possession, but did nothing except maintain a small garrison at Kykoveral, abandoning the Pomeroon entirely. Two years passed, and yet no one could be found to again undertake the management of the "Colony." Late in 1668 it was offered to the three Walcheren cities, but they declined it.† Another two years elapsed and still no taker. Finally, in 1670, the Zeeland Chamber of the Dutch West India Company was induced to once more receive "the Fort and the Colony of Essequibo."‡

Zeeland Estates take possession.

Zeeland Chamber W. I. Co. again takes the Colony.

The outlook for the colony was now very gloomy. When Hendrik Rol, the new governor, arrived, in 1670, there appear to have been no private planters whatever.‖ During the first year of his administration three plantations were started.§ But Rol's energies seem to

Hendrik Rol's administration.

* "Just when the last European of the Nova Zelandia colony left the Pomeroon can not be learned. The Dutch admiral, Crynssen, on taking possession in 1667, is said to have left a garrison in that river as well as in Essequibo (Hartsinck, *Beschryving van Guiana*, i, 224); but this was doubtless only until the wish of the Zeelanders could be learned as to the resumption of the colony. We hear no more of Europeans there." [U. S. Commission, Report, i, 218, note.]

"Essequibo and Pomeroon, first taken by the English, then plundered by the French," and now "by the whole world abandoned"—to use the phrases of the Zeeland Estates themselves—passed again into the hands of the Netherlands. [U. S. Commission, Report, i, 197.]

† They [the Zeeland Estates] at last (late in 1668) offered them to the three cities; but these, dismayed at the expense of a fresh beginning, would no more of them, and thought of selling the colony. [U. S. Commission, Report, i, 197–198.]

‡ U. S. Commission, Report, i, 198.

‖ "There does not appear to have been any private planters in Essequebo at the commencement of his administration [*Rol's, 1670*], but with the improved prospects two or three Zeelanders came to Essequebo and commenced clearing land. Rol proposed that estates should be cultivated on behalf of the Company. . . . On their arrival [arrival of some negro slaves], land was cleared and the Company's plantations were commenced, being principally laid out for cane cultivation." [Rodway (J.) History of British Guiana. 8°, Georgetown, 1891, i, 13, 14.]

§ U. S. Commission, Report, i, 199, 348.

Hendrik Rol's administration.

have been given to trade rather than to agriculture. This policy was in line with that which had first brought, and which still kept the Dutch in Essequibo. His policy was, therefore, not new. It differed from that of his predecessors merely in degree. He maintained the Essequibo as a trading post; but he also converted it into a trading center. He sought, beyond the confines of his island home, to attract and build up trade with the Spaniards and with remoter parts of Guiana. Pursuant to and as a result of this policy, trading stations came later to be established at points more or less distant from the Essequibo itself.‡

‡ But while the territory thus actually occupied by the colony for purposes of cultivation, whether in the neighborhood of Fort Kykoveral or in the coast district, was confined within such narrow bounds, there was another colonial activity, which laid far wider regions under tribute. This was the colony's trade; for this trade was mainly a trade with the natives.

As we have seen, this was at the outset and for more than a quarter century of its existence its exclusive function. Even after plantations had there been established by its proprietors and the colony thrown open to private planters, it was alone this trade with the Indians which the Company retained as its own monopoly; and for many decades this remained its chief source of income and the object of its most jealous care. This it was in defense of which it built its forts, planted its outposts, maintained its garrisons. [U. S. Commission, Report, i, 203.]

The natural supply of these [dyes, oils, precious woods, balsam, etc.] was, therefore, at best, but constant, and the increasing demand made it necessary to seek them ever farther afield. The means employed to this end by the colonial authorities were of two sorts, which must be clearly distinguished. They had, first, the agents whom they called outrunners (*uitloopers*). These, who must have existed from the very beginning of the colony, scoured, by canoe or on foot, the whole country, stirring up the Indians to bring in their wares and barter them at the fort or themselves carrying into the wilderness the trinkets for exchange and bringing back the Indian produce. The outrunners were regular employés of the Company—in the later time usually half-breeds or old negroes familiar with the Indian dialects—and seem to have been sent on definite tasks. "All the old negroes," wrote the Essequibo governor to the Company in 1687, "are off for their several old trading-places among the Indians, to wit, six for annatto, two for balsam copaiba, and two for letter-wood and provisions." Later these outrunners regularly appear in the muster-rolls of the colony. The districts or routes of their activity are, however, never named. Occasionally in the correspondence of the colony one hears of them in this region or in that, but too vaguely to infer their exact whereabouts. [U. S. Commission, Report, i, 204.]

By 1673 Rol was trafficking in the Orinoco with the Spaniards as well as with the Caribs of Barima.* Hendrik Rol's administration.

These efforts toward more extended commercial relations with the Spaniards and Indians, and the establishment of a few plantations in the immediate neighborhood of Kykoveral, constitute the only advance made by the Colony prior to the dissolution of the old Company in Extent of Colony in 1674.

In addition their *outrunners* (*uitloopers*) they came also to have their *outliers* (*uitleggers*). It was by this title, as we have seen, that the employés first sent to the Essequibo were known; and, in truth, the relation later borne by the posts of the outliers to the central fort of the colony was not unlike that borne for long by the colony itself to the home land. It was somewhat more than half a century after the beginning of the colony when a beginning was made of this new method. The suggestion may very possibly have come from Berbice. In 1671, when the neighbor river of Demerara passed into the control of the Essequibo colony, the Berbice authorities had in that river a post of 15 or 16 men, and the commander of this force had been stationed there some fifteen or sixteen years. [U. S. Commission, Report, i, 204–205.]

* The chief external trade of the colony, and the only one of interest to the present research was that with the Spaniards of the Orinoco. Begun as early as 1673, it seems always to have been carried on by that inland water route connecting the Moruca with the Barima and must have involved more or less of intercourse with the Indians of this region. [U. S. Commission, Report, i, 210.]

But it is from that event and from the arrival of the energetic skipper, Hendrik Rol, in 1670, as the first governor under the new régime, that a new era of prosperity for the colony seems to date. In his first year there were but three private plantations in Essequibo, two of them worked by 12 or 14 slaves apiece, the third, lying an hour above Fort Kykoveral (doubtless on the Mazaruni), by 28 or 30. In 1671 he won from Berbice the control of the Demerara. By 1673, if not earlier, he was trafficking with the Caribs in the Barima, as well as with the Arawaks, and he was also just opening a trade with the Orinoco. [U. S. Commission, Report, i, 199.]

July 20, 1673.—There was read the private or secret letter from the Commandeur Hendrik Rol, from Rio Essequibo under date of 16 March, 1673, wherein the following points were noticed, which it was resolved to insert here:

Peace had been made between the Caribs in Barima and the Arawaks, and they now had intercourse with each other, and he was going to send a boat after carap-oil, intending in the meantime to make trial of linseed oil.

He had sent some wares to Orinoco for the purpose of trade; by mistake these were carried to Trinidad, and, no opportunity being found to trade there, they had come back home.

Since that time the people of Orinoco have requested that we go there to trade, whereupon he has resolved to send thither Steven Tornaelje with an old negro who knows the language well. [Appendix to Case ii, 86.]

Extent of Colony in 1674.

1674. When that Company passed away, the Colony, with the exception of the plantations referred to, was still confined to a small island; its occupation was still limited to the very banks of the Essequibo; and its condition was little, if any, better than it had been in 1660.

Results of 26 years, 1674.

To summarize the results of 26 years (1648-1674): The Dutch, in an attempt to improve their precarious position on the Essequibo, had planned a settlement on the Pomeroon; had attempted it; had been too weak to maintain it, or even to complete the erection of its projected buildings; had abandoned it; had withdrawn to their little island on the Essequibo; and, except for a few plantations on the banks of that river in the immediate vicinity of the fort, found themselves, after the lapse of more than a quarter of a century, no further ahead than they had been when the treaty of Munster was signed in 1648.

VII.—HISTORY OF THE ESSEQUIBO DUTCH POST. 1674—1700.

In 1674 the old Dutch West India Company was dissolved.* A wholly new West India Company took its place;† and with this infusion of new blood hopes for a brighter future were kindled.

End of the old and beginning of the new W. I. Co.

The policy of trading to distant points, initiated by Hendrik Rol in 1670, was continued by his successor Abraham Beekman who, in 1679, sent one of his soldiers to the Pomeroon to barter for annatto dye.‡ At this time the Pomeroon was entirely deserted.§ For the purpose of facilitating this trade with the Pomeroon he built there a little hut as a shelter for two or three men.‖ As early as 1673 Hendrik Rol had, as already stated, begun to trade with the Spaniards and Caribs of the Orinoco,¶ a trade carried on *via* the Möruca, the

---

* In 1674, the old West India Company, so long in the agonies of death, at last expired. To take its place there had already been created (by charter of September 21, 1674) one wholly new, with territorial limits widely different. Instead of the entire coast of America, there were granted to the new one on that continent only "the places of Essequibo and Pomeroon." Of the situation or limits of these places there was no other definition than the phrase "situate on the continent of America." [U. S. Commission Report, i, 199.]

† Appendix to Case, iii, 22.

‡ The river Pomeroon also promises some profit; for, in order to make trial of it, I sent thither in August last one of my soldiers to barter for annatto dye. [Appendix to Case, ii, 87.]

§ On receiving the aforesaid ill tidings I called in to the fort the above-mentioned outlier in Pomeroon, both to save him from being surprised, along with the Company's goods, by these savages and to strengthen ourselves in case of attack. Accordingly he came to the fort on the 8th inst. with all the goods, bringing with him a barrel of annatto dye which he had there bought up. [Appendix to Case, ii, 38.]

‖ If the trade prospers, it would not be a bad idea to build there a hut for two or three men, so that they may dwell permanently among the Indians and occupy that river. [Appendix to Case, ii, 38.] Of this post, which was speedily established, one hears often in the letters of the next few years. [U. S. Commission Report, i, 219.]

¶ Appendix to Case, ii, 36; *also* U. S. Commission Report, i, 260.

French and Surinam Dutch in the Barima, 1684.

Waini and the Barima.* But Beekman, continuing Rol's policy, found rivals in that quarter competing for the trade.† The Dutch from Surinam and the French were both strong competitors there; and in view of that fact, he determined, in 1684, to see whether he could not gain advantage by having one of the Company's servants take up his abode at Barima.

Barima shelter, 1684.

Accordingly, in 1684, he put up a "a small shelter"‡ there for the use of the Pomeroon outlier when he should from time to time visit the place.§ This action he re-

* U. S. Commission Report, i, 262.

† That this Carib traffic was not yet in Dutch hands is clear from Commandeur Beekman's letter of January, 1683, which cautions the Company that the Indians must not be repelled by too shrewd bargaining, since when offered trash for their wares they only meet you with the tart answer that they can swap for plenty of such things in Barima and elsewhere—"and there is some truth in this," he adds, "on account of the traffic which the French from the islands carry on there." [U. S. Commission Report, i, 262.] Beekman says: "This trade must as much as possible be kept secret that strangers may not spoil it." [Appendix to Case, ii, 38; also *same*, pp. 43–46, 51–52.]

‡ Note by Prof. Burr. As to what sort of a shelter (*pleisterhuisje*, literally "little resthouse") this probably was, we need not be in doubt. Adriaan van Berkel, writing of these Guiana colonies only a few years before (1672), gives us a vivid description of one (p. 16). He is speaking of a trip down the Berbice. "This night for the first time I slept on land, in the forest, with my hammock made fast to two trees. Just before I was ready to go to rest our slaves had built for me a *pleisterhuisje*—so called by both Christians and Indians—at the place where the hammock was to be stretched. There are four posts, the front ones somewhat higher than the rear ones, covered over with a roof of leaves, leaves uncommonly large, being usually 4 or 5 feet long and some 2 feet broad. Neither sun nor rain can here vex one, for the leaves lie so close upon each other that not even the rays of that great luminary can penetrate. Such *pleisterhuisjes* one sees along the entire river; and one has them built in a moment wherever one will, for an Indian is like the turtle—everywhere at home." And, for that matter, one meets them constantly in the records. (See, for example, the journals of the Surinam expedition of 1714, and of Hildebrandt, the mining engineer—U. S. Commission, Report, ii, pp. 224–228, 285–301.) Such one must have wherever one stayed over night. It is possibly worth noting that, while *pleisterhuisje* means a "little shelter," this on the Barima was only a "*small* pleisterhuisje"; yet it is quite as likely that the commandeur was only belittling the importance of his own action. On the other hand, when proposing a *dwelling* for a postholder he calls it a *huysken*, a hut. (See his letter of October 20, 1679, U. S. Commission, Report, ii, p. 145.) [U. S. Commission Report, i, 265, note.]

§ Pomeroon begins to furnish annually much and good annatto, and

ported to the Company; but for his pains he received a caustic reply attacking his financial honor and his good sense; and he was ordered by the Company to stop forthwith all trade to the Orinoco.* For years no more is heard of this trade.

Barima shelter 1684.

The year 1686 marks a second futile attempt by the Dutch to expand the limits of their Essequibo settlement beyond its original island home. In that year Jacob de Jonge, a planter of Essequibo, was appointed Commandeur of a proposed colony on the Pomeroon.† A beginning

Pomeroon Colony of 1686.

---

much was brought from Barima, as appears from the enclosed list under No. 7, from which you will see how much has been got by barter here at the fort as well as by all the outliers. But Gabriel Biscop and other searovers from Surinam not only spoil that trade, but buy up all the letterwood, which is there fairly abundant and good, and also all the carap oil and hammocks, so that this year I have got only a very few, and they old and wretched. They traverse and scour the land even into the river Cuyuni. In order somewhat to check this, I have had a small shelter made in Barima: and Abraham Boudardt, who is stationed there [*i. e.*, in Pomeroon] as outlier in place of Daniel Galle, who is going home, shall sometimes visit that place, etc. [U. S. Commission Report, i, 263, and Appendix to Case, ii, 45.]

* The correspondence of the Zeeland Chamber, in whose hands was the immediate direction of the Guiana colonies, is preserved in full; but in their long reply to Beekman's letter there is from beginning to end no mention of Barima. That reply is, however, a mere string of reproaches. The poor commandeur's financial honor, his justice, his commercial good sense, are in turn discredited. He is accused of transcending his powers. Even the Dutch of his letters is found fault with. Amid this array of charges is one which may suggest why the matter of the Barima is ignored. "Concerning the trade to the Orinoco," which up to this time, as we have seen, had been constantly encouraged by the Company, they now write, "We find it advisable that you stop it, and neither trade thither yourself nor permit trade thither, directly or indirectly, until further orders—since we are of opinion that the Company bears all the expenses and burdens, while others help themselves to the profits." This charge of bad faith in his trade to the Orinoco is repeated in even more explicit terms in a later letter; and the reopening of this trade was not again urged until Abraham Beekman had given place to a successor. [U. S. Commission Report, i, 268; see *also* Appendix to Case, ii, 48–51.]

† There was read the petition of Jacob Pietersz. de Jongh, whereby he requests payment of a sum of £42 13s. 4d. Flemish, according to the balanced account given him by the Commandeur Abraham Beekman on April 10 in Rio Essequibo; and furthermore that he be allowed to settle as a free planter on the river Pomeroon, together with other planters who have also made a request to this effect, and that for this purpose the rivers Essequibo and Pomeroon be thrown open, * * * * *

Destruction of omeroon Colony by French and Caribs.

was made, but barely three years elapsed before this new colony was completely destroyed by the French. These, coming from Barima under the guidance of the Caribs, fell upon the colony and utterly dispersed it.* The French were at this time temporarily established on the Barima.† No attempt was made to re-establish this

---

And it was furthermore resolved to throw open hereby the rivers of Essequibo and Pomeroon to each and everyone who shall desire to navigate and trade thither, or to settle and dwell there. [Appendix to Case, ii, 58.]

The Board of Ten has decided that the river of Essequibo, together with that of Pomeroon, shall be thrown open, and that henceforth each and everyone who shall desire to found plantations there shall be permitted to do so, and under not unfavorable conditions, as you will see from the missive written you by the Board of Ten aforesaid concerning this matter, and from the commission given to Jacob Pietersz. de Jonge as Commandeur of the river Pomeroon. [U. S. Commission Report, ii, 181.]

* Noble, Honourable, Worthy Lords,

My Lords, July 6, 1689.

This letter of mine humbly to service to make Y. N. acquainted with what has happened since my last, as to how that we in the River Bourona have been suddenly attacked and overpowered by 33 French and about 300 Caribs the one party by water with 10 canoes and 3 coriáls, and the other party by land out of the wood (since we had no cannon and were but six men strong), to wit, the last day of last April; but I effected my escape, accompanied by some red slaves. The Caribs of the French party pursued me vigorously, so that I was compelled to hurry through the wood to escape them with my clothes all thrown off, and came at last with great distress into Essequibo to the fort, to give them warning of our miserable experiences. They had on the next day, being the 1st May, taken their departure from there, and had taken, moreover, with them everything that was there, and had used strong threats to the people that they would burn everything, unless they sought me out. * * *

* * * A few days after this I left again for Bourona to inspect what was the state of things, because not otherwise did it appear whether they should have murdered everyone, since they had so many Caribs with them. But I found my people all still alive, and continued my sojourn with my people there, until I received a letter from the Commandeur of Essequebo telling how the French were in the River Berbice engaged in hostilities against the other settlements; whereupon I straightway determined with my people to hasten to Essequebo, since we besides had no provisions to live upon. The bread that the Caribs had left there, not cut level with the ground, was very little, so that we in a body have departed for Essequebo, since the people of Berbice had warned the people of Essequebo, that they firmly believed that the French would also make attack on Essequebo. [Appendix to Case, ii, 60–61.]

† But it is the French of the Caribbean islands who seem to have been, in the seventeenth century, the especial patrons and allies of the Caribs

Pomeroon colony; and in November, 1689, the Company formally resolved to abandon it, removing to Essequibo the employees, slaves and commodities, and leaving only two men at the former site.* Pomeroon abandoned 1689.

Thus were the Dutch again driven back to the Essequibo. The year 1691 found them confined to its muddy banks, the whole colony containing not more than 100 Europeans, with their slaves.† This number re-

---

of the Barima. Father Pelleprat, the Jesuit missionary, tells us that they had invited the French to plant a colony there, and that in March, 1654, he was informed by Indians of that river "that they had already built a fort in which the French could be quartered as soon as they should arrive." And no sooner do we have reports from the Dutch colony of Essequebo than we find in them complaints of French rivalry in this region. It was, as will be seen, a rivalry not without results to the Dutch. In 1684, when the French of these neighboring West India Islands raided the Orinoco and occupied Santo Thomé, the Caribs in the Barima showed their loyalty by murdering the crew and scuttling the ship of a Dutchman from Surinam, who had come thither for trade; and already they threatened to come with the French and lay waste the Dutch colony of Essequebo. [U. S. Commission, Report, i, 259.]

"The French come into the Barima, and fetch them [*sic*] to above on the Cayuni, and have burned there the houses of the Pariacots, and have driven them away; the latter collect the balsam from the trees, and this is the reason that Daentje, the negro, has come back two weeks ago without bringing with him a single pound of balsam (maraen)." [Blue Book, 3, 60.]

This undoubtedly, according to all indications, will happen, as the French are daily sojourning in Barima with the Caribs, often with two or three barques, and the English from the islands may do likewise. [Appendix to Case, ii, 59.]

* Appendix to Case, ii, 62; *also* U. S. Commission, Report, i, 207.

No attempt was ever made to re-establish it. The West India Company, on receiving full tidings, only instructed (November 15, 1689) the Essequibo commandeur to leave there the Company's flag, with three men, in order to retain possession. The post was established and maintained, though, as would appear, with but two men instead of three. [U. S. Commission, Report, i, 219–220.]

The energy and perseverence of the founders of the Pomeroon colony had been entirely wasted, and now the few planters had abandoned the place in despair. [Rodway (J.) History of British Guiana, Georgetown, 1891, vol. i, p. 10.]

† Rodway (J.) and Watt (T.) Chronological History, etc., Georgetown, 1888, vol. ii, pp. 12, 86, 88.

His (Samuel Beekman's) first report, dated April 8 [1692], stated that there were at Kyk-over-al and on the three Company's plantations, 48 Europeans, including soldiers, 58 Indian slaves, 14 coloured people, and 165 negro slaves. On the private estates there were several hundred slaves. [Rodway (J.) History of British Guiana, Georgetown, 1891, vol. i, p. 48.]

Pomeroon abandoned, 1689.

mained the same through the remaining years of the 17th century.*

The desertion of the Pomeroon in 1689 was not merely temporary: that river was not again occupied during the 17th century. The light in which it was regarded by Samuel Beekman in 1695 is well illustrated by the fact that, on receiving intelligence in that year that the French were in the Pomeroon, he made no effort whatever to dislodge them; but limited himself to fortifying Kykoveral against a possible French attack there.†

Trade into the interior.

Before closing this period, from 1674 to 1700, it is proper to refer to the Dutch trade into the interior. Mention of this is first found in 1680.‡ Between 1680 and 1693, this trade seems to have been with the Indians and confined principally to "hammocks, balsam and other Indian products."§ It is to be noted, however, that this trade was in no sense exclusive, and that it was participated in not only by the Spaniards, but by the French as well.‖

* The entire population in 1691–98 did not exceed one hundred Europeans and "several hundred slaves." [Rodway (J.) and Watt (T.) Chronological History, etc., Georgetown, 1888, vol. ii, pp. 12, 86, 88.]

† We have been kept here in continuous alarm, since at various times we have had tidings that some French, aided by Caribs from Barima, are staying in the mouth of the river Pomeroon, who say that they will come here to visit us. In view of this I have at once sent order to all the planters to send down all the male slaves, in order to strengthen the fort, so that we may defend ourselves well in case of an attack. [Appendix to Case, ii, 64.]

‡ The earliest mention of the river I have found in the Dutch records is that in Commandeur Abraham Beekman's letter of June 28, 1680, when that river, temporarily closed by an Indian war, is called "our provision chamber." [Prof. Burr in U. S. Commission Report, i, 306; see *also* Appendix to Case, ii, 40–41.]

§ It appears that not provisions alone were gathered there by the Company's "old negroes," but hammocks, balsam and other Indian products. [U. S. Commission Report, i, 306.]

By reason of the Accoway war in Cuyuni, of which you know, the trade in hammocks, especially in new ones, has resulted badly, for no one dares venture among that faithless tribe. As a result, no more than six of the common kind could be sent; the others were too small and not fit for you. [Appendix to Case, ii, 41; see also *same*, pp. 52–53.]

‖ Just as I am closing this, Daentje, the Company's old negro, comes

In or about 1693 the Dutch began the trade in horses up in Cuyuni—a trade which could only have been carried on with the Spaniards;* and this trade was continued through the remaining years of the 17th century.

Cuyuni horse trade.

The close of the century saw the following state of affairs:

Results of twenty-six years. Condition in 1700.

All efforts of the Dutch to extend the area of their actual occupation had been foiled. A second attempt at establishing a colony on the Pomeroon had ended disastrously, owing to the weakness of the Dutch and their inability to defend their possessions against attack: having thus been driven back to the Essequibo, the Company had formally determined to acquiesce in its ejectment from the Pomeroon. It is true it made a pretence of keeping two men there; but, excepting for

---

from the savanna up in Cuyuni, from the Pariacotten. He has been away for fully seven months, and was detained quite three months by the dryness of the river. Because the French scour the country up there and buy up everything, he was able to get but little carap-oil and a few hammocks. [Appendix to Case, ii, 58–59.]

The French in the Barima likewise come even to the upper Cuyuni to get them, and have there burnt the houses in the Pariacotten, [and] driven them away. These gather the copaiba from the trees, and [this] is the reason that Daentje, the negro, came back two weeks ago without bringing with him a single pound of copaiba, bringing only thirty hammocks, among them eight small new ones not fit to be used by any man, much less worthy of your service. [Appendix to Case, ii, 52.]

The copaiba and curcai are much bought up by the Spaniards. The war which various nations there carry on with one another has been the cause that Daentje the negro has not been able to get so far among that nation, and, therefore, has made a fruitless journey, and could get only a few bad hammocks for the negroes. [Appendix to Case, ii, 46; see *also* Blue Book, 3, 62.]

*No slight advantage, moreover, has been brought the Company through you [Samuel Beekman] by your having found out, up in the river of Cuyuni, a trade in horses, which here cost the Company much money for their purchase and involve it in heavy expenses for their transportation thither. We are confident, too, that the native horses are better used to the nature of the country. You are therefore most urgently recommended and instructed to retain this trade for the Company alone. We give you, however, permission to dispose of them to the private planters at a reasonable profit. [Appendix to Case, ii, 63–64.]

Results of twenty-six years. Conditions in 1700.

this, its actual occupation in 1700 did not go beyond Kykoveral and a few plantations on the adjacent banks. The Dutch trade to the Orinoco and to the regions forming its delta had been forbidden by the Company itself in 1684; and had not been thereafter resumed. Trade with the Cuyuni was being carried on; but, so far as the Indians were concerned, it was a trade shared in by both Spaniards and French; and as for the rest, it was a trade with the Spaniards themselves settled in that region.

Except, therefore, the two men in the Pomeroon, and the extension of plantations in the immediate vicinity of Kykoveral, the lapse of another twenty-six years (1674–1700) brought no change, and seems to have witnessed no enlargement of Dutch possession or control. After more than half a century the colony was little, if any, further ahead than it had been at the time when the Treaty of Munster was signed.

VIII.—HISTORY OF THE ESSEQUIBO DUTCH POST. 1700–1725.

It will be convenient to group the events of the next quarter of a century according to location and character.

Trade to points west of Essequibo.

First.—As to the trade of the Company to points west of the Essequibo.

No trade to Barima.

As regards the Barima, there is no record of any attempt whatever to trade there during this period.* The prohibition of 1684 against trading to the Orinoco continued in force, certainly until 1717, at least so far as private settlers were concerned, for in that year these settlers addressed a protest to the Company against its continuance.†

Suggestions regarding Barima ignored by W. I. Co.

The only other connection of the Essequibo Dutch with the Barima during this period seems to have been a suggestion made in 1722 by the Engineer Maurain-Saincterre‡ with regard to the establishment of planta-

---

* But the French seem to have maintained for years their alliance with the Barima Caribs against the Dutch, and no more is heard of the Barima in Dutch records of the seventeenth century.

In the muster-rolls of the Company's servants in Essequibo for 1691 and 1701 no Barima post appears among the others. And when, in 1703, he Essequibo commandeur had occasion to speak of the exclusion of Surinam traders "here in our district," he defined the phrase by "Essequibo, Pomeroon, and Demerara," with no mention of the Barima. [U. S. Commission Report, i, 270.]

The pay-rolls of the Essequibo colony, which from 1700 on give us, year by year, full information as to the staff of every outpost, know no post on the Barima. [Same, p. 272.]

† It is not till 1717 that I again find mention of that river in the documents of that colony. Then the private settlers of the colony addressed to the West India Company an indignant remonstrance against the restrictions put upon their freedom of trade, protesting that thus an unfair advantage is given the colonists of Berbice and Surinam, who may trade as they will, whether in Pomeroon, Moruca, Waini, Barima, Orinoco, or Trinidad. [U. S. Commission Report, i, 272.]

In October, 1701, the Essequibo Court of Policy justified the purchase of horses from a Rhode Island trader by the plea that "all the lands where we carry on our horse trade are under the King of Spain, as we know by experience from the prohibitions we have already met in the trade to Orinoco. [Same, p. 309; see also Appendix to Case, ii, 77–78.]

‡ U. S. Commission Report, i, 272–273.

Suggestions regarding Barima ignored by W. I. Co.

tions there, a suggestion never acted upon or even considered by the Company.* What does appear is that during the period referred to (1700–1725) the French and the Dutch from Surinam and Berbice were allowed by the Spaniards to trade in that region.† In 1711 a Surinam party passed that way and found it entirely deserted.‡

Attempt to trade to the Waini, 1699.

An ineffectual attempt at trade nearer home was made by the Essequibo Dutch late in 1699. In that year a bark was sent to the Waini to salt fish and to trade for victuals, but it returned six weeks later "without having done any trading."§ Coming

---

* Appendix to Case, ii, p. 79.

† But as regards the balsam oil, the same has, together with the trade in red slaves, according to the direction of the Noble Chamber of Zeeland, been first forbidden by me to the inhabitants of this Colony on the 24th July in the past year [1712], since this trade has been permitted to the free [inhabitants] because that it took place outside the district of the Noble Company, and was but carried on solely on Spanish ground in the River Orinoco, where likewise trade was done by the inhabitants of the Colonies of Berbice and Surinam. [Blue Book, 8, 74.]

Saint-Trond is the only one of our people who is capable and familiar with the Indians and acquainted with their language; also, although from Brabant, he is of proven fidelity, and this is the reason why he was employed. [U. S. Commission Report, ii, 229.]

No whites are allowed to enter the Orinoco except with a pass. The thing we have in view could be accomplished only under pretext of trading with the Indians, for which we would need the permission of the commander of the Orinoco. He was favorably inclined towards us, and if he had remained in command we might have expected everything from him; this was why Mollinay had orders to address himself to him. Now there is another commander, who is not willing to allow anyone there; but possibly this may change with time, and I shall therefore continue to exert myself elsewhere in order to attain our object. [Appendix to Case, ii, 73–74; *see* also, same, p. 75.]

‡ The Surinam expedition sent to the Orinoco in 1711, stopped at the mouth of the Barima, both in going and coming, and makes no mention of a shelter there, though its journal always mentions one when found. That site would have been a more natural one for the French, who, on their way from the islands to the Barima, would here first reach the mainland, than for the Dutch of the Guiana colonies, who came through the Moruca and reached the Barima by the Mora Passage. [U. S. Commission Report, i, 271, note.]

§ And because our barque which we sent to Waini on November 11 last, in order to salt fish and to trade for victuals, has arrived here on December 29 with a very bad catch and without having done any trading, etc. [Appendix to Case, ii, 65.]

nearer home still, even as far away only as the Pomeroon, trade was forbidden by the Company to private settlers of the colony at least as late as 1717.* On the other hand the French and Spanish had so little regard for any supposed Dutch jurisdiction there that, in 1712, a party of them in the Pomeroon, meeting a Dutch agent there, drove him away with impunity.† The shelter put up on the Pomeroon for two servants in 1689, when the attempt to establish a colony on that river was abandoned, was probably kept up as a matter of form. It later came to be known as the Wacupo post.‡ An attempt, however, to establish and maintain a post in that region higher up on the Pomeroon and nearer home came to naught; and if a post was in fact started there in 1703, as seems barely possible, its existence certainly came to an end not later than 1705.§ So much for trade with the Orinoco and the coast region generally.

Trade to Pomeroon forbidden.

French and Spanish in the Pomeroon.

Shelter at Pomeroon, 1703–1705.

As regards the interior, trade was hardly more flour-

Trade to the interior.

---

* Appendix to Case, ii, 77–78.

† Appendix to Case, ii, 75.

‡ The post was established and maintained, though, as would appear, with but two men instead of three. At least, according to the muster-roll of September 6, 1691, there were there only a postholder and a single assistant. In 1700 it was on the same footing; but in this year we begin to hear a new name for its site: where the pay-roll for this year makes Jan Debbaut "postholder in Pomeroon, at the Company's trade house," the muster-roll makes the same soldier "postholder in Wacupo." By 1704 the pay-roll, too, adopts the new title for the post, calling Jan Debbaut "postholder in Wacupo." [U. S. Commission Report, i, 220.]

§ It would appear, however, that there was now for a year or two a second post on the Pomeroon; for we learn from the pay-rolls that on July 14, 1703, Paulus Veefaart was made "postholder in Pomeroon," and both the pay-roll and the muster-roll for 1704 register him there, with an assistant, while Jan Debbaut and his assistant are still accredited to Wacupo. On April 6, 1705, however, he was discharged from the Company's service; and, although on the muster-roll for June 18, 1705, his assistant, Dirk Schey, still appears in the Pomeroon, it was perhaps only to finish out the year. In the following year we find him serving as bylier in Demerara, and the name Pomeroon does not again occur among those of the posts. [U. S. Commission Report, i, 221.]

Trade to the interior.

ishing. By 1701 the horse trade had begun to fall off.* By 1702 it had grown more difficult.† In 1703, probably with the idea of fostering this horse trade, it was proposed to establish a "post" up in the savannas of the Cuyuni, six weeks by water from Kykoveral. A "postholder" was actually appointed on May 20, but whether the post was ever established or not is very doubtful.‡ Certain it is that on the first of the following October, this same postholder was removed and nothing more is heard of any post. The trade gradually came to an end, and the year 1707 is the last in which mention is to be found of it.§ The reason is not hard to guess. Already the Dutch governor had written home:

End of Cuyuni horse trade, 1707

> "I am very sorry to be obliged to inform you that, owing to the present war, no horses are to be got above here as hitherto, inasmuch as those Indians think themselves to stand under the crowns of Spain and France; and this trade is thereby crippled."‖

Even while it lasted it was carried on in what was confessedly Spanish territory.¶

---

* The trade in horses up in Cuyuni does not go as briskly as it used to; still the negro traders brought, on March 24th of this year, 12 fine ones, 8 head of which I have disposed of to the plantation "de Vrijheid," and inclose the bills of exchange therefor. [Appendix to Case, ii, 65-66.]

† That truly is a great loss to the Colony, the more so since the Spaniards will no longer permit any trafficking for horses on their territory, so that I shall be perforce compelled to make use of an English barque, or other vessels such as those which came in this river, to go and fetch horses, or else Y. N. will be obliged to send out the same to me from the mother-country, because it is impossible to deliver sugar without horses. [Appendix to Case, ii, 68-69.]

‡ U. S. Commission Report, i, 312-316.

§ In October, 1707, the commandeur complained that they could no longer be got thus from above so conveniently and in such quantity as need required. It is the last mention I have found of the importation of horses by this route. [U. S. Commission Report, i, 316.]

‖ The mention of France here along with Spain is to be explained, doubtless, by the fact that under its Bourbon claimant Spain was now virtually in the hands of France. The phrasing is perhaps, only the commandeur's own, and chosen for Dutch ears.

¶ For long one hears no more of the upper Cuyuni, save now and

Second.—As to the extent of actual settlement during this period. Extent of Settlement.

The only growth which the Essequibo colony enjoyed during the first quarter of the 18th century was confined exclusively to the banks of the Essequibo itself, and to those portions of the Mazaruni and Cuyuni which lie below the first falls of these latter rivers.*

As showing the exact extent of the Colony in 1701 may be cited its division in that year into two districts for purposes of military organization; one district comprising the plantations on the Mazaruni, the highest of which was below its first falls; and the second comprising the plantations on the Essequibo, all on tide water.† The two districts comprised but a dozen plantations. Essequibo divided into two districts, 1701.

In 1706 we have another definition of limits in the map of Abraham Maas‡ sent to the Company by the governor Samuel Beekman. According to this the plantations at that date were all limited to the immedi- Extent of colony, 1706.

---

then of the pursuit and capture there of an escaping slave. [U. S. Commission Report, i, 316.]

That truly is a great loss to the Colony, the more so since the Spaniards will no longer permit any trafficking for horses in their territory. [Appendix to Case, ii, 68-69.]

The more so because all the lands where we carry on our horse-trade are under the King of Spain. [Appendix to Case, ii, 68.]

In October, 1701, the Essequibo Court of Policy justified the purchase of horses from a Rhode Island trader by the plea that "all the lands where we carry on our horse trade are under the King of Spain, as we know by experience from the prohibitions we have already met in the trade to Orinoco." [U. S. Commission Report, i., 309.]

* The attempt in 1704 to move the plantation of Poelwijk above the falls could not have been a success, since the map of 1706 shows it below them.

† Item, two Commissaries shall every one or two months, or at least four times a-year, time undefined, be sent off to go and visit all plantations, and to give instructions to the new planters, to wit, those dwellings in Maseroene; the plantations lying in the river being the first district: since they find it good to divide the Company's river into two districts: as from the plantation Poelwijk down as far as Van Rump's Court. The second district is the river Essequebo and stretches from the plantation Bosbeek to the plantation New Cortrijk. [Appendix to Case, ii, 66-67.]

‡ Appendix to Case, atlas, map 50.

Extent of colony, 1706. ate banks of the Mazaruni and Essequibo, and were all below the first falls of those rivers.

Cartabo, 1716. "In 1716 the Commandeur got permission to build a new government house on the mainland just opposite the island, on the Mazaruni side of the point formed by the two streams."* The hamlet of 12 or 15 houses which grew up around it came later to be known as Cartabo.†

Colony in 1722. By 1722, the Colony had not materially changed, and we have the evidence of the engineer Maurain-Saincterre that up to that time no European had established a sugar plantation above the falls.‡

Results of 25 years, 1700–1725. To sum up the results of 25 years from 1700 to 1725:

Trade to the Orinoco, the Barima and even the Pomeroon had been forbidden to the Dutch of Essequibo and no attempt was made to undertake it. In the Cuyuni the horse buying station of 1703, after a possible existence of a few months had been abandoned and forgotten, the Indians there claiming to be Spanish, and little or no thought was given to that region.

The only posts west of the Essequibo were those on the Wacupo and the Pomeroon. The first of these, composed of two servants and a shanty, served to prevent the running away of slaves; the second lasted but two years and was then abandoned. The colony itself spread along the banks of the Essequibo, the Mazaruni and the Cuyuni, but did not go beyond tide-water.

* U. S. Commission, Report, i, 202.

† U. S. Commission, Report, i, 202.

‡ The ground is even better above in the rivers Essequibo, Mazaruni, and Cuyuni than below; but because they are full of rocks, falls, and islands, and much danger is to be feared for large sugar canoes, this is the reason why up to this time the Europeans have not been willing to establish sugar plantations there. [Appendix to Case, ii, 79.]

IX.—HISTORY OF SPANISH SETTLEMENT BY WAY OF ORINOCO. 1648-1725.

Introduction.

The history of the Dutch Colony for three-quarters of a century has thus been sketched: it will be well to consider the progress made by the Orinoco Spaniards during the same period.

To properly appreciate this progress it is necessary to distinguish between the character, purposes and methods of the Dutch and of the Spanish respectively.

Dutch methods and purposes.

As has been before stated, the objects which first brought the Dutch to America, were to plunder the Spanish settlements, and to rob the Spanish treasure on its way across the ocean. When the treaty of Munster put an end to this system of robbery, the Dutch relations with Guiana became those of mere trade; and the possessions of the Dutch on the Guiana coast stood out as merely so many trading establishments. The Spaniards, on the contrary, came to America to conquer the land, to found an empire, to gather its treasure, to christianize and civilize its people. The history of Spanish settlement on the Orinoco is therefore a history, first, of political control over all the surrounding region, and second, of missionary activity and settlement among the Indians.

Purposes and character of Spanish colonies.

Spanish control of the Orinoco Delta Region.

As to political control, it was general throughout the territory now in dispute. In proof of this let us look first at the Orinoco delta region between the main mouth of that river and the Moruca. The trading of the Surinam Dutch and of the French in and about Barima during the closing years of the 17th century, the continued trading of these two and of the Dutch

Spanish control of the Orinoco Delta Region.

from Berbice during the first quarter of the 18th century, like trading on the part of the Essequibo Dutch from 1673 to 1684, the sojourn of the French at Barima in 1689, and the ineffectual attempt of the Essequibo Dutch for a few weeks in 1700 to trade in the Waini, are the only known instances of the presence of foreigners in the Orinoco delta between 1648 and 1725.

Spanish control recognized by the Dutch.

As to the sovereignty and exclusive political control by the Spaniards in that region, it was distinctly and repeatedly recognized by the Dutch.*

Seizure of Dutch vessels by Spain.

During this period the Spaniards repeatedly seized and confiscated Dutch vessels in that region; and the Dutch submitted to these acts without protest.†

Spanish presence between Moruca and Essequibo.

Beyond the Moruca, and between that river and the Essequibo, the Spaniards constantly made their presence felt; driving out Dutch agents, and attacking the embryo colonies which the Dutch attempted to plant, but which they finally abandoned.‡

---

* Thus, *e. g.*, in 1685 and in 1712:

The Spaniards have resumed possession of Oronoque. The dispersed and hunted-away Caribs from the Copename River are flying to leeward near about Barima, Weyni, Amacoora, often alarming the coast, and sometimes slaying some unlucky Arowaka Indians or Christians, as happened to Bishop and the men from Berbice. [Blue-Book 3, p. 60.]

Concerning the 600 to 700 stoops of balsam (oil), of which I spoke in my former despatch that I would have in readiness with this same merchandize, I am obliged, to my vexation, to say that this past year not a single pound has been procured for the Noble Company, since they in Orinoco had all at once prohibited the traffic in it to the Hollanders, these changes having come to pass with the arrival of a new Governor at Trinidad, who, with this object, has caused several manned vessels to cruise in the River Orinoco, so as to confiscate and bring in as good prizes all Dutch vessels who should wish to come thither; that has forced me to put a stop to the journey, since of necessity, I dared not hazard and put in danger on such like a journey the Company's cargoes, slaves, vessels, and other goods, the which I hope Y. N. will take well; yet some however, have undertaken to send thither with small vessels, but at how great risk! But at the present moment the traffic is again free, so that shortly I shall send thither, as before, a proper vessel, and I think that next year I shall have about 600 stoops ready for the Noble Company. [Appendix to Case, ii, 74.]

† Appendix to Case, ii, 74.

‡ Appendix to Case, ii, 74–76; *also* U. S. Commission Report, i, 229–230.

In the interior Cuyuni-Mazaruni basin, the Spaniards for a time permitted both the French* and the Dutch to trade. French and Dutch trade in Cuyuni.

Turning now to the question of settlement and missionary activity, we find a growth and development which is in marked contrast with the weakness of the hemmed-in Dutch post on Kykoveral. Spanish settlement and missionary activity.

Even as early as the Treaty of Munster we find the Jesuits active in this region. In their "Annual Letters" for 1652, recounting the history of this province during the decade preceding, they write:

> "In the Mission of Guayana, where scarcely any harvest responds to labor, however distressing, Father Andreas Ignatius, head of that mission, a man of obedience and heroic zeal, and a professed of the four vows, fell at that glorious and most destitute post."†

As early as 1659 missions were already established in the *llanos*, that is to say in the savannas of the upper Cuyuni. Missions in the *llanos* in 1659.

In that same year Father Antonio de Monteverde persuaded the provincial authorities in Santa Fe to take religious possession of the lower Orinoco; and in consequence Fathers Vergara and Llauri were sent there.‡

---

* Appendix to Case, ii, 45–46, 52, 58–59.

† U. S. Commission Report, i, 55.

‡ Cassani, the historian of the Jesuit province, begins the story of Jesuit activity in the regions of the lower Orinoco with the year 1659. He relates how in that year Father Antonio de Monteverde, a Fleming, came from Cayenne to the Orinoco and then made his way up the river to the mission of his order in the llanos. He persuaded the provincial authorities in Santa Fé to take religious possession of the lower Orinoco, and Fathers Vergara and Llauri were sent thither in 1664. Monteverde and Mesland, "a tried man," were in the same year assigned to the mission in the llanos. Llauri and Vergara found the Spaniards of Guiana in a condition of spiritual destitution. (Cassani, "Historia de la Provincia de la Compañia de Jesus del Nuevo Reyno de Granada," 1741, pp. 81, 82, 110, 114, 128.) Gumilla, in his "El Orinoco Ilustrado" (p. 11), also a Jesuit, has no earlier origin of Jesuit missions in Guiana to suggest. [U. S. Commission Report, i, 55–56.]

Spanish missions, 1664.

By 1664 the missions had so far advanced that registers of baptisms began to be regularly kept.

From this time on Dominicans, Augustinians, Jesuits and Capuchins vied with each other in their efforts at christianizing the natives, and in their willingness to die for the cause.*

Spanish missions, 1677.

In 1677 the Governor General of Trinidad and Guayana asked the Prefect of the Missions of Cumaná if he could send him missionaries; to which the Prefect answered that he had eight priests only, but was expecting ten more from Spain, and would gladly do as requested.†

Spanish missions, 1680.

In 1680 ten Capuchins arrived from Spain for the missions of Trinidad; that island and Guayana constituting, at that time, a single government.‡

Spanish missions, 1681.

By 1681, work had progressed so far that the Indians had begun to form regular settlements; and there is

* They [the missions] were *established* in the year 1724, notwithstanding that other Missioners had undertaken the same work before. This conclusion is derived from the contents of a book of baptisms, showing that from the year 1664 several other Priests at different times had tried the pacification and reduction of these Indians, such as Father Joseph Sanpayo, a Reverend Father of the Dominican order, and Father Manuel de la Purification, of the Bare-footed order (descalzos) of Saint Augustine; the Clergymen Don Francisco de Rojas, Don Miguel de Angulo, Don Joseph de Figueroa, and the ration canon, Don Andres Fernandez; the Father Jesuit Juan de Vergara, Dionisio Mestand, Francisco de Ellauri and Ignacio Cano, the Catalan Capuchin Father Angel de Mataro and Father Pablo de Blanes, the Capauchins and others. The Fathers of the Company made an assignment of said Missions, and the act was authorized by the Governor of Trinidad, Don Tiburcio de Harpe y Zúñiga, in the year 1681, as shown by the Royal Cedule of the 7th of February, 1686, and the 29th of April, 1687, by which His Majesty approves the assignment made by the Jesuits, and sends the Catalan Capuchin Fathers to attend the Missions of the Province of Guayana. These two Cedules are kept in the Archives of the Community. From said year 1687 they took charge of the Missions and commenced their work, but the miseries and deaths, without any help in their wants, were so discouraging, having nobody to replace those who died, many long interruptions of the Apostolic ministry followed, losing at the same time whatever advancement had been made previously for the good of the souls and the pacification of the natives. [Appendix to Case, ii, 344.]

† Appendix to Case, ii, 270.

‡ Appendix to Case, ii, 268.

record of at least two villages with their churches near Santo Thomé: these were under the care of the Jesuits of the Province of the New Kingdom of Granada.* In addition to these, the Jesuits had other missions higher up on the Orinoco.† Spanish missions, 1681.

In the same year, the Jesuits, finding their hands full with their missions on the Upper Orinoco, transferred to the Capuchins the missions in the vicinity of Santo Thomé.‡

By 1682 the Governor General of Trinidad and Guayana could state, in a formal official document, that there were 24,000 Indians who had been subjected to Spanish rule in Guayana and Trinidad.¶ Spanish missions, 1682.

In that year two Capuchins arrived at Trinidad to take part in the missionary work in Tierra Firme; and having made objection to Guayana as a destination, because of their ignorance of the Spanish language, were informed by the Governor that the Indians there were in general familiar with Spanish; and that such as could not understand it could be reached through other Indians who spoke it. The friars accordingly went to Guayana.§

In 1686 twelve Capuchins arrived from Spain for the missions of Cumaná, and twelve more for Trinidad and Guayana.‖ Spanish missions, 1686.

---

* Appendix to Case, ii, 269.

† Appendix to Case, ii, 269.

‡ The Jesuits solemnly renounced these Missions in favour of the two aforesaid Capuchins and others on the authority of the Governor of Trinidad, Don Tiburcio Arpe y Zuñiga, in the year 1681, and he intrusted them to the aforesaid Capuchins of Catalonia, being commissioned by the Royal Audiencia of Sante Fé to provide missionaries for the Province of Guayana, as appears from the Decrees which remain in the Government Office of Trinidad, as also the Royal "Cedulas" of the 7th of February, 1686, and 29th April, 1687, by which His Majesty grants the Missions of the Provinces of Guayana to the said Catalonian Capuchins, who took charge of them from thenceforth. [Appendix to Case, ii, 338–339.]

¶ Appendix to Case, ii, 269–270.

§ Appendix to Case, ii, 270.

‖ Appendix to Case, ii, 271.

Spanish missions, 1693.

By 1693, the stock raising had grown to such proportions, that the Essequibo Dutch were travelling six weeks up from Kykoveral to the savannas of the Cuyuni to buy horses.*

Spanish missions. General results.

The result of all this missionary activity was that roads were opened through apparently impenetrable forests; towns and churches were founded; plantations laid out, and stock farms established.†

Dutch Cuyuni horse-trade prohibited by Spain, and abandoned.

This trade in horses in the Cuyuni continued without restriction until 1702. In that year the Spaniards prohibited it; and though it was attempted to be kept up by the Dutch, they were compelled to abandon it altogether by 1707.‡

Spanish missions. Results in fifteen years.

All this time missionaries continued to pour in; and as a result of the settlement in Guiana in 1686–87 of a number of Capuchin Fathers, five thousand Indians were baptized in fifteen years, five towns were founded in Trinidad and three more in Guiana.§

Spanish missions, 1724.

Finally in 1724 an entire reorganization of the missions was effected, and the plan of specific missions, each with a definite foundation, was initiated.¶

Suay and Caroni, 1724.

In accordance with this reorganization, two missions were formally "founded" in this year, Suay and Caroni.‖

* Appendix to Case, ii, 63–64.

† Strickland (*Rev.* J.) Boundary question, Rome, 1896, Appendix, p. 72.

‡ In October, 1707, the commandeur complained that they could no longer be got thus from above so conveniently and in such quantity as need required. It is the last mention I have found of the importation of horses by this route. [U. S. Commission Report, i, 316.]

§ Caulin (*friar* A.) Historia, etc., Madrid, 1779, p. 9; see *also* Rodway (J.) and Watt (T.) Annals of Guiana, Georgetown, 1888. ii, 64; and Documentos para la historia de la vida pública del Libertador. [Bolivar]. 4°, Caracas, 1875, vol. i, p. 421.

¶ It is true that ever since the year 1724 the Indians of the Province of Guayana began to show some perseverance in the Catholic Faith preached to them by the Capuchin Missionaries of Catalonia, and it may therefore be said that their true foundation dates from that time. Although the preaching of the Gospel in that Province was not begun in that year, it may be inferred from the old register of Baptisms that from the year 1664 various priests at different times attempted their pacification and conversion. [Appendix to Case, ii, 338.]

‖ U. S. Commission, Report, iii, 215.

To sum up the results of Spanish growth from 1648 to 1725: Summing up and contrast with Dutch.

In the delta of the Orinoco and in the interior Cuyuni basin there had been trading both by French and Dutch, the latter principally from Surinam and Berbice; but the Spaniards had throughout maintained exclusive political control of both regions. Over by the Moruca and Pomeroon they had made their presence effectively felt, and Spain claimed both of these rivers as her own. Along the Orinoco, and over the sloping savannas of the Cuyuni, Spanish missions had gradually spread, their stock farms raising horses in such numbers that they not only supplied the home needs but had a surplus for export.

The Dutch Essequibo post, on the other hand, scarcely maintained itself at Kykoveral and on the adjacent banks.

X.—HISTORY OF THE ESSEQUIBO COLONY. 1725-1803.

Returning to the Essequibo, the story of that colony, from 1725 until it was finally taken by the British in 1803, will now be taken up. History of Essequibo colony.

In 1725, as has before been seen, the Dutch possessions were limited to the Island of Kykoveral, to a few plantations on the adjacent banks of the Essequibo, Mazaruni and Cuyuni, and to a shanty on the Wacupo. Dutch possessions in 1725.

Prior to 1725, such limited tendency to growth as the Essequibo colony may have had, had been up-stream from Kykoveral, on the Essequibo, the Mazaruni and the Cuyuni: there had, however, never been any plantations above the first falls of those rivers.

Subsequent to 1725 the tendency was all the other way. Indeed, this tendency became so marked that, little by little, the whole colony moved down nearer the mouth of the Essequibo, abandoning Kykoveral, deserting former plantations, and apparently giving up all thought of the interior except as a place for trade with the Spaniards and Indians. Tendency of colony downstream.

In 1739-40* the garrison and seat of government were transferred from Kykoveral to Flag island (afterwards known as Fort island)† at the mouth of the Essequibo.‡ Garrison transferred to Flag island.

* Appendix to Case, ii, 89; *also* U. S. Commission Report, i, 201; ii, 283.

† On Flag Island, now coming to be called Fort Island, there likewise grew up a cluster of buildings; the fort, the public offices and warehouses, the quarters of the garrison, the dwellings of the officers. [U. S. Commission Report, i, 202.]

‡ But as these upper lands became exhausted, the more fertile lower reaches tempted even those who were already established above; and at

Cartabo abandoned.

In 1740 the dozen houses which composed the hamlet of Cartabo were abandoned and fell to ruin.*

By 1748 the Cuyuni could be counted very remote.†

As early as 1764, Storm van 's Gravesande could speak of "the few colonists who still live up the river,"‡ meaning, as the context shows, at the old site of the colony, about the junction of the Cuyuni and Mazaruni.§

By 1773 all demands for grants of land up the river at the former site of the colony had ceased.‖

No plantations above Flag Island in 1777.

By 1777, there was, with one exception, not a sugar, coffee, or cotton plantation above Flag island; in fact, no culture whatever except a few cassava grounds.¶

---

the completion of the new fort on Flag Island, near the mouth of the river, and the transfer thither from Kykoveral (in 1739-40) of the garrison and the seat of government, the exodus had already become general. [U. S. Commission Report, i. 201.]

* After 1740, when the colonial government was removed to the new fort on Flag Island, Cartabo fell to ruin. According to Hartsinck [*Beschryving van Guiana*, i, p. 263], writing in 1770, when it was "now in ruins," it had consisted of "twelve or fifteen houses." [U. S. Commission Report, i, 202.]

† We have the honor to report that in fulfillment of your salutary intention, we have caused to be posted everywhere the announcements of the sale, on January 8 last, of the burdensome and unprofitable indigo plantation. But, to our sorrow, we must report that in this matter we could in no way attain the desired end, inasmuch as, although the conditions were arranged very favorably, not one person was willing to bid a single stiver thereon, presumably on account of the great distance and the insalubrity of the river Cuyuni. We had therefore to keep it for the Company, to whom, even for bread-grounds alone, it is worth at least two hundred rix-dollars and more. [Appendix to Case, ii, 100.]

‡ "Nog boven in de riviere wonen." [U. S. Commission Report, i, 201, note.]

§ I have received a report from the few colonists who still reside in the upper reaches of the rivers that a few weeks ago they had seen a white man with a few Indians proceeding down the falls of the River Cajoeny and proceeding up the River Masserouny. I reproached them very much for not apprehending and sending the man to the fort, and expressly charged them that if they caught sight of others they should immediately apprehend them and send them to me, which they promised to do. [Appendix to Case, ii, 158-159; *also*, atlas, maps 66 and 67.]

‖ It is now an opportune moment for closing the Court, because there are no longer any grants of land to be made; no one will ask for lands in the upper reaches of the river, and most of them are already annexed as timber grounds for the plantations below. [Appendix to Case, ii, 221.]

¶ Thus one finds above this island (which is distant only one tide from

By the close of the century the original site of the colony had become a wilderness.*

Original site of Colony a wilderness.

But while the movement of the colony was thus down-stream, the general movement was also toward the *east* bank and around the coast *toward Demerara.*†

With the exception of a single transient squatter on the Pomeroon, and an isolated short-lived plantation on the Moruca, there were no settlements upon those rivers, or on the Wacupo, at any time during the 18th century.‡

The year 1800 found them in practically the same condition that the year 1700 had left them.

1700-1800 remained in *statu quo.*

Except for purposes of trade, for the intercepting of runaway slaves, for fishing, for occasional wood cutting, and, from time to time, for the temporary sojourn of a Dutchman, these rivers were in no way utilized by the Dutch. Indeed, the Essequibo colonists, so far from needing more land, were not sufficiently numerous to

Pomeroon region not utilized by the Dutch, except for trade, etc.

---

the mouth) not one sugar, coffee or cotton plantation except only that of the ex-Councilor, S. G. van der Heyden, situated a great tide above this island, at the mouths of the two rivers Mazaruni and Cuyuni.

In these rivers, likewise, just as in the river of Essequibo, properly so-called, there can be found not one plantation which furnishes any products except a little cassava bread, and this of so slight importance as not to deserve mention. [Appendix to Case, ii, 233.]

* U. S. Commission Report, i, 201.

† Flag Island hugs the east of the river, and whether it was due to this fact or to the opening and rapid colonization of the Demerara, while the Pomeroon remained closed, or only to the greater attractiveness of the lands, the center of gravity speedily transferred itself to the east of the Essequibo. Before the plantations on the west had reached the mouth of that river, those on the east formed a solid row clear around to the Demerara. [U. S. Commission Report, i, 201; *see* also Appendix to Case, atlas, maps 66, 67, 68, 70.]

‡ After lying a score of years unpeopled, it [the Pomeroon] was again colonized in 1686; but only to be laid desolate by the French in 1689. Thereafter the river was never again thrown open to settlement until the very last years of Dutch occupation. [U. S. Commission Report, i, 226.]

From the seventeenth century until the very end of the eighteenth it [Moruca] had no settlers, save for a single plantation during a few years; but before its final loss to the Dutch its lands may have been once more coming into occupancy. [U. S. Commission Report, i, 247; *see* also U. S. Commission Report, i, 201, 222, 224, 226, 243, 244; *also* same, ii, 612-632; *also* Appendix to Case, atlas, map 69.]

Pomeroon region not utilized by the Dutch, except for trade, etc.

take up the land immediately available on the banks of the Essequibo and Demerara.*

In 1794 there was some talk about establishing settlements on the Pomeroon: the river and adjacent territory were surveyed, and a map of them prepared;† but it was not until after the close of the eighteenth century, and after the British had taken possession of the colony, that cultivation extended as far as the Pomeroon.‡

In delta region, between Moruca and Orinoco, Dutch were mere traders.

As for the delta region beyond the Moruca, between that river and the main mouth of the Orinoco, the only relations of the Dutch to it, during the eighteenth century, were the relations of traders; and even these relations ceased soon after the middle of the century.§

There should possibly be excepted from this last statement a gang of Essequibo thieves who sojourned in Barima about 1766; yet their presence in that region, for a brief period, can be of no possible importance. They were denounced by the Dutch Governor himself; and shortly after were cleared out of the river entirely.‖

Summary of preceding.

It has been stated that, except for purposes of trade;

---

*. . . [I regard] the river of Pomeroon as a district bringing no earthly profit to the Company; and I am, moreover, convinced that, if once we should be so fortunate as to have this river [Essequibo] and Demerara completely settled (which cannot be expected inside of fifty years, for a considerable number, possibly even more than 300 plantations, can still be laid out if some pains be taken), no one would then be kept from settling in Pomeroon by the fact that there is no bourewey wood left there. [Appendix to Case, ii, 120.] As to the cessation of Dutch trade, see U. S. Commission Report, i, 210, 211.

† Appendix to Case, atlas, map 69.

‡ Appendix to Case, atlas, map 70. See also U. S. Commission Report, i, 225.

§ Down to this time (1764), indeed, there is in the records no mention of any Dutchman's sojourning in the Barima for any purpose save that of trade. [U. S. Commission Report, i, 283.]

‖ At the same time I shall write to the Governor of Orinoco concerning the state of affairs in Barima, which would become a den of thieves, a gang, rag-tag and bobtail, of our colonists staying there under pretense of salting, trading with the Indians, felling timber, etc. They live there like savages, burning each other's huts and putting each other in chains, and I fear that bloodshed and murder will yet come of it. [Appendix to Case, ii, 164–165.]

for the intercepting of runaway slaves; for fishing; for occasional wood-cutting; and for the temporary sojourn of some Dutchman; the Orinoco delta, from the main or "Great" mouth as far as the Moruca, and even the region beyond, between the Moruca and the mouth of the Essequibo itself, was in no way utilized by the Dutch. In order to show how entirely this statement is borne out by the facts it máy be well to refer to this in rather more detail.

Summary of preceding.

1. As to Trade.

Dutch trade to the Orinoco.

Trade with the Spanish colonists of the Orinoco, though forbidden by the laws of Spain, began in the last quarter of the 17th century to be encouraged by the Dutch authorities. For a brief period (1684-1690) it was forbidden on account of distrust of their own governor; but it was resumed after his dismissal.* At first the conduct of this trade may have been largely in the hands of the Dutch; and their passage through the rivers—the Moruca, the Waini, the Barima—which were its route, must have resulted in considerable traffic with the Indians of that quarter. But the Dutch of Essequibo had serious rivals in their neighbors of Berbice and Surinam;† and yet

* U. S. Commission Report, i, 260-270.

† Puzzling questions are raised as to the notions of the West India Company regarding the district lying beyond its northwestern post of Wacupo by its attitude toward the traders of the neighboring Dutch colonies of Berbice and Surinam, whose trade "in the district lying under the charter" they restricted or forbade, while their trade west of this post was tolerated, and it was even proposed to legalize it by a toll The Surinam traders carried on, indeed, on the testimony of the Essequibo governors, a larger trade with the Indians west of the Moruca than did the Company's colony itself. What bearing, if any, this fact may have upon the territorial claims there of the Company or of the Dutch is a problem. Not to be overlooked in this connection is the evidence from a later period that the passes granted by the Surinam governors for this trade were recognized by the Essequibo postholders. To be noted, too, is the Company's assertion, in answer to the request of the Essequibo col-

French trade to the Orinoco.

more serious in the French of the islands, who from 1685 to 1700 cut off this trade altogether, and continued thereafter to be troublesome competitors.* Before the middle of the eighteenth century the Spaniards themselves were beginning to take this trade into their hands.†

Spanish trade to the Essequibo.

By this time, too, and perhaps long before, these Spanish

onists to be allowed freedom of trade in the neighboring Spanish territory, that "although Orinoco, Trinidad, etc., is under the power of the Spaniards, still it also lies within the charter of the Company, where nobody has the right to trade except the Company and those to whom the Company gives permission to do so—so that it all is the territory of the Company, even though we have no forts there." It is, of course, the trade provisions of the charter which are here in thought. [U. S. Commission Report, i, 362-363; see *also* same, pp. 271, 272.]

* But it is the French of the Caribbean islands who seem to have been, in the seventeenth century, the especial patrons and allies of the Caribs of the Barima. Father Pelleprat, the Jesuit missionary, tells us that they had invited the French to plant a colony there, and that in March, 1654, he was informed by Indians of that river "that they had already built a fort in which the French could be quartered as soon as they should arrive." And no sooner did we have reports from the Dutch colony of Essequibo than we find in them complaints of French rivalry in this region. It was, as will be seen, a rivalry not without results to the Dutch. In 1684, when the French of these neighboring West India Islands raided the Orinoco and occupied Santo Thomé, the Caribs in the Barima showed their loyalty by murdering the crew and scuttling the ship of a Dutchman from Surinam, who had come thither for trade; and already they threatened to come with the French and lay waste the Dutch colony of Essequibo. The threat was no vain one, for in 1689 the French, aided by the Caribs of the Barima, made their way in canoes from that river through the Moruca passage and utterly destroyed the new Dutch colony on the Pomeroon; then, returning to the Barima, fortified themselves in that river. In 1695, aided by the Caribs of the Barima, they were even stationed in the mouth of the Pomeroon. [U. S. Commission Report, i, 259-260; see *also* same, pp. 274, 275.]

† Business with the Spaniard begins to grow better as time progresses, and we should have advanced somewhat better if the absence of goods through the long-deferred arrival of ships had not been a very great obstacle thereto. Some Spanish merchants have been obliged to wait here nine, ten, yea eleven months, to their great inconvenience. [Blue Book, 3, p. 90.]

There should sometime be some profit gained with the Spaniards, though the attempt is made as far as possible to pay attention thereto. But many Spaniards, come and go out of the river without coming under my observation. [Appendix to Case, ii, 102.]

It gave us especial pleasure to learn through a subsequent letter from you, dated September 9, how, by the zeal you have shown, the trade of the Spaniards in the river of Essequibo begins to develop more and

traders were making their way into the Dutch colony via the Cuyuni.*

Spanish trade to the Essequibo.

The Orinoco authorities found it easy to favor their own people in this competition by merely enforcing against the Dutch traders the Spanish laws and thus making the Orinoco too hot for them.† Both to avoid this danger and to lessen the risk of smuggling on their own side, the Dutch West India Company and the Essequibo government made it, from the middle of the 18th century, their settled policy to transfer this trade to Spanish hands.‡

No Dutch trade to Orinoco after 1761.

From about 1761 on, the trade was exclusively in the hands of the Spaniards; and from this time forward one scarcely hears of Dutch traders to the Orinoco; the current was all the other way; and the Spaniards were induced to come to the Essequibo to sell their products there. ¶

By 1794 the Governor-General, though himself a son

more, and we hope that all further means will be put in operation to make it altogether flourish there. [Appendix to Case, ii, 101.]

* That furthermore they, the members of the Committee, were of opinion, that the Company's shop there should again be started especially if some new colonists were to be sent thither, because not only would it in that case be extremely necessary for supplying the needs of those colonists, but also in view of the increasing Spanish trade it was not unlikely that a reasonable profit might be made by it; especially so, if it could be brought about that the Spaniards no longer, as heretofore has usually happened, tarry with their wares and articles of trade among the private settlers living up the river, but come with them farther down and as far as to the fort. [U. S. Commission, Report, ii, 333.]

† See *e. g.* U. S. Commission Report, ii, 335, 336.

‡ I have always imagined that it was best for our inhabitants to send few or no boats to Orinoco, and so compel the Spaniards to come here with their merchandise; in this way our people would not be exposed to the least danger, and the arrangement began to work very well. [Appendix to Case, ii, 120.]

¶ Not even a Dutch trader is again heard of in the Barima. The West India Company, which theretofore had always encouraged the colonial trade to the Orinoco, issued in 1761 its instructions that so far as possible this trade be transferred to the Spaniards and carried on, not from Essequibo to Orinoco, but from Orinoco to Essequibo. This policy was loyally and effectively carried out; and within two years the current of trade was flowing the other way. [U. S. Commission Report, i, 289.]

No Dutch trade to Orinoco after 1761.

of the colony, was seemingly ignorant that this trade had ever been in other than Spanish hands. *

Former Dutch trade relations with Barima a tradition by 1800.

By the end of the century the former trade relations of the Dutch with the Barima had become a mere tradition, subsequently distorted, knowingly or ignorantly, to serve as a supposed justification for a claim to territory far beyond the limits which Dutch occupation ever reached.

2. Capture of Runaways.

Dutch slave trade.

Slaves were extensively used by the Dutch, and it was essential to the life of the Essequibo Colony : *first*, to obtain them ; and *second*, to prevent their escape.

The demand for Indian slaves, which had been great and constant ever since the beginning of Dutch plantations in Essequibo, was much increased toward the middle of the 18th century by the influx of planters of other nationalities to whom the colony was now opened. In order to obtain these slaves the Caribs were induced to make raids into Spanish territory through the country in the immediate vicinity of the Spanish Mis-

Dutch slave raids into Spanish territory.

* A very noteworthy thing is that in the rainy season the Spanish lanchas come from Orinoco as far as Moruca by an inland way, passing from one creek into another, and they transport in this fashion their horned cattle and mules, and find on the way the necessary sustenance for the cattle, both grass and water.

Those inland voyages are made through the following creeks and rivers : from Moruca one comes into the creek Habon [Itaboe?] and Barimani, then into the river of Waini, which, from the point where one reaches it, is as large and deep as the river of Demerara. Two tides away from the mouth of the river Waini, to wit, on the southwestern side one finds a creek named Mocra which one goes up a couple of hours, when one passes into Rio Barima, about three tides from the mouth of the sea. That river is much larger than Rio Demerara and is reckoned twenty hours distant from the post of Moruca. From the mouth of the Rio Barima to Rio Orinoco one counts 3 [Dutch] miles distance ; between these two rivers there is again a creek named Amacura.

This report was made to us by the postholder Bartholy, who in for-

sions.* The Dutch themselves assisted in these raids, disguising themselves for that purpose as Indians.†

Dutch slave raids into Spanish territory.

The trade became so all-absorbing to the Caribs that in 1746 the Dutch Governor could say that their whole livelihood depended on it.‡ In 1758, the Prefect of the Spanish Missions wrote:

---

mer times has made various voyages to Orinoco. The navigation of the Spanish lanchas being disposed of, I shall again go on with my journal. [Appendix to Case, ii, 248; see, *also*, U. S. Commission, Report, i, 211, 289.]

* After invoking the name of God, the Commandeur Laurens d'Heere, informed the Court that, according to reports received, the Magnouw nation were killing all whom they could lay hands on up in Essequebo, and that they were driving away all other nations who were our friends. His Honour maintained that it was very necessary for the protection of the whole Colony to extirpate and annihilate these rebels if possible. This having been taken into consideration, it was unanimously agreed to order Jan Batiste, the Postholder at the Company's trading-place, Wacquepo, to come up the river about the beginning of next month, December, with as great a force of Indians, well armed with bows and arrows and the necessary ammunition of war, as he shall be able to collect, and that he shall be ordered by the Commandeur and Court to proceed against the said Magnouws, and to kill or capture all he can find, on the condition that for each head which he and his men take they shall receive two large axes, and for every slave taken and brought here as much in cash as such slaves are worth in public sale. [Blue Book, 3, 78.]

† Sire, the harvest is great, the soil of many pagan nations well-disposed and fertile for the reception of the Holy Gospel, and the labourers (though few) would produce much fruit if the enemy of souls did not avail himself of the avarice of the Dutch, and the bloodthirsty and inhuman character of the Caribs, to destroy in a day the apostolic labour of a whole year. They come up from the sea (both these nations) to rob and burn the villages of the Missions and carry off as many captives as they can, and sell them at Essequibo, Berbice, and Surinam, colonies of the aforesaid Republic established (not on the Orinoco), but a good distance to the east of its mouths. Besides the profit from slaves the Dutch are moved to keep up their strong alliance with the Caribs, by the value of the balsam of Tolu (Aceite de Maria), and of a species of bixwort found on the Orinoco. To procure these some Dutch introduce themselves among the fleets of these Indians, painted according to the custom of the said savages, by which they encourage them, and add boldness to the lamentable destruction which they work. Added to which many Caribs receive a great supply of arms, ammunition, glass beads and other trifles, with the understanding that they are to be paid for within a certain time with Indians, which they must take prisoners on the Orinoco. And when the time has elapsed, the Dutch creditors encourage and even oblige the Caribs to their bloody raids against the defenceless Indians of the Orinoco. [Appendix to Case, ii, 294-295.]

‡ I have it from a reliable source that they have been thinking of founding next year yet another nearer, whereat the inhabitants are much

Dutch slave raids into Spanish territory.

"it will not be an exaggeration to estimate the yearly sale by the Caribs at more than 300 young Indians, killing the old ones, over 400, which are not salable to the Hollanders, because they run away." *

These slave raids were not confined to the region between the Essequibo and the Orinoco, but extended into the very heart of Spanish territory, into the Caroni, the Caura, and even north of the Orinoco.†

Measures for retention of slaves.

The slaves once captured, it became necessary to adopt measures for their retention. From Essequibo

---

aggrieved, and the Carib Indians much more still, since thereby the slave trade in that quarter, from which alone that nation derives its livelihood, is wholly shut off. [Appendix to Case, ii, 97.]

* Appendix to Case, ii, 305.

† On these occasions Aruacas, Caribs and Dutchmen disguised come, for they are not likely to be detected. These last-named are accustomed to go ashore at the River Caura, and whilst the others are engaged in fishing for turtle, they occupy themselves in buying from the Caribs, in that and other rivers, Indian slaves. The fishermen also engage in the same traffic, and buy from our Indians other Indian slaves, and both the one and the other take a large number with them on their return journey. [Blue Book, 1, p. 89.]

It is not unlikely that the Hollanders stopped their purchase of Poytos at Cuyuni, because they do not hesitate to continue doing this illicit trade in the neighborhood of the Missions. Your Honor knows well that Captain Bonalde, within a day's journey from the Missions, arrested a Hollander who used to buy Poytos or Indians, who were sold to them by the Caribs, and although he was not actually found in the Carib's house, three Indian Poytos were rescued and several machetes and bugles were found in his ranch and distributed among the Miamo Indians. We know, besides, that very often the Hollanders pass by Paraba, Caura, and the sources of the Carony. They do that every year. [Appendix to Case, ii, 304-305.]

Tolerated now on the Maruca, they will next pass on to Barima, which empties into the same mouth, and later on they will come to the Aquire river, whose mouth is on the Orinoco itself, some leagues from the ocean. By this river the neighborhood of the Palmar Missions is reached, and by it they accomplish free communication with the other Missions in the interior of the country, as they have already done, owing to the indifference of Father Friar Bruno, of Barcelona, who for this reason was removed therefrom by his Prefect, and reduced to serve as a companion in another Mission, and deprived of active or passive part in the meetings. [Appendix to Case, ii, 301.]

On such occasions Aroacas, Caribs and Dutch come registered in order not to be molested. The latter are accustomed to land on the Caura river and other rivers to buy Indian slaves from the Caribs while the others fish for turtle. These fishermen also buy Indian slaves from our Caribs, and they all on the return take a large number of them. U. S. Commission Report, vol. viii (3), p. 167.]

Measures for retention of slaves.

there were two roads by which these unfortunates might make their way back to liberty. One was by the Cuyuni, the other by the inland waterway *via* the Pomeroon, Moruca, Waini and Barima.* For the purpose of capturing these runaways, the Dutch stationed sometimes one man, sometimes two or three, at strategic points.†

In March, 1767, Storm had earnestly suggested the advisability of putting "two good, armed, and well-manned coast-guards, one in the mouth and one outside the river, to put an end to all the desertions."‡

Moruca shanty

In 1726 or 1727, for example, the shanty on the Wacupo was moved to the Moruca, as a more suitable location for this purpose.§ (In April, 1770, Centurion

---

* As to taking efficacious measures against the running away of slaves to Orinoco and elsewhere, we are as much as anybody convinced of the necessity thereof. [Appendix to Case, ii, 172.]

With much greater sorrow we have learned of the outcome of the Mission on which the Secretary Rousselet de la Jarie was sent to Orinoco, so little advantageous to the colony, in spite of the hope of a favorable result which Don Hieronimo Fernandez de la Penna, Secretary to the Governor of Guayana, had so shortly before given you; and we with you fully appreciate the unpleasant results which sooner or later are to be expected therefrom, to the ruin perhaps of the whole colony, or at least of many planters in it, if the running away of the slaves cannot in some way be effectually stopped and prevented. [U. S. Commission Report, ii, 422-423.]

† Following the example of the States General, we hereby ask that you give us, at earliest opportunity, your detailed considerations in regard to this point—in the same way as you have already proposed to us, as an efficacious means against the desertion of the slaves, the manning of an outlier, which, as in Surinam, would have to remain lying outside to cut off their way on that side just as the postholders do on land. We confess that this expedient seems to us very apt, and in case of necessity it will be only a question of finding the amount required for its cost. [U. S. Commission, Report, ii, 424-425.]

And as regards the means of prevention to be set on foot yonder, namely, the fitting out and manning of two outliers, to wit, one in the mouth of the river and one outside, we refer you in this connection to what in our aforesaid missive we said in relation to an outlier, which we consider as here repeated. [U. S. Commission, Report, ii, 435.]

‡ Appendix to Case, ii, 170.

§ In October last the Commandeur informed the Court of his intention to Proceed to the Post of Wacquepo, lying between Orinocque and this river, at the end of the aforesaid month, and to inspect the same in com-

Moruca shanty. spoke of this post on the Moruca as having been tolerated 40 years).*

By 1754 these runaway slaves had discovered a new route from Essequibo back to their Orinoco home. It was by the outside sea current, which, running always along the coast from southeast to northwest, could carry their boats along with ease and safety.† The Dutch accordingly, in 1757, built a new watch-house at the mouth of the Moruca river.

It was a mere shelter, unmanned; but by granting land to one Beissenteufel, he was induced to settle at this place, and to take charge of this lookout.‡ His stay was short, for only a year or two after his arrival

Moruca hut abandoned. he had the misfortune to blow himself up with gunpowder, and the watch-house then fell into decay.§

The station at the mouth of the Moruca having thus come to an end, the older station, higher up on the

---

pany with the Councillor and Secretary; knowing that the said Post lies far out of the ordinary course of boats which come hither through the inland waters, it was his intention to choose a fit place in the River of Marocco to which he might transplant the house and Post, since all vessels which come through the inland waters must pass that way. Everything having been closely examined by the said gentlemen, they decided that the fittest place was where the horse-dealers from Orinocque generally moor their boats in the River of Marocco (called in the Indian language Accoujere), it being possible to build a house there so close to the river side that a hand grenade can be thrown into the boats, the river being at its narrowest there. The unfortunate state of affairs in Europe having been taken into consideration, it was resolved to establish the house and Post of Wacquepo upon the aforementioned site as soon as possible, and thus have an opportunity of being kept well informed of the hostile boats that had any intention of coming to disturb this river, and so enable us to place ourselves in a position to resist the same. [Appendix to Case, ii, 80.]

* For, as it appears from Document No. 1 of the "Autos," the Dutch are not, nor have they ever been, in possession of the rivers nor of the creeks which flow into the sea from Essequibo to the Orinoco. Nor have they any other settlement there than a guard in a thatch-covered house on the east bank of the River Marucca which they established there, and has been tolerated since about forty years, for the purpose of preventing the desertion of their slaves. [Blue Book, 1, p. 114.]

† U. S. Commission Report, i, 232-233

‡ U. S. Commission Report, i, 236.

§ U. S. Commission Report, i, 236.

river, continued for some time to serve the purpose, the postholder going down from time to time to the coast to intercept fugitives.* Moruca shanty.

In 1783, however, this higher station, too, during the occupation of the Colony by the French, was entirely abandoned; and it was not thereafter occupied.† Abandoned in 1783.

About 1785, after the restoration of the colony to the Dutch, a new station was put up at the mouth of the Moruca. After the expiration of the West India Company, in 1792, this was the only Dutch station which continued to appear on pay or muster rolls.‡ The British, during their occupation of the colony allowed it to fall into a very dilapidated state. In 1802 it was resumed by the Dutch during their brief occupation of the colony.§ Moruca trading station of 1785.

* Yet in 1765 the Moruca postholder, who had apparently come down to the coast in the effort to intercept certain fugitives, could report, "I am lying between the mouth of Moruca and Pomeroon, so that I can see everything that passes the seacoast"—language which certainly does not imply the presence there, at that date, of a regular lookout. And the historian Hartsinck, writing in 1770, after mentioning the post's erection there in 1757 at the joint cost of the Company and the planters, declares that [*Beschryving van Guiana*, i, 258-9] "it has since fallen to ruin." [U. S. Commission Report, i, 236; see *also* Blue Book, 3, 137.]

† Whether or no the English maintained the post, the French, who succeeded them in the possession of the colony, abandoned it; for on December 5, 1783, the Spanish officer, Inciarte, who had made so successful a reconnoissance here in 1779, reported the abandonment to his superiors, urging them to take advantage of the opportunity by occupying the place. This, however, so far as is known, was never done. [U. S. Commission Report, i, 238; see *also* Appendix to Case, ii, 440.]

‡ After the expiration of the West India Company and the assumption of the colonies by the State, in 1792, the only post which continues to appear on pay and muster rolls is that of Moruca. [U. S. Commission Report, i, 242.]

§ While I am finishing this letter, the Postholder of the post of Moruca comes to report that the detachment for that post arrived there three days ago, but that everything is in ruins and that the battery cannot stand for six weeks more; that an entirely new dike of some sort must be made there and all the buildings set back; that the few cannons found there are lying flat on the ground; that the gun-carriages are rotten, and that the English have cut and slashed everything to pieces; in a word, that things are in a hopeless state. I have not yet received a report from the officer who was ordered thither, and we shall have to await it;

No Dutch occupation of the interior.

As to the interior, apart from the ineffectual attempts of the Dutch in 1754-58 and in 1766-72, (to be referred to later), there was at no time any Dutch occupation whatever above the lowest falls of the Cuyuni.*

Dutch pursuit of fugitive slaves.

Of course the pursuit of runaways and their capture

---

but according to these details there is not much of good to be expected. [Appendix to Case, ii, 254.]

* Turning now, my Lords, to the matter of the River Essequebo, it is now about two years since I myself with Mr. van der Kaey proceeded up the river to find out whether it was not in any way possible to successfully set on foot some enterprise up above the falls, but we found the river very dangerous, so that in some places we were obliged to be drawn up in a corrial through the falls, with great danger to our lives. It is absolutely impossible to navigate the river with large boats, such as canoes, and it is equally impossible with barques, because above the plantation Nieuw Cortrijk there is fall upon fall. With regard to the land out there, it seems to me very good, but having inquired how high the water rose in those parts, it was pointed out to me in different places that it rose in the rainy season between 25 and 30 feet, so that nearly all the land is then under water, and there are also many great hills there which are nearly all rocky and very steep at the river side.

I have also carefully inquired, my Lords, what kind of trade might be done there with the Indians, and have up to the present not been able to discover any other trade but a little maraen which is brought thence, and sometimes a few red slaves. To this end two creoles went up the river only last year, who, having been out for seven or eight months, brought very little home. The only profit that this Colony derives from the River Essequebo is that the latter is very rich in fish, and is therefore visited annually both by the Company and by the private colonists for the purpose of salting, to which end two boats have again been prepared for your Lordships, which will be ready to depart in the month of October. I see no profit for your Lordships in sending any man up the river, because I can discover nothing of the savage nation. [Appendix to Case, ii, 81.]

Concerning the advantages of the trade in the rivers of Masseroeny and Cajoeny for the Honourable Company alone, this consists only in red slaves, and the order has been renewed because the veto was one kept up by all former Commandeurs. But most of the Indians having left those parts that trade is now of less profit, except for the orange dye. The plantation Poelwijk, lying up in the first-mentioned river, sometimes buys one or two red slaves in a whole year, but they are mostly children of about 8 or 10 years old, who are bought for about twelve or thirteen axes and choppers, together with a few provisions. The red slaves, too, cannot work together with a black slave, and are mostly used on the plantations for hunting and fishing, the women looking after the cassava for the daily consumption of the plantation. The great number of rocks which lie in these two rivers, and which occasion the falls by reason of the strong stream rushing over them, makes these rivers unnavigable for large vessels, wherefore it is impossible to establish any plantations there, although the soil is very well fitted for it. [Appendix to Case, i, 84-85.]

extended beyond the Moruca on the coast, and beyond Kykoveral in the interior; but such captures were always effected either without the knowledge, with the connivance, or by the express permission of the Spaniards.

Dutch pursuit of fugitive slaves.

Slave-Trading Cuyuni Stations of 1754 and 1766.

The two ineffectual attempts of the Dutch in 1754, and again in 1766, to establish slave and trading stations on the Cuyuni merit more than passing notice—not because of any importance on the part of the stations themselves, but merely because they furnished to the Spaniards signal opportunities for proving to the Dutch how thoroughly Spain was mistress of the Cuyuni-Mazaruni basin.

Failure of the Dutch to occupy interior.

In 1750 the acting Dutch Governor in speaking of the Spanish missions deprecated the opening of the trade in cattle with them "unless a good post were established" on the route.* In 1754 or 1755 such a station was actually established at some place on the lower Cuyuni, possibly as high up as the mouth of the Quive-kuru creek.

Proposal in 1750 to establish a trading post.

Its purpose was threefold: 1st, to foster trade with Indians and Spaniards; 2d, to capture new slaves, and

Purpose of the post.

* The aforesaid Persik has also informed me that the Fathers up in Orinoco were inclined to open a trade with this colony in cattle, which they, if able to obtain permission, could transport overland. If permission be asked and the Commandeur be still absent, I shall refuse it, until you shall be pleased to frame the necessary orders thereon, which I hereby request. On the one hand, this would contribute very much to the encouragement and stimulation of trade, but on the other hand it would be a safe and open way (not to mention times of war) for the slaves who might come to run away from this colony, unless a good post were established thereon. On account of the consequences, I have thought it best simply to mention this to you, that you may be pleased to deliberate thereon in your high wisdom as you may deem most proper, trusting that, as the Commandeur in person is with you, he will doubtless have spoken thereof also. [U. S. Commission, Report, ii, 335.]

Purpose of the post.

intercept runaways; and 3d, to keep an eye upon Spanish movements in that quarter.*

Post destroyed by the Spaniards in 1758.

When its purposes became known to the Spaniards, in 1758, they quickly descended from the savannas, made prisoners of the few persons whom they found, and laid waste everything about the post.†

No attempt to re-establish it.

No attempt was made by the Dutch to re-establish the post, and their remonstrances upon the subject remained unheeded by the Spaniards.‡

Some post required.

The importance of *some* post in the Cuyuni for the prevention of smuggling and for intercepting runaway slaves became each year more urgent.§ In 1763 the

* Appendix to Case, ii, 118–119.

† Having had the honour of writing to your Lordships but a short time ago respecting the state of affairs in Essequibo, I should have very little to say in this letter were I not obliged to inform your Lordships at the earliest opportunity of an occurrence that caused me not only great surprise but also great embarrassment. Nearly all the Caraiban Indians living on the River Cuyuni came down the stream last week, and informed the creoles of your Lordships' living just below the great fall of that river that the Spaniards of Orinoco, according to their computation about 100 strong, had come down the stream, and made a successful raid upon your Lordships' Post; that they had carried off as prisoners the Post-holder and his assistant, and a creole belonging to your Lordships, together with his wife and children; that they had laid waste the Post and all round it, and had threatened to come down stream again and serve the whole Colony in the same way. [Appendix to Case, ii, 125.]

‡ The destroyed post was not at once restored. Both the colonial authorities and the West India Company hoped that the Spanish Government would make reparation for the act of violence. But they waited in vain. [U. S. Commission Report, i, 336–337.]

The extract from the map of Mr. D'Anville, enriched by you with indication of the post in question and of many other places, and transmitted with your letter of March 18th, pleases us exceedingly. We shall not fail, when opportunity offers, to make the necessary use of it in the affair of Rio Cuyuni, of which we are by no means losing sight. [Appendix to Case, ii, 146.]

Concerning the affairs of Cuyuni we shall in the near future present a further memorial to the States-General. [Appendix to Case, ii, 147.]

Up to this time not the least answer has been received from the Court of Madrid to the memorial about Cuyuni presented by us to the States-General. In view of this, it is our intention to present one of these days a further memorial upon that subject to the States-General, with addition of what has happened since, and especially of the matter of the colonist I. Dudonjon. This further memorial will probably now be of more influence and effect, because of the war with England. [Appendix to Case, ii, 149.]

§ The Cuyuni was now, however, too familiar a route to be left open

Dutch Governor suggested to the Company that quietly and "without exercising the least violence," possession should be again taken of the post in Cuyuni.* *Some post required.*

This suggestion was approved.†

In 1766 a new post with three, soon after reduced to two, and finally to a single man, was established on the Cuyuni, probably at a different site from the post of 1758, but certainly not above Tokoro island. Cuyuni trading post of 1766.

The Dutch were, however, too weak, and the Spaniards too strong for this post to continue.‡ In 1769 it First site abandoned and post moved down in 1769.

with impunity. A rascally colonist went up the river and misused the Indians under pretence of authority. Spaniards or Spanish Indians repeatedly came all the way down to the Dutch plantations. The Caribs, in dismay, were all withdrawing to the Essequibo. Smugglers availed themselves of this door. Runaway slaves found the river an open road; they even began establishing themselves there. [U. S. Commission, Report, i, 337.]

* "I could greatly wish that your further memorial to the States-General might finally have the desired effect, and that an end might be reached of that matter, for which I very much long. But could you not find it good that meanwhile, without use of the least violence, possession should be again taken of the post in Cuyuni?" [U. S. Commission, Report, i, 337-338, note 10.]

† U. S. Commission, Report, i, 338.

‡ As early as March, 1767, there was a rumor that the post had been sacked by the Spaniards. This proved a false alarm; but Spanish influence over the Indians was such that they would do nothing for the postholder, and even passed the post in their canoes in defiance of his summons to lie to for inspection. In September there was again rumor that the post had been raided. This was again an error; but the governor a few weeks later declared to the militia officers of the colony that there were no Indians left there, and that the new postholder could scarcely maintain himself. In December the postholder, who had suffered much there from illness, asked on this pretext to be relieved; and in February, 1768, on the ground that the Indians would have nothing to do with a Frenchman, he was allowed to withdraw, and was stationed elsewhere. His place was never filled, nor were soldiers found for the post; the two byliers alone remained there, the elder in charge. [U. S. Commission Report, i, 339.]

I am anxious [writes Gravesande, March 23, 1767,] to have some tidings from Cajoeny, because I received a note from Director Van der Heyde yesterday in which he informs me that the creole, Tampoko, had been to see his son at Old Duynenburg, and had reported that he had heard from a few Indians that a party of Indians had been sent by the Spanish Mission to make a raid upon the Post, and had completely sacked it, and that he was going to find out how true that was. That Post is a terrible eyesore to the Spaniards, and there is no doubt that it stands in the way of their attaining some important aims. As soon as I

Cuyuni abandoned by the Dutch.

was abandoned; and the bylier in charge moved down to a place among the lower falls of the Cuyuni, at least as far down as Tonoma rapids. At this place the byliers led a solitary life until 1772, when the senior died. With his death all thought of posts on the Cuyuni was forever and definitely abandoned by the Dutch.*

---

have reliable tidings I shall deliberate with the Court what is to be done in the matter. [Appendix to Case, i, 169.]

At the same time [again wrote Gravesande, June 27, 1767,] I received a report from the Post in Cajoeny that the Indians are being bribed and incited to such a degree that they are unwilling to do the least thing for the Postholder, and that even when he orders the passing boats to lie to to see whether there are any runaways in them, they obstinately refuse to do so, and when he threatens to shoot upon them they reply that they have bows and arrows with which to answer. [Appendix to Case, ii, 170-171.]

The Assistant Gerrit Van Leuwen [again writes Gravesande, February 9, 1769,] has reported to me concerning the Post in Cajoeny, that he had heard from the fugitive Indians that a detachment of Spaniards had come to just above the Post, and had captured and taken away a whole party of Indians; that they had threatened to come again during the next dry season and proceed as far as Masseroeny to capture a party of Caraibans there, and that they would then sail down the Masseroeny and again up the Cajoeny and visit the Post on their way. I immediately sent him back again (after having provided him with gunpowder and other things), and charged him to use the oars as much as possible, and to find out through the medium of the Indians the time about which they would commence their expedition and to inform me of the same, when, in order that they may have a fitting reception, I will send a commando to Mr. Van der Heyden upon Old Duynenburg (with whom I have already spoken on the matter, and arranged what measures are to be taken), past which plantation they must go. [Blue Book, 3, 158.]

* Anxiety was now constant; and early in May [1769] there came once more tidings of a Spanish attack on the Post. This news was speedily corrected by a letter from the senior bylier, reporting not an actual but only a threatened attack. There was added the important information that he intended to remove the Post to an island named Toenamoeto, lying between two falls, where it would be better and healthier, and that he had already begun a clearing there; and he inclosed a bill for the expenses of this clearing. Though both the Company and the governor were annoyed at this high-handed action of the bylier, the step was not reversed. Fear, remarked the governor, often leads to mistakes; but "he is now there, and is much better protected against surprises"—though he adds, "this is wholly contrary to my intention, since for good reasons I would gladly have had that post gradually farther up the river." In June, 1770, the senior bylier, Jan van Witting, announced that the Indians were still drawing off from the Cuyuni; and in the same note asked for his own discharge at New Year's, when his time would be up. He remained there, however, through the following year and into

These ephemeral attempts at establishing posts on the Cuyuni, and an unsuccessful attempt in 1741-3 to mine for copper in the Cuyuni below Moroko creek, located somewhere near the head of what is now known as Suwaraima island, were the only attempts made by the Dutch during the 18th century to actually occupy land in the Cuyuni-Mazaruni basin above the lowest falls of those rivers.*

These, the only attempts at Dutch occupation of Cuyuni.

---

the next, apparently undisturbed by the Spaniards. Then his service was cut short by death; in the pay-roll for 1772 his decease is chronicled by the secretary, who adds that he could not learn the exact day of its occurrence. The second bylier, Gerrit von Leeuwen, seems to have served out his year and then returned to the ranks of the garrison. Thus quietly, but forever, the post in the Cuyuni disappeared from the records of the colony. [U. S. Commission Report, ii, 340-341.]

Yesterday evening Bont received a letter from Mr. Van der Heyde, in which that gentleman informs him that the Indians up there have told him that the Post in Cajoeny had been attacked by the Spaniards; that Jan Wittinge had been killed, and Van Leuwen carried off. Mr. Van der Heyde at the same time states that he is doing his best every day to hire Indians to send up the river in order to see whether this is true, but has up to the present not been able to persuade any Indians to go. If this be true it is insufferable, and it is too bad that a cat should allow itself to be eaten up by a small mouse. If we only had the soldiers we would make them pay for it well. [Appendix to Case, ii, 189.]

I shall not dwell upon this further, and shall try to obtain full information concerning it. I shall send the Postholder, G. Jansse, to Demerary as soon as possible. [Blue Book, 3, 166.]

* Early in 1741 this miner, one Thomas Hildebrandt, arrived; and until the middle of 1743 investigations were carried on vigorously under his direction, both in the Mazaruni and in the Cuyuni. His letters, and especially his journals, transmitted to the Company, give with prolix minuteness the method and the place of his researches. In the Mazaruni he went no further up than a little above the plantation Poelwijk, scarcely to the lowest rapids. In the Cuyuni, which promised better, he pushed his explorations much farther. The highest point reached by him was a creek called "Moroko-Eykoeroe" (Moroko Creek), where he opened a copper mine. The place was some two days distant from Kykoveral, and, so nearly as can be determined from his description, was on the right or south bank of the river, probably somewhere near the head of what appears in modern maps as the island of Suwaraima.

To facilitate his work and "to escape the great danger of the falls," Hildebrandt constructed a road through the forest from the indigo plantation, at the head of tide-water, to the still water above the first great series of rapids, and planned to build another stretch yet higher up stream.

The mines, however, did not speedily pay. Hildebrandt's brutal manners alienated superiors and subordinates, and drove the slaves to desertion. In 1743, after an alleged attempt to run away himself, bag and baggage, up the Cuyuni to Orinoco, he was packed off home to

Results of three-quarters of a century.

To sum up the results of three-quarters of a century: The colony, which in 1725 had clustered about Kykoveral, had abandoned that site and had moved down to the very mouth of the river, spreading little by little along the eastern bank of that river, and finally stretching over into the Demerara. The interior had been entirely abandoned except for purposes of trade and slave raiding. Two efforts at actual occupation in the Cuyuni-Mazaruni basin had proved failures, and that region had been abandoned to the Spaniards. The only Dutch post west of the Essequibo was at the mouth of the Moruca; but, except for that post, the Moruca, the Wacupo and the Pomeroon were entirely deserted.*

Europe. This was the first and the last of Dutch attempts at mining in the Cuyuni. [U. S. Commission Report, i, 317-318.]

That it is not true that the Hollanders had had, nor have now possession of the Cuyuni river (called by them Cayoeny), because when they established a Guard and Barrack, like that of Maruca, in the year seventeen hundred and forty-seven (1747), to facilitate the inhuman traffic and capture of Indians, whom they surreptitiously enslaved, within the dominions of the King our Lord, for the culture of the plantations and improvement of their Colony, as soon as it came to our knowledge, in the year seventeen hundred and fifty-seven (1757), they were dislodged from there, so that neither in the Cuyuni, Mascrony, Apanony nor any other rivers emptying into the Esquivo, have the Hollanders any possession; nor could it be tolerated that they should have it, because those rivers embrace almost all the territory of the Province of Guayana in their course from their western termini, where their headwaters originate, down to the eastern limit emptying into the Esquivo river. From that fancied possession it should result that the Hollanders would be the owners of the extensive Province of Guayana and that we, the Spaniards, had no more part of it than the said margin of Orinoco, which is an absurdity. [Appendix to Case, ii, 372.]

* Surinam, belonging to the Dutch, borders Berbische, on our right, and a little further up the coast is the French colony of Cayenne. With such restless neighbors about us we shall require to be watchful and alert. On our left we *approach* the river Orinoco, and what is termed the Spanish main. [Pinckard (*Dr.* Geo.) Notes on the West Indies. 2nd ed. London, 1816, i, 357.]

By inspecting the map you will find that our situation upon this coast is now rendered peculiarly interesting. The Spaniards are on our left, to leeward; the Dutch and French to windward on our right;—close in our rear are heavy and impenetrable forests, inhabited by wild and naked tribes; and our whole front is bounded by the open sea. [Same, ii, 115.]

Demerara, Feb. 11, 1797. A considerable time has now passed since

DUTCH WEAKNESS AND SPANISH CONTROL.

But what has been said shows merely the *limits* of Dutch *occupation*. It gives no idea of the weakness of the colony, nor of the frequent danger it was in of total extinction at the hands of the Spaniards, nor of the political control which Spain exercised throughout the region now in dispute up to the very banks of the Essequibo. It was a control which served to limit the growth of the Dutch colony; which, in great measure, shaped its policy; and which confined it always to the mouth of the Essequibo and to the region east of that stream. Effects of Spanish control.

The weakness of the colony and its danger of extinction was due mainly to three causes: 1st, to lack of population; 2d, to military weakness; and 3d, to fear of the Spaniards. Causes of Dutch weakness.

1st—Population.—In 1733, after a century's existence, the colony numbered less than two hundred Europeans.* Population.

our arrival upon this coast, and, having remained so long without any interruption, we had almost believed that the many foes upon our borders meant to leave us in quiet possession of the colonies we had taken; but we have, at length, been assailed from the quarter, whence we least expected it, having had a skirmish with the Spaniards to leeward, instead of the Dutch or French, who in more imposing aspect, threatened us from windward. Fixing upon a favorable moment when they expected that the garrison might be sunk in repose, after the festivities of the Queen's birthday, a party of Spaniards crossed [over from] the river Oronoko in the night of the 19th inst. and made an attack upon our outpost at Moroko, the remotest point of the colony of Essequibo. [Same, ii, 165.]

Pinckard, whose writings should have authority, and who came to Guiana in 1781, in the fleet under Sir George Rodney, which took Guiana from the Dutch, distinctly says, in his admirable letters on Guiana, that the most northern outpost of the Dutch colonies at the time of their first capture by the English was on the Morooca. [im Thurn (E. F.) Boundary pamphlet of 1879, in U. S. Commission Report, ii, 716; see *also* Appendix to Case, iii, 152.]

* There were then in Essequibo 66 Europeans, servants of the Company, and 854 slaves, distributed at the fort, Cartabo, the five Company's plantations, and the trading posts. The private estates numbered 25 to 30, averaging three Europeans and about sixty slaves on each; the whole population may therefore be estimated at about three thousand, besides the free Indians. [Rodway (J.) History of British Guiana. Georgetown, 1891, i, 73.]

Military weakness.

2D—MILITARY WEAKNESS.—The military condition of the Dutch is thus referred to in letters of the Essequibo Governor:

June 8, 1734

In a letter to the West India Company, written on June 8, 1734, the Commandeur in Essequibo speaks of the Spaniards as "formidable" and of the Dutch as "very feeble." He submits the following question for their Lordships' consideration:

"First, as the Spaniards are making themselves so formidable by the collection of a considerable number of troops, and we on the contrary are very feeble here, whether it is not of the greatest necessity to send a militia reinforcement hither, since the real design of the Spaniards is unknown to us."*

Sept. 2, 1754.

Again on September 2, 1754, Gravesande, then Commandeur in Essequibo, wrote to the Company:

"With the small number of soldiers I cannot repel the least aggression in those quarters. It is even impossible for me (however necessary at this conjuncture) to detach eight or ten men to garrison and defend as far as possible the post of Moruca, which will, I fear, see trouble. All that I can do is, with the aid of the Carib nation, whose flight from Barima I daily expect, to cause all possible hindrance to the undertaking; but then I should want ammunition and food and have none of either."†

Aug. 15, 1758.

In 1758, August 15, Gravesande writes to the Company:

"In the current year many people have died in this Colony, and the garrison is in a very lamentable state; one soldier dies after another, and, of those who fall ill, there is scarcely one who recovers. We have, therefore, not more than fourteen men at present who are capable of doing duty, none at all in Fort Kijkoveral, which I have had to leave unprotected, and one solitary man in Demerary."‡

* Appendix to Case, ii, 86.

† Appendix to Case, ii, 112-113.

‡ Blue Book, 3, 109.

Again in 1760, October 24, he writes to the Company: Oct. 24, 1760.

"The River Cajoeny is still unguarded, and presents an easy road to fugitive slaves." *

In 1761, May 28, he writes to the Company: May 28, 1761.

"The two soldiers there (in Demerara) could not prevent him from going, and I could not send more because I have only seventeen more privates here, of whom but very few remain when there is some patrol to be sent out, as has frequently been the case lately." †

In 1764, December 28, after describing some details of the plans and acts of the French on the east (i. e., on the Amazon side of the Dutch colony) and the Spaniards on the west, he says: Dec. 28, 1764.

"Thus, what with the French on the east and the Spaniards on the west, we are really like a little boat between two men-of-war.

I shall not attempt to give my masters advice in a matter which it is in no one's power to prevent or to circumvent. My only aim in this is to respectfully submit to your Lordships what is our humble opinion concerning this in all our Colonies situated on the mainland, and our well-grounded fears concerning the consequences.

I, for my part, see no remedy for this matter except by populating the Colony and establishing good Posts in the interior, from which a sharp and careful lookout can be kept upon all movements." ‡

In 1766, December 8, speaking of the soldiers, he says: Dec. 8, 1766.

"Herewith I will again reiterate my request that no French or Flemish be sent, but as many Protestants as possible. The proximity of the Spaniards, and especially of the Spanish Missions, renders it impossible to place the slightest trust in Catholics." §

* Appendix to Case, ii, 143.

† Blue Book 3, 116–117.

‡ Appendix to Case, ii, 159.

§ Appendix to Case, ii, 168.

Feb. 18, 1768. In 1768, February 18, he writes to the company thus:

"I was very pleased, my lords, on reporting the arrival of the twelve men to the Director-General to hear from him that, according to your lordships' letter, they were all Protestants and that there was not a Frenchman, Fleming, Portuguese, or Spaniard amongst them. But when I mustered them I found to my great surprise that out of these twelve men there were only three who were not French, these being the corporal, who comes from Utrecht, and has served in the State troops for some years, and a German, a native of Zweibrucken, and a French deserter. The others are all French deserters, so that I conclude that your lordships have been scandalously deceived by the recruiting agents, who are infamous scoundrels."*

Sept. 15 1768. In 1768, September 15, speaking of the desertions of the soldiers in considerable bodies, he says:

"Even if they went away before our eyes, in a manner of speaking, what could we do? To have them pursued would be going *ex Scilla in Charibdim*, for the pursuers would very probably join them, and the more so because they would be well armed and well furnished with provisions.

"Therefore, my Lords, be pleased not to take it amiss if as long as I have the honour to be in your Lordships' service (which I trust will be but a short time) I send back to Europe by the first ship all recruits who come here and turn out to be French. Necessity compels me to do this, and I would no longer be answerable to God or man for the danger into which the Colony would be brought by this."†

In this same letter he protests again his weakness, and says:

"Must we, my lords, regard all this quietly and endure all these insults and hostile acts? Must we see our posts raided and ruined and our boats attacked upon our own coasts?"

March 15, 1769. In 1769, March 15, speaking of the Spanish attacks, he asks:

"May I ask once more whether all this must be borne quietly

---

* Appendix to Case, ii, 175.

† Appendix to Case, ii, 178.

and whether your lordships' patience has not yet come to an end? With me it is *Patientia lesa tandem furor fit.* March 15, 1769.

What can I do with such a small garrison? The burghers are not yet ready for service—the letters to the burgher officers calling them together on the last day of March have been sent off—the general meeting is at hand, and there is *periculum in mora*—three clerks are continually at work writing commissions, instructions, and orders, but everything is so spread about that it will take twelve or fourteen days before everyone can be warned.

With the exception of the rebellion of Berbices this is one of the most critical matters I have been in during my long years of service. Had I the power and were my hands free I should not feel embarrassed and would be quite willing to risk my grey head in the affair."*

In 1769, May 12, he again writes: May 12, 1769.

"According to the last reports from the Postholder and from the Caraibans, they are still all in Barima, having sent their prisoners to Orinocque, and they threaten to come again at an early date, and not only carry off all the Indians from Powaron, but even to attack and plunder our plantations." †

On July 26, 1769, the company wrote to the Commandeur that they were willing that he should secretly incite the Caribs to murder the Spanish missionaries and their flocks, but added, July 26, 1769.

"We do not as yet think it advisable to use direct retaliation, for more than one reason, but especially on account of the weakness of the garrison."‡

Finally came this wail from the Governor:

"It is finished now, my lords; neither Postholders nor Posts are of any use now. The slaves can now proceed at their ease to the Missions without fear of being pursued, and we shall in a short time have entirely lost possession of the river Cajoeny." §

It is not strange that a Colony so inherently weak Relations of the Dutch with the Caribs.

* Appendix to Case, ii, 184.
† Appendix to Case, ii, 190.
‡ Appendix to Case, ii, 197.
§ Appendix to Case, ii, 180.

Relations of the Dutch with the Caribs.

should endeavor to strengthen itself by getting outside assistance. This, and the slave trade, explain the relations of the Dutch with the Carib Indians, whom they bribed, coaxed and incited into becoming at times their slave catchers, and at times their protectors against the Spaniards.

In 1748, December 2, Storm van 's Gravesande wrote:

"The Spaniards were beginning to approach more and more up in Cuyuni but a war having some weeks ago arisen between the Carib nation and that of the Warrows, which is carried on very obstinately, this will stop their further progress, and possibly, if the Caribs obtain the upper hand, they will be driven somewhat farther away, without our having in the least degree to meddle therewith."*

The "Chief of the Spaniards" he quotes as saying

"That the whole of America belonged to the King of Spain, and that he should do what suited himself without troubling about us;"

And then adds:

"Seeing that all my remonstrances and letters to the Spaniards are of no avail, and that no redress is obtainable, I intend to tell the chiefs of the Indians, when they come to me, that I can provide no redress for them, and that they must take measures for their own security. Then I feel assured that in a short time no Spaniard will be visible any more above in Cuyuni."†

In 1754, September 2, Gravesande, writing of reported silver mines between the Orinoco and Moruca, and possible aggression there, says:

"I cannot repel the least aggression in those quarters. It is even impossible for me (however necessary at this conjuncture) to detach eight or ten men to garrison and defend as far as possible the post of Moruca, which will, I fear, see trouble. All that I can do is, with the aid of the Carib nation, whose flight from Barima I daily expect, to cause all possible hindrance to the undertaking."‡

* Appendix to Case, ii, 101.

† Appendix to Case, ii,102.

‡ Appendix to Case, ii, 112–113.

Relations of the Dutch with the Caribs.

Again in 1754, October 12, writing of the attack of the Caribs upon the Spanish Cuyuni missions, he says that this attack "has covered us on that side, so that we have nothing to fear from that direction."*

In 1755, Gravesande, to protect himself against the Acuway Indians, thought his only recourse might be to fan the standing feud between them and the Caribs.†

In 1764, February 28, he wrote:

"The Caraibans, about whom mention is made above, have come back, bringing with them a large quantity of right hands from the rebels whom they killed, for which I paid them this morning, it being the custom in the Colonies to pay as much for a runaway's head or hand as for a slave." ‡

In 1768 he wrote:

"The expedition of the Caraibans, thank God, turned out very successfully. * * *. The negroes were attacked and seven, together with two women, were killed, whilst three men and four women escaped; the Acuways are after these. §

---

* Appendix to Case, ii, 115.

† The nation of the Acuways, which is very strong in the interior, and some of whose villages both in Essequebo and in Mazaruni and Demerary are situated next to our plantations, commenced [the war] with attacking the dwellings of some free creoles belonging to the plantation Oosterbeek, and massacreing those they found there. Thereupon they spread themselves and caused terror everywhere. Most of the planters living in Masseroeny retired to an island with their slaves and their most valuable goods, and none of them dared to stay at night on their plantations. A few days after that the aforesaid Acuways attacked the plantation of a certain Pieter Marchal (who, according to general report, is the chief cause of this revolt) at half-past five in the morning, killing two of his people and wounding five, most of whom have since died.

Many of the colonists, and amongst them several Councillors, have requested me to send out an invitation to the Caraiban Indians to take the field against the Acuways, but as there are many difficulties connected with this, I have not yet decided to do so, and am of opinion that such measures should not be taken until absolutely necessary. Because, if the Caraibans come (which they will certainly do at the first invitation), they will come several hundred strong, and ask for bread and other provisions, of which we have none.

But if I am unable to succeed in so doing, and if, as I hear, they assemble in large numbers and persist in their hostilities, I shall be compelled to choose the lesser of two evils and set the Caraiban nation at work, which I cordially hope will not be necessary, and which step I shall only take in the last extremity. [Blue Book, 3, 104–105.]

‡ Blue Book, 3, 127.

§ Blue Book, 3, 152.

Relations of the Dutch with the Caribs.

"The Carnibans were not at work very long, having killed seven men, one woman and one girl. * * * They have brought the seven right hands to me, and I am just now occupied in paying them."*

The Dutch dependence upon the Caribs is excellently depicted in a letter written by Gravesande on May 12, 1769, in which he says "the outlook is daily becoming blacker for the colony," and adds:

"I asked the Caraiban Owl this morning whether the Caraibans were no longer men and whether they had no hands with which to defend themselves, whereupon he replied, 'Indeed, they have; but the Spaniards have guns, and we only bows and arrows. Give us rifles, powder, and shot, and we will show you what we are.' Even had I been inclined to do so I could not, having no further supply of these than just sufficient for the garrison."†

Dependence of the Colony on its Indian allies.

This dependence of the colony on its Indian allies and the submission of the latter to the Spaniards, is shown by the following extract from a letter of Gravesande, January 6, 1772. He says:

"The former Postholders in Maroco were able to do something to arrest the progress of this evil, they having at least six or seven hundred Indians around that post, some of whom they could always have out at sea, but the unauthorized attacks of the Spaniards have driven these natives away, and the Spaniards even came to the post, as your lordships know, sword in hand, to drive away or carry off the few that still remained, and succeeded only too well in doing so."‡

* Blue Book, 3, 154.

† Appendix to Case, ii, 191.

‡ Appendix to Case, ii, 218.

XI.—SPANISH CONTROL AND SETTLEMENT IN THE DISPUTED TERRITORY. 1725-1800.

With such scanty defence no wonder that the Dutch were in fear of the Spaniards. No doubt they had reason for this: a statement of Spanish strength and activity during this period will show it. Dutch fear of the Spaniards.

Turning to this it will be convenient to consider:

1.—THE COAST REGION.

From the Orinoco to the Essequibo the Spaniards claimed dominion. They also exercised exclusive control there. Spanish control of disputed territory.

This control of the Orinoco itself, which can hardly need demonstration, is evidenced by their repeated seizure of Dutch craft found trespassing there—both those entering for the purposes of trade and those attempting to carry on fishing at the mouth of the river. Spanish control of the Orinoco.

Thus, in 1701, the Dutch Governor mentions, as a thing well known by experience, "the prohibitions we have already met in the trade to Orinoco."*

In 1712 his successor in this governorship reported that the Spaniards would not allow the Dutch to enter the Orinoco;† and in the following year he wrote of the Dutch traffic there that "it took place outside the district of the Noble Company, and was but carried on

* U. S. Commission, Report, ii, 201.

† Blue Book 3, 74.

Spanish control of the Orinoco.

solely on Spanish ground in the River Orinoco."* And commenting again on this subject in 1714, he admitted that "Orinoco, Trinidad, etc., is [sic] under the power of the Spaniards."†

In 1717 the Dutch colonists of Essequibo begged to be allowed to trade there, declaring that "the Orinoco is a river which is accounted as the property of the King or Crown of Spain, and hence that nation master there."‡

In 1719 the Spanish Commandant in the Orinoco arrested a Dutch trader who attempted to pass up the river; and the Dutch authorities of Essequibo were so sensible of the justice of Spanish complaints on this point that they not only made stricter the passes granted for this trade but thought of prohibiting it altogether.§ In 1727 a Dutch trader from Essequibo was seized by the Spaniards, who told him that "they had orders from the Governer of Trinidad to stop the trade in that river."‖ In the following year the same fate befell a Surinam Dutchman who was but fishing in the neighborhood of that river.¶

Policy of the Dutch to change current of trade.

In fact, this danger came to be so well understood as to terrify Dutch commerce, and from the middle of

* Blue Book 3, 74.

† U. S. Commission, Report, ii, 241.

‡ Blue Book 3, 76.

§ U. S. Commission, Report, ii, 245–247.

‖ Blue Book 3, 80.

At the end of August last year twenty-three red slaves ran away from the plantation belonging to Pieter la Rivière to Orinocque, and he having sent his son there to claim them, but without any results, resolved to go there in person, but on arriving at the usual mooring place in that river he was attacked by a vessel flying the Spanish flag, and was unfortunate enough to be killed. Those with him begged for quarter, whereupon the Spaniards took all their merchandize, and told them that they had orders from the Governor of Trinidad to stop the trade in that river. [Appendix to Case, ii, 80–81.]

¶ Blue Book 3, 81.

The Secretary, H. Gelskerke, having communicated to us a certain

the century it was the Dutch policy to transfer this intercolonial trade to Spanish hands. Yet the Dutch smugglers were still often seized there.* Policy of the Dutch to change current of trade.

During 1767 the following property was seized and confiscated by the Spanish: A launch and contents from Essequibo, a boat and contents from the same, 4 mules loaded with foreign goods, several goods, 16 small barrels of brandy, an Indian boat with Dutch goods from Essequibo, one English sloop and Spanish schooner, 2 Spanish launches, an English boat and French schooner and French sloop, another French schooner. These were all tried and adjudged good prizes at Guayana.† Spanish seizures in the Orinoco.

---

letter written by Jan Batiste from the Post in Wacquepo, and opened by him (the Secretary) in the absence of the Commandeur, in which information was given that the Spaniards of the Orinocque had with armed force taken possession of a Suriname vessel fishing in the neighborhood of the aforesaid river. [Appendix to Case, ii, 82.]

* See, *e. g.*, the list of such seizures reported by the Spanish Contador of Guayana on Jan. 28, 1769. [Appendix to Case, ii, 366-368.]

† Don Andres de Oleaga, Official Royal Accountant of this City of Guayana and its Province for his Majesty (whom God preserve), etc.

I certify in the best manner I can, for whatever purpose, and before the Señores that may see it, how, after the arrival of Señor Don Manuel Centurion, Captain of the Royal Corps of Artillery, and Commandant General of this said Province, pursuant to his great energy and zeal in the Royal service, the following confiscations and seizures were made: On the twenty-seventh of January of the past year of seven-seen hundred and sixty-seven, in a closed port of the Presidio of old Guayana, a launch coming from Esquivo, Dutch Colony, with two slaves, and cargo of Taphia rum and merchandise, from Don Vicente Franco. On the sixth of March of said year, at the same Presidio, various goods from Bernardo Montes, who was coming from the same Colony in a felucca. On the eleventh of April of the said year, on the land within the said Presidio, four mules loaded with different kinds of foreign clothing, without permit or license. On the twenty-second of said month and year, above the port of this city, different articles, without permit or license, from Lorenzo Yeguas. On June sixteenth of the said year, at the Presidio aforesaid of old Guayana, sixteen kegs of brandy, from Master Gazpar Vidal, who was introducing them clandestinely and left them buried on an islet in the Orinoco. On September twenty-eighth of the same year, at the port of Piacoa, below the aforesaid Presidio, a canoe laden with Dutch goods from Esquibo, from Pedro Sanchez.

And by the Sergeant of the Company of Pioneers, Ciprinno Maiorga,

Dutch prevented from fishing in Orinoco.

The Dutch effort to fish in the mouth of the Orinoco was more persistent; and was the cause of repeated arrests by the Spanish officials. In November, 1769, the Dutch Governor reported the ruin of their fisheries; and before 1770 the Essequibo Dutch finally abandoned them.*

---

with the pirogue he commanded, one of the Orinoco corsair canoes from the aliens engaged in the clandestine extraction of mules, horses, cattle, and other products, through the Guarapiche and Theresen rivers, which empty in the interior of the Golpho Triste de la Paria. An English sloop named the *Sevillana*; a Spanish schooner, the *Esperanza*; two launches, also Spanish; an English boat with four lately-imported negroes, some animals, and different foreign articles, besides (in the same campaign and before returning to this city) a French schooner named *Maria Louisa*, with two newly-imported negroes; two barrels, one of claret and the other of *Taphia* rum, and ten *arrobas* (250 lbs.) of *chinchorro* thread; and, also, on the same occasion, in company with the cruiser armed at the Island of Trinidad, a French sloop and schooner with various goods and newly-imported negroes, of which, after deducting all expenses and the sixth part, which the officials retained, they delivered to him the half, which amounts to seventeen hundred and ninety-two *pesos*, twenty-four *maravedis*, which brought in this place two-thousand and eighty-five *pesos*, three *reals*, one and two-fourths *maravedis*. Which seizures were declared to be legal and belonging to His Majesty on March 26th, April 30th, and July 29th of last year—1768. [Appendix to Case, ii, 366-367.]

* Appendix to Case, ii, 216.

The principal fishery, my Lords, has always been in the mouth and between the islands of Orinoque, near the Warouws, to which we send salting markott twice every year. This has never been prevented until recently, to the inexpressible injury of the Company's plantations and Colony, because there now being a want of that fish, and the slaves being obliged to have their rations, salt cod has continually to be bought, which even in one year runs pretty high, and sometimes brings me into difficulties with the payment. Only this week I paid over 300 guilders to Captain Andrew; the twelve casks of meat which each plantation gets annually are of little use, and 1,000 lbs. of fish is soon gone. [Appendix to Case, ii, 176.]

A report which I received after the closing of my letters compels me to add these few lines. A Spanish privateer from Orinocque cruising along our coast made an attempt to capture your lordships' salter before the River Wayni (indisputably the Company's territory) and fired very strongly upon him. The latter was cautious enough (not being able to escape otherwise) to run his boat high and dry upon the bank so that he could not be reached by the privateer who, having continued to fire upon him for some time, and seeing that he could do nothing, finally departed.

They are not content with most unreasonably keeping our runaway slaves and with hindering us from carrying on the fishery in Orinocque, which we have always been free to do, but they now wish to prevent us from salting along our own coasts, and will in this manner end by closing our river and no boats will dare to go out any more. Is this proper

Assertion of Spanish authority in coast region.

In the coast region between the main mouth of the Orinoco and the Essequibo the Spanish assertion of authority was not less clear. In 1732 the Swedes conceived a project of settling in the Barima. This being reported by the colonial authorities to Spain, a royal order enjoined prompt and thorough resistence. Careful investigation was made, and a force of soldiers was gathered for the purpose of expelling the intruders. All this was communicated by the Spanish governor to the governor of Essequibo, who not only made no protest, but furnished supplies to the Spaniards; and the Dutch West India Company, to whom the matter was reported with a request for instructions, did not so much as deign to reply.*

In 1755 the Spanish Prefect of the Capuchin missions, in whose province this district lay, demanded of the Dutch postholder of Moruca some Indians who had for "already over ten years been dwelling under the Post; adding that, in case of reluctance, he would come

behaviour on the part of our neighbours and allies? [Appendix to Case, ii, 177-178.]

Meanwhile our fisheries are ruined, and we have lost all our runaway slaves. [Appendix to Case ii, 213.]

The fishery in Orinocque still being closed, I am compelled to buy cod for the plantations and for the rations of the slaves." [Appendix to Case, i, 216.]

* On his return he reported that he had put to sea by the principal river of the Orinoco, and entered the creek called Barima, where, according to the Caribs, the Swedes were established. Having considered this matter in my Council of the Indies, and taken the advice of my Attorney-General, and deliberated thereupon, seeing that the information sent by the aforesaid Alcaldes, though not to be despised, is not full enough to warrant my making any order in the matter, I have resolved to command, and hereby do command, that soon as you receive these despatches you do forthwith verify the facts of the matter, and, in case any orders should be necessary, you do forthwith make such orders as you think advisable, giving me an account of your proceedings in this matter with all dispatch, remembering that I have also instructed the Governors of Caracas and Margarita by despatches sent this day. [Appendix to Case, ii, 283. See *also* same, ii, 257-266; *also* Blue Book **1**, 64-65; **3**, 84-85, 224-226.]

Assertion of Spanish authority in coast region.

with sufficient force to fetch them, and take them away in chains."*

Two years later, in 1757, there came to the Spanish general commanding in the Orinoco tidings that the Dutch were building a new fort on the Moruca. He at once ordered a reconnoissance to be made. The new fort proved to be only a watch-house at the mouth of the river to prevent the escape of slaves, and it was not interfered with.† But the occurrence gave occasion for vigorous protest to the governor of Guayana against the toleration of the Dutch in this quarter, lest, being suffered to stay in the Moruca, they pass on to the Barima, and even to the Aguire.‡

Barima ordered to be cleared of Dutch slave traders.

In 1760 the Spanish Governor ordered the arrest of certain Dutch slave traders whom he learned were lurking in the Barima.§

*After the despatch of my last, the Postholder of Marocco has come, and has brought me a letter from a missionary Father written to him from Oronoque, wherein he has requested him to deliver up and send to him some Indians of the Chiama nation, by us called Shiamacotte, and who have already (over ten years) been dwelling under the Post, adding that, in case of reluctance, he would come with sufficient force to fetch them, and take them away in chains. [Appendix to Case, ii, 119; see *also* Blue Book, 3, 105.]

†I inform Y. H. that I have performed the duty entrusted to me to reconnoitre the waters of the Moroca channel, and the fortification you were informed of, from which reconnoissance it results that the information is incorrect, for on the whole of that channel and the other channels communicating therewith there is no fortification to be found, and all there is is the news that the Dutch of the Esquivo Colony intend to move the guard which, under the name of post, they maintain on the Moroca channel, taking it down to the mouth thereof, emptying into the ocean, which will be about a distance of six leagues, for which purpose they have cut down trees and made many clearings for sowing that site, and built the houses necessary for the Aruaca Indians and the Dutch, which news I have been unable to verify with certainty, and I have only heard it said that the purpose is to prevent the negro slaves of the Company and residents of the said Colony from running away so easily to these Dominions, for the said guard being at the mouth of the Moroca, it can watch the boats that, without entering it, may pass by the coast to take the main mouth of this river. [Apppendix to Case, ii, 301-302.]

‡U. S. Commission Report, viii (3), 175.

§Whereas, on account of a report received from the Most Reverend Prefect of the Missions of this Province, I have become aware of the information received by him from four fugitive Poyto Indians about the tyrannic power of the Hollanders inhabiting the neighboring Colonies of Esquivo and

As a result of this two launches and two Indian boats were captured.*

Barima ordered to be cleared of Dutch slave traders.

The officer in charge of the expedition also reported that near the point between Waini mouth and Barima,

---

Surinam, at the mouth of the Barima creek, coming out from this river, where five Hollanders from said colony are staying and carrying out the inhuman and lucrative commerce they maintain with the wild Indian tribes who trade in the Orinoco, buying from them the infidels taken in their wars, making them prisoners and trading them for iron utensils, clothing, and munitions of war; and as said Hollanders are awaiting for a party of Indians, they have sent Carib agents to purchase said Indians and bring them to their Colony.

Such an illicit traffic in human beings is already going on. The four Indians who escaped were included as victims and came in quest of protection to the said Missions. As the service of our Lord and of His Catholic Majesty requires the stopping of this illicit trade, and the punishment of the Hollanders of the above-mentioned Colony, who possessed them in their own country, (if they had any right for this kind of possession), [a better translation would be: *to keep the Dutch of the said colonies by chastisement within their own possessions (if so be that they can hold them lawfully)*], they ought not to be allowed to communicate through the rivers and dominions of the King. Therefore, in virtue of the powers granted to me, I order and command that the Lieutenant of Infantry and second officer of this place, Don Juan de Dios Gonzales de Flores, without any delay whatever, depart on board the Royal vessel that he will find in Port Royal with a crew of ten men and manned in the ordinary way, armed with two light guns, and the necessary stores for twenty days. He will take Spanish river pilots and the fugitive Indians, and go to the place where said Hollanders are staying. He will proceed straightway, navigating night and day, and as soon as he reaches the place, he will attack the ranch, after having surrounded it. He will imprison the Hollanders, French and Spaniards found there, at the words, "Long live the King!" and will employ his arms in punishing and apprehending the same persons, as well as the Caribs that he may find in their company, carrying out this inhuman trade. He will likewise seize every vessel he may meet, going up or down the river, and the foreigners as well as Spaniards unprovided with the lawful and proper papers of navigation. The masters and crews of the same will be brought along to this place, well secured. The full cargoes as well, without allowing the least fraud or disorder by the troops of his command. [Appendix to Case, ii, 327-328.]

*As a consequence, said Lieutenant Don Juan de Flores has seized and brought along with him a schooner and two launches which were anchored under the artillery of the Castle of San Francisco de Asis, which is the chief port of this city. [Appendix to Case, ii, 328.]

Inventory of Seizures.—In the first place, there was a schooner with her main and foremast, and rigging without sails.

One small anchor, with its corresponding rope.

Five barrels of salt fish.

One launch, with a mast, canvas shrouds and a round sail of coarse cloth.

Four barrels of powdered salt.

One curiara (a small Indian boat) for the service of the launch, with wash boards. Six hatchets, ten short coarse Indian drawers, eight knives, six bundles of beads and an old case.

Barima cleared of Dutch traders.

he had captured one vessel with ten Arawak Indians from Essequibo colony on their way to fish in the Orinoco.*

In 1761 the Spaniards cleared the Barima of Surinam traders. †

In this same year, 1768, the Spanish marine police cleared out, by order of the Spanish authorities, certain Dutch plantations which, without the knowledge of the Dutch Government of Essequibo, had just been established in the Barima. Their occupants escaped by flight; but the property was confiscated and sold at auction by the Spanish officials.‡

Another launch, with its mast, canvas shroud and a round sail.
A small anchor with its corresponding hemp rope.
One curiara, answering as a boat. [Appendix to Case, ii, 329.]

* Lieutenant Don Juan de Dios Flores testified, that having left this port, under orders of the Commander, to proceed to the Barima creek, and having reached and tacked about the mouth of it, on the eleventh instant [Sept., 1760] at about four o'clock in the afternoon, he descried a sail towards the point of Guani, that was coming in the direction of the mouth of the Orinoco, and he went after it and having met her and fired a small gun, she stopped immediately, and having boarded her he found ten Aruaca Indians who came from the Esquivo Colony to fish in the river, three of whom ran away, throwing themselves into the river, and on the following day he continued his journey and went through the mouth of Barima, going up the creek for about three leagues, when he descried a vessel that was left aground by the low tide, at a long distance, finding no means to reach on board the same, until it was full tide, when he could draw near. The people and the crew on board, as they had seen and recognized his vessel, had left theirs, carrying away their sails and cutting the best part of the rigging. Although he tried his best to reach them, he could not succeed. Through the Aruaca Indians who had been seized he was informed that that schooner belonged to the Esquivo Colony, and came there for the purpose of fishing; that finding himself with these two vessels without any crew, he had only four men in their charge, two men in each one; that he had only six men left, and being informed that five days at least were necessary to reach the place where the traders in Poytos were reported to be, it was natural to suppose they had been warned of his visit by those who had left the vessel; that he found [it] necessary to return at once, as he did, finding that his order was only to reach the same mouth (Barima). [Appendix to Case, ii, 330-331.]

† I am also informed on very good authority that the canoes were taken by an armed boat, commanded by Captain D. Flores, who was sent out expressly to catch the Surinama traders in Barima, and who captured everything that came in his way. [Appendix to Case, ii, 121.]

‡ That the Commandant-General there present having received information that in the Creek called the Creek of Barima, which is close to the great

In the following year, 1769, the Spanish did more than merely visit the neighborhood of Essequibo. It was an eventful year along the coast. In March, the Spaniards, with two Capuchin fathers, a detachment of soldiers, and a large party of armed Indians, were capturing and taking prisoners all the free Indians between the Barima and Pomeroon. They next overpowered the Moruca post.*

Spanish control of coast regions.

In that same month (March) Gravesande wrote that "they (the Spaniards) have the audacity to go to work as if they were sovereigns of this whole coast."†

Again he wrote:

"They have captured and taken away all our people that were on the sea-coast. The salter of Luyxbergen has luckily escaped

---

mouth of the River Orinoco and falls into it, sundry Dutch families were established, dispatched him with instructions to warn them once, twice and thrice to quit the whole of that territory because it belonged to the said Province, in virtue whereof the Declarant went in his vessel, with another accompanying him, in search of the said Creek, and having arrived at the mouth he saw several Indians of the Carib nation, and these, before the Declarant could reach the establishments and farms of the said foreigners, gave them intelligence, and thereupon they took to flight without giving an opportunity for the notification; and they only found the deserted houses and the effects, implements and utensils contained in the inventory, which they put on board the two vessels and then set fire to the said houses, in order that they should not form settlements in future, and destroyed the farms as far as they possibly could. [Appendix to Case ii, 361; see, *also*, same, p. 396; *also* U. S. Commission Report, viii, (3) 232; *also*, and especially, as to this, U. S. Commission Report, i, 285, 286.]

* The 10th March I received two consecutive letters from Councillor M. Buisson, which gave me information that an Indian named Adahouva, from Pomaroon, had come to his house and related to him that the Spaniards, with two Capuchin Fathers, a detachment of soldiers, and a large party of armed Waykiers, were capturing and taking away as prisoners all the free Indians between Barima and Pamaroon, and that they had actually overpowered the Company's trading place, Marocco, and that they were now there, but that he had as yet no further knowledge of the circumstances. On the 11th came the assistant from Marocco with a letter from the Postholder. From his written Report, copy whereof is here annexed, your Honours will perceive to what pitch the insolence of our neighbors goes. [Appendix to Case, ii, 183–184.]

† But I should as soon have expected heaven to fall, as that they, in so high-handed a manner, openly (as if in open warfare), in breach of the right of nations, in breach of all Treaties of Alliance with his Catholic Majesty, should attack us from another side, and have the audacity to go to work as if they were sovereigns of this whole coast. [Appendix to Case, ii, 183.]

Spanish control of coast region.

them, but his Indians, his vessels, two large canoes and three single canoes, which he had got by barter, they have taken away."*

And he adds:

"The alarm in the river is great. If they come to Pomaroon as they have threatened they can be in three hours overland in Essequebo, and can ruin our lowermost plantations." †

Only a few months later, in May of the same year, (1769) he wrote again:

"According to the last reports from the Postholder and from the Caraibans, they are still all in Barima, having sent their prisoners to Orinocque, and they threaten to come again at an early date and not only carry off all the Indians from Powaron, but even to attack and plunder our plantations." ‡

That the Spaniards did not remain idle is shown by the following words of Gravesande, written also in the same month:

"The depredations of the Spanish from Barima to Powaron continuing daily, we must acknowledge that they are capable of anything, and that we must expect all kinds of violent and piratical acts from them." §

And he adds:

"The poor colonists on the west coast below Essequibo are in a terrible state of alarm, and are on the lookout night and day." ‖

Dutch cut off from the Orinoco.

The Dutch continued cut off from all communication with the Orinoco.¶ The Spaniards for the purpose of once more visiting Moruca and Pomeroon fitted out two privateers.**

Dutch excluded from coast.

In fact, the policy of the Spanish Governor at this time was to keep the Dutch out entirely, even as traders,

* Appendix to Case, ii, 184.

† Appendix to Case, ii, 184.

‡ Appendix to Case, ii, 190.

§ Appendix to Case, ii, 191.

‖ Appendix to Case, ii, 191.

¶ We have as yet not had the slightest tidings of this, all communications with Orinocque being still cut off. [Appendix to Case, ii, 218.]

** I take this opportunity of informing your lordships that Pedro Sanchez, having been in chains in Orinocque for some months, had the good fortune to escape. He has informed me that two privateers are again fitted

fishers or settlers; and to that end, he constituted a strong watch to patrol the coast.* Dutch excluded from coast.

This state of things continued, with the result that the Dutch colony was "on the brink of total ruin." † Spanish rights openly exercised.

All this exercise of sovereign rights by the Spaniards was done openly and without the slightest effort to disguise their acts or motives. Gravesande speaks of this himself saying, that they "go to work openly like a proud nation." ‡

But the Spaniards were now to go much further. Stirred to action by the projects of the French for the settlement of the interior of their Guiana colony, the Spanish Government of the Indies issued instructions for the occupation of all eastern Guiana, to the very borders of the French and Dutch. In obedience to its orders there was drawn up in 1778, by the Intendant of Caracas, a definite and detailed plan for this occupation. An official map of Guiana, defining the Spanish Spains plans for occupying all eastern Guiana. Instructions to Intendant of Caracas.

out, with a much stronger crew than the former one, and that in about five or six weeks from now they would come to Maroca and, further, into Pomeroon to carry off all the Indians whom they could get, and that they would probably come as far as the mouth of this river. [Appendix to Case, ii, 214.]

* It is related here that a new Governor has arrived in Orinocque. Should that be true, I hope that he will not be such a Turk as his predecessor. With the latter there was not the least chance of getting anything out of Orinocque, and he even forbade the usual salting in the mouth of the river, and set a strong watch to prevent it. [Appendix to Case, ii, 219.]

† The very dangerous condition of the Colony, which has been and still is [1772] on the brink of total ruin, compels me to report the same to His Serene Highness as speedily as possible, which despatch, being enclosed, I take the liberty of humbly requesting your lordship to forward to him at once. [Appendix to Case, ii, 220.]

‡ If we ever desired to follow the example of the English and French, the Posts of which I have spoken would be absolutely necessary and indispensable and (be it said) if this matter is not taken in hand, our neighbours will quietly approach and surround us, and finally, without exercising any violence, drive us from the country. This is already beginning to be observed, and what can we expect from the numerous arrivals of settlers in Cayenne and the removal of the Spanish colonies in Guayana so much nearer to our boundaries? The latter go to work openly, like a proud nation, and they can therefore be better opposed, an open enemy never being so dangerous as a secret one. [Appendix to Case, ii, 157-158.]

Instructions to Intendant of Caracas.

boundaries, was put in the hands of the Governor of Guiana as a basis for action; and the latter was commissioned to make an armed reconnoissance of the entire territory.

Reconnoissance of Moruca and Pomeroon by Inciarte.

This reconnoissance in the summer of 1779, as early as the fall of the rivers made a survey possible, was carried out on behalf of the Governor by his deputy, the young officer Inciarte, who with an escort, carefully examined the whole coast region, not only as far as the Moruca, but far into the Pomeroon; selected a site for a village and fort on the Moruca, which were to displace the post of the Dutch, and another site for a fortified village in the upper Pomeroon, which was to bear the name of San Carlos de la Frontera. The Dutch Governor of Essequibo was informed of the presence of the Spaniards in the Pomeroon, and even of his intention to build a fort there; but he not only made no effort to arrest him, but reported the matter to the Company without so much as a protest; and no protest was made by that body to the Dutch government or through it to that of Spain.

Inciarte's report and orders for expulsion of the Dutch from Moruca.

Inciarte meanwhile reported his results first to the Spanish colonial authorities, and then in person to the King of Spain and to his Council of the Indies. A royal order commissioned him to proceed at once with the expulsion of the Dutch from the Moruca and the erection of the projected Spanish establishments on that river and on the Pomeroon, instructing him in case of Dutch complaint to reply that the "laws of Spain do not allow such intrusions of foreigners in the Spanish dominions." All preparations were made for the execution of the project, and the granting of lands actually begun. The troublous times brought on in Europe by the French Revolution delayed its progress, but it was never abandoned. With a view to its better accomplishment Inciarte was himself made Governor of

Guiana, and held that post for thirteen years. And though, owing to the continuance of the revolutionary wars, its execution was not actually pushed further, the the project was never given up, and was receiving the attention of the Spanish government to the very end of its control of these South American colonies and to the very eve of the Dutch cession of Essequibo to Great Britain.*

Plan never abandoned by Spain.

So much for the coast.

2.—THE INTERIOR.

Turning now to the interior, it will be seen that there the Spaniards exercised exclusive control; and that the Dutch were in terror of them.

Spanish control of interior.

As early as 1733 the Capuchin missions pushed over into the basin of the Cuyuni, and with their herds took firm possession of the savannas which stretch to the banks of that river.† These missions, let it be noted, were no mere private attempts on behalf of Capuchin missionaries to christianize Guiana. They were in every way representative of Spanish political and military authority. Each mission was provided with its armament and quota of soldiers, and either the missionary in charge, or some attendant functionary, was vested with all necessary political powers.‡

Early Capuchin missions in the Cuyuni.

The shining sands of this region, too, soon attracted Spanish attention, and a royal order gave rise to the mines of Cupapuy. By 1755 they knew by investigation that "gold and silver are found at every step, in the districts of all" these missions, even to the Curumo.§

Spanish mining in the Cuyuni.

* Blue-Book 3, 305–314; Appendix to Case, ii, 434–441; iii, 380–399, 414–424.

† U. S. Commission Report, I, 382.

‡ Appendix to Case, ii, 370, 372.

§ Blue Book 1, 84-85.

Spanish missions in the Cuyuni.

On December 7, 1746, Gravesande wrote:

"I had the honor to inform you *via* Rio Berbice of a mission, together with a little fort, erected by the Spaniards up in Cuyuni, in my opinion on your territory; and I have it from a reliable source that they have been thinking of founding next year yet another nearer, whereat the inhabitants are much aggrieved, and the Carib Indians much more still, since thereby the slave trade in that quarter, from which alone that nation derives its livelihood, is wholly shut off. They wanted, too, to surprise that mission and level it to the ground, which I, not without trouble, have prevented; for, since they belong under our jurisdiction and carry on all their trade in the Dutch colonies, such a step would by the Spaniards surely be charged to us. It is very perilous for this Colony to have such neighbours so close by, who in time of war could come and visit us overland; and, above all, the making of fortifications upon our own land is in breach of all custom. I say upon our own land: this [assertion], however, I cannot put forth with full certainty, because the boundaries west of this river are unknown to me." *

Spanish control of the Cuyuni.

Of the Spanish raid on the Dutch station in the Cuyuni in the year 1758, mention has already been made.

In 1759 the Dutch Governor acknowledged that the Spaniards were "remaining in possession of Cuyuni."†

* Appendix to Case, ii, 97.

† The despatches received from Orinoco having been translated by Mr. Persik, I found one to be from the Commandant Don Juan Valdez, in which he informs me that, being forbidden to enter into any correspondence concerning the matter of Cajoeny, he is obliged to send back my letter unopened; he adds that he has brought the matter to the notice of the King of Spain, and that he has no doubt that I, too, have informed their High Mightinesses of the same, and that, therefore, the case would have to be decided not by ourselves but by our respective Sovereigns. This matter is of very great importance to the Colony, because if the Spaniards remain in possession of Cajoeny, which is one of the arms of this river, and in which there were coffee and indigo plantations belonging to your Lordships, as well as the estates of Old Duynenburg (now allotted to private holders), there will be no safety at all in this Colony. A way for all evil-doers, deserters and bankrupts will be quite open and free, and the Colony will be ruined immediately there is the least misunderstanding with Spain. Your Lordships will therefore see that this matter is fully deserving of your attention. The Spaniards continue to stay where they are, and to entrap and drive away all the Caraibans living there. [Appendix to Case, ii, 132–133.]

Spanish control of the Cuyuni.

In 1761 the Spaniards were "down to the lowest falls" of the Cuyuni "where your Lordships' indigo plantation is situated"; and were driving all hostile Indians out.* In 1762 they were still recognized by the Dutch as in control down to the "lowest falls close to the dwelling of your Lordships' creoles."† The sending out of Spanish patrols over the region had become a "daily" matter.‡ By 1763 the Cuyuni had been entirely cleared, not only of Dutch but of Caribs as well.§

The year 1764–5 saw the same state of affairs; the

*Everything in the upper part of the river is in a state of upset, the people who live there bringing their best goods down the stream. This is because a party of Spaniards and Spanish Indians in Cajoeny have been down to the lowest fall where you Lordships' indigo plantation was situated, driving all the Indians thence, and even, it is said, having killed several. The Indians sent in complaint upon complaint. [Appendix to Case, ii, 145.]

† They are not yet quiet, but send detachments from time to time, which come down as far as the lowest fall, close to the dwelling of your Lordships' creoles, by which both the settlers and our Indians are continually being alarmed, and take refuge each time down stream. [Appendix to Case, ii, 147.]

‡ From the reports received from the upper part of the river, I learn that the Spanish Indians of the Missions continue to send out daily patrols as far as the great fall (just below which your Lordships' creoles live); all the Caraibans have also left that river, and gone to live above Essequibo. [Appendix to Case, ii, 149.]

§ The Indians have also informed me that the Spaniards up in Cajoeny are engaged in building boats. Where will all this end, my Lords? I fear that this may lead to the entire ruin of the Colony (which God forbid) unless rigorous measures are taken. Our forbearance in the matter of Cajoeny makes them bolder and bolder. At the time of that occurrence the Caraibans were full of courage and ready for all kinds of undertaking; now they are all driven away from there and have retired right up into Essequebo. [Appendix to Case, ii, 151.]

The fourth, and last, is the still abandoned Post in Cajoeny, abandoned since the raid of the Spaniards, a Post of the very greatest importance, because the Spaniards, in order to get to this river, and the slaves in order to escape to them, have a free and open road, and the more so because the Spaniards have driven away the Caraibans who lived there, and who could apprehend and bring back the runaways. [Appendix to Case, ii, 154.]

It is certain, your Lordships, that this [is] not the time to think of the re-establishment of the Post in Cajoeny. That matter will give us plenty of work to do when, with the blessing of God, all is at rest and in peace, because, the Spaniards having driven all the Indians out of the river, it will be no small matter to get [all] the necessary buildings, etc., in readiness there. [Appendix to Case, ii, 155.]

Spanish control of Cuyuni.

Spaniards establishing themselves more and more firmly.*

Caribs afraid to venture there.

By 1765 even the Caribs were afraid to venture into the Cuyuni; and only after repeated promises from the Dutch could they be induced to do anything for the protection of the Essequibo colony.†

By 1766 the proximity of the Spaniards had rendered even the foreign soldiers of the Essequibo colony useless.‡

* In addition to this, there is also the fact that . . . . this river[1] is a tract of land along which the Spaniards spread themselves from year to year, and gradually come closer by means of their missions, the small parties sent out by them coming close to the place where the Honourable Company's Indigo plantations stood, and being certain to try and establish themselves if they were not stopped in time. [Appendix to Case, ii, 156–157.]

This is certain, that so long as no satisfaction is given by the Court of Spain concerning the occurrence of the Post in Cajoeny, the Spaniards will gradually become more insolent, and will gain ground on us from year to year. [Appendix to Case, ii, 161.]

Thus, what with the French on the east and the Spaniards on the west, we are really like a little boat between two men-of-war.

I shall not attempt to give my masters advice in a matter which it is in no one's power to prevent or to circumvent. My only aim in this is to respectfully submit to your Lordships what is our humble opinion concerning this in all our Colonies situated on the mainland, and our well-grounded fears concerning the consequences.

I, for my part, see no remedy for this matter except by populating the Colony and establishing good Posts in the interior, from which a sharp and careful look-out can be kept upon all movements. [Appendix to Case, ii, 159.]

† We are entirely of your opinion that it is of the greatest necessity to restore the post in Cuyuni, and in consequence we were very much pleased to learn that you had at last succeeded in getting Indians to give a helping hand in that work, on condition that assurance should be given them of protection against the Spaniards. This it was easy to promise them. [Appendix to Case, ii, 162.]

‡ Herewith I will again reiterate my request that no French or Flemish be sent, but as many Protestants as possible. The proximity of the Spaniards, and especially of the Spanish Missions, renders it impossible to place the slightest trust in Catholics. [Appendix to Case, ii, 168.]

[1] Note.—The reading of the Blue Book "the bend of" is an impossible translation. There is no such Dutch word as that the British translators have rendered "bend." What it does mean is not so certain. It is a document of van 's Gravesande, which has been copied by a secretary and then corrected by the Governor's own hands. It looks as if van 's Gravesande had written "bezit" ("possession") so that it should have read "There is, moreover, the possession of this river, a tract of land," etc., but that the secretary had misread it "bent" (which in Storm's handwriting it looks for all the world

By 1767 the weakness of the Dutch had reached such a point that even their Indian protectors scoffed at them and refused to obey their orders. These Indians, fearing the Spaniards, refused even to halt their passing boats at the summons of the post.* Spanish control of Cuyuni.

In 1767, and again in 1768, the Spaniards raided the river, captured a lot of hostile Indians, and so terrified the rest that they all abandoned the Cuyuni.† Hostile Indians driven from Cuyuni.

By 1769 the Cuyuni had been so thoroughly cleared that there were no Indians left to give the Dutch warning of approaching danger.‡

The Spaniards were now completely masters of the entire Cuyuni—recognized as such by the Dutch.§ Spanish control of Cuyuni.

like). Storm, then, in reading it over could make no sense of it, and struck out the words "bent van" and wrote "dat" (that) above them without noticing that this left it nonsense.

* At the same time I received a report from the Post in Cajoeny that the Indians are being bribed and incited to such a degree that they are unwilling to do the least thing for the Postholder, and that even when he orders the passing boats to lie to to see whether there are any runaways in them, they obstinately refuse to do so, and when he threatens to shoot upon them they reply that they have bows and arrows with which to answer. [Appendix to Case, ii, 170–171.]

† There is a rumor here that the Post in Cajoeny has again been raided. I do not know whether it is true, because I have as yet had no direct tidings from above. The old negro Abarina, who always looks after the turtle business up in Cajoeny, and who is well acquainted with all the roads there, went up stream yesterday to get information. [Blue Book, 3, 147.] [The Blue Book does not tell us definitely whether the rumor was true or not. It seems, however, that it was true.] Matters up there are not so bad as the Indians had reported; the Manoas have not been in those parts, and indeed I could hardly believe it, because it seemed to me improbable that they would have come such a long distance without being discovered by the Caraibans, their inveterate enemies, and the more so since, after the raid upon Cajoeny by the Spaniards, Essequibo swarms with Caraibans, who have all flocked there after having asked me for permission to do so. [Blue Book, 3, 148–149.]

‡ But this is certain, that the road for the runaways is now quite open and free, it being impossible for the Post in Cajoeny to stop them, there being a number of inland paths; nor can we be warned in any way by Indians, there being no more of these in that river. They did begin to settle there again when the post was re-established, but the raid made by the Spaniards last year, when a large party of Indians were captured and taken away, has filled the rest with terror, and they are gradually drawing off. [Appendix to Case, ii, 182.]

§ In my previous despatches I had the honour from time to time to inform your Honours of the secret doings of the Spaniards and especially

Cuyuni free of both Dutch and Caribs.

In 1770 the river still remained free of both Dutch and Caribs.*

In 1788 Antonio Lopez de la Puente was able to descend the Cuyuni to tide water, and then seize and bring away the principal Carib chief employed by the Dutch, without encountering any Dutch post nor a single Dutchman, and without resistance from the Indians, so thoroughly had these been cowed by the Spaniards whose armed expeditions had constantly come down to the same point before without trouble or opposition.†

---

in my second letter by the "Vrouw Anna," and in my letter by the "Geertruida Christiana," did right circumstantially concerning the fatal and, for the Colony, most highly-perilous news of the River Cayuni. My opinion has always been that they would gradually acquire a foothold in Cayuni, and try to obtain the mastery of the river, as they now practically have none at the end of the past year. [Appendix to Case, ii, 183.]

* This is to inform Your Excellency that I am sending down with Gerrit Van Leeuwen a female slave with her child belonging to Diderik Neelis, the Postholder of Maroco, and who were taken from him by the Spaniards, and also some free Indians who were also living in Maroco, who have run away from the priest. I understand from these same Indians that there are more coming on behind, but that in the bush they got separated from each other. I hope that they may come to light, and then I do not know how they will come home, because I have no boat and people to send them down, because the greater part of the Caraibans have departed from Cajoeny to Masseroeny to make dwelling places there, and some have gone to Upper Siepanamen to live there. [Blue Book, 3, 176.]

† On the tenth day we departed from Capachi, and after passing some rapids, not of the largest, we passed the night at the mouth of the Creek Tupuro, having rowed ten hours' journey to the head of the Rapid Camaria, which is two leagues long, and ends at the mouth of the Cuyuni, a short distance, about a quarter of a league, before the Cuyuni flows into the Masuruni, in the fork of which a Dutchman lives, named Daniel, with four companions, very many negroes and Indian slaves, all his.

From the mouth of this Creek Tupuro there is a road to the foot of the rapid where the Carib Manuyari has his house, and he it is who keeps up this road opposite Daniel's house. The tide reaches above this rapid. From this to the fortress of Essequibo there are only two floods on the southern part of the River Cuyuni. There is a road which comes out at the Masurini, where there are some Dutchman with a Carib village. We arrived at the said mouth of the Tupuro at daybreak.

On the eleventh day I dispatched the corporal, three of the militiamen, and fifteen Caribs to apprehend the Indian Manuyari, and we, with the others, remained to guard the canoes; and at twelve o'clock at night they returned with the said Manuyari, whom they found in his

In 1792 the Spanish completed the construction of a fortified post on the southern bank of the Cuyuni opposite the mouth of the Curumo.* This continued to be the main Spanish post in the Cuyuni basin until long after the acquisition of Essequibo by the British.† Spanish Curumo post.

This post was maintained for the purpose of exercising exclusive political control of the basin; and the instructions to its commander were clear upon that point.

But apart from all this military and political control, there was, during the period under consideration (1725–1800), a great growth of Spanish population, and spread of mission villages, not only as far as the Curumo itself, but far into the interior of the Cuyuni-Mazaruni basin, and even beyond, into the Potaro region and as far as the headwaters of the Siparuni.‡ Spanish growth.

Quite apart from this, again, the "entradas," as they were called (that is to say, the expeditions of the missionaries into the unsettled lands for the purpose of converting the Indians and bringing them back to reside in towns and villages), were constant throughout the region west of the Essequibo from the coast far into the interior, even beyond the Pacaramia mountains.§ *Entradas* by the missionaries.

The spread of these missions was really remarkable. By 1734 they had so increased, and the various orders of friars found their fields of work so overlapping, that in that year the Prefect and the Governor met at Old Guayana, and definitely and legally apportioned the territory among the different religious orders. The Spread of missions. Division of mission territory.

---

plantation three leagues distant from the port, having taken the Indian woman from Panapana, named Josefa, and ten others. [Appendix to Case, ii, 464–465.]

* Through unofficial information, it is known that a beginning has been made of a foundation of the new town on the site by the junction of the Cuyuni with the river Curumo. [Appendix to Case, iii, 400.]

† U. S. Commission Report, iii, 212.

‡ U. S. Commission Report, atlas, map 15.

§ Appendix to Case, iii, 377.

Division of mission territory.

agreement gave the region south of the lower Orinoco to the Catalonian Capuchins.*

Spanish missions, 1743-1813.

There were many missions during the 18th century which were never formally "founded." Of these, of course, no official records exist. There were others formally "founded" which have left no record behind them. By 1743 we know of seven Capuchin mission-villages in existence, beside one just being established. They contained a population of some 2,000 souls.† A decade later, in 1753, eight new villages had been established; and although four missions had just been destroyed by the Caribs and one by a raid of the English, nine were in existence, with four more under way.‡ In 1755 their population was nearly 3,000.§ There were 16 missions in the year 1761, containing 4,392 domesticated Indians and 1,081 men capable of bearing arms, as well as 15,000 head of cattle.‖ Besides these, there was the Spanish civil town of San Antonio de Upata.¶

In this same year it was estimated that to build at

* Appendix to Case, ii, 291-294.

†Appendix to Case, iii, 369-372.

‡Appendix to Case, iii, 373-375.

§Appendix to Case, iii, 426.

‖The 16 Missions established at present [1761] are those of Capapui, Altagracia, Suay, Amaruca, Caroni, Aripuco, Aguacagua, Murucuri, San Joseph de Leonisa, Guarimna, Carapu, Miamo, Guazapatl, Palmar, Avechica, and Piacoa, as shown in the map, in the corresponding statement of the men of arms, families, souls, houses, and churches existing in every one of the said 16 settlements. [Appendix to Case, ii, 345.]

One thousand and eighty-one men of arms; 1,031 families; 4,392 souls; 408 houses; and three churches. [Appendix to Case, ii, 345.]

The same certificate shows that the cattle estate of the Community contains from 14,000 to 16,000 head of bovine cattle for the maintenance of the settlements and the Missioners. The cattle has been placed on new grounds in proportion of its increase, and to-day it is kept in the Mission of Guarima, where the fields and mountains are most abundant in grass and water, in a cool climate. On account of these circumstances, the multiplication of the cattle has been incredible. [Appendix to Case, ii, 346.]

¶ If the settlements in distant places, deserted and not reduced, are difficult, their establishment, after the Indians are pacified, is very easy, and of no expense to the Royal Treasury, as it is shown to-day in the same Province of Guayana with the new settlement of San Antonio de Upata, which commenced in the year of 1762. [U. S. Commission Report, viii, (1) 80-81.]

Angostura a town large enough to hold the people of Santo Thomé alone would cost $300,000.

Spanish missions, 1743-1813.

In 1766 the Capuchin villages had a population of 5,273 Indians; and by 1773 this number had risen to 6,832.*

Meanwhile the province, as a whole, including the missions of other orders, had grown not less strikingly.

In 1779 the province of Guayana contained 80 villages and 18,000 inhabitants.† How many of these villages were Capuchin missions does not appear; but in 1788, there were 29 or 30 of these "missions" with 14,012 persons and 180,000 cattle.‡

In 1799 there were 28 missions with 15,908 persons.§

In 1813 there were 29 missions and 21,246 persons.¶

Definition of Dutch and Spanish territories in 1803.

It is now possible to state exactly the extent of the territories belonging to the Netherlands and to the Kingdom of Spain respectively at the time of the acquisition by Great Britain of the colonies of Essequibo, Demerara and Berbice.

Dutch limits of occupation.

The Dutch were confined, on the west, to the mouth of the Essequibo. Their occupation up-stream did not reach even to Kykoveral. In the Cuyuni they had made two attempts to penetrate beyond the lowest falls, and both attempts had proven failures. Although originally

---

* Appendix to Case, iii, 382, 383.

† There were also civil towns. Caulin (who lived in Guiana) says that at his date of publication, 1779, "the settlements which the Spaniards hold to-day in the province of Guayana are 80 villages and 18,000 inhabitants." [Caulin, (*friar* A.) Historia Coro-Graphica, etc., Madrid, 1779, p. 12.]

‡ The stock of cattle is reckoned at about 220,000; 180,000 head in the cattle farms of the Community of the Capuchin Fathers, although a very accurate estimate cannot be made, owing to the difficulty of counting them, and the remaining 40,000 among the private settlers. [Blue Book 3, 819;] see *also* Appendix to Case, ii, 447, for list of 29 missions.]

§ Appendix to Case, ii, 485.

¶ Appendix to Case, ii, 487.

Dutch limits of occupation.

permitted by the Spaniards to trade in the Cuyuni basin, even this had been long forbidden them; and they, as well as the Caribs upon whom they relied for protection, had been driven out so that not one remained.

On the coast, the little trading station at the mouth of the Moruca was as far as they dared to venture; and even to that point they went only by the permission of the Spaniards. The colony itself was utterly weak, on the verge of ruin, and entirely cowed by the Spaniards.

Spanish growth and control.

Spain, on the other hand, had spread until she could count her towns and villages by the score, her inhabitants by the tens of thousands, and her herds of cattle by the hundreds of thousands. The whole Orinoco delta from the Barima to the Moruca she had cleared of Dutch, Caribs, English, French and Swedes, policing these regions to beyond the Pomeroon, and exercising dominion under a claim of right from the Orinoco to the very banks of the Essequibo.

Over the interior savannas her settlements had spread to beyond the banks of the Cuyuni and Caroni. In the fairest region of that great basin, and south of the Cuyuni, she had erected and was maintaining a military post; exercising from that center exclusive political control down to the lowest falls of the Cuyuni and Mazaruni. Through the great forests of the Cuyuni-Mazaruni basin, and over the Pacaraima mountains into the Potaro region and beyond, her missionaries had penetrated and settled; and, at the moment that the Dutch colony passed into British hands in 1803, she was exercising undisputed and exclusive control of every acre of land west of the Essequibo, except where the Dutch were actually settled upon its very banks.

XII.--DUTCH REMONSTRANCES.

Before passing to the 19th century, there is a subject whose intimate connection with Dutch-Spanish relations during the 18th century entitles it to special mention:

Uselessness of Dutch remonstrances.

The story of Dutch remonstrances is one of Spanish aggression and assertion of sovereign rights in the territory now in dispute, followed by repeated protests of the Dutch, and memorials to the Spanish Court, all of which were treated with contempt—answered only by a continuance of these aggressions, by further acts of political control, by further grumblings on the part of the Dutch, by further complaints to which the Spanish Government did not deign to reply, and by final acquiescence by the Dutch in the inevitable.

Remonstrance of 1746.

The first recorded remonstrance of the Dutch Essequibo Colony was in 1746. The Dutch Commandeur complained to the West India Company of the encroachments of the Spaniards in the Cuyuni river, and of the capture by the latter of three canoes of the Dutch colony engaged in fishing in the Orinoco. In his letter to the Company the Dutch Commandeur said that on the arrival of the new Spanish Governor he would "send there to claim the boats and cargoes," but was "certain that such would be in vain," having profited by a previous example.*

What may have been the language of his remonstrance, or of the Spanish Governor's reply, does not appear. The practical result, however, is well known: the Spanish control of both regions continued; and the

* Blue Book, 3, p. 87.

Remonstrance of 1746.

growth of the Spanish missions on the Cuyuni savannas was in no way affected.*

Remonstrance of 1759.

The second Dutch remonstrance had reference to the Spanish attack upon the slave-trading post that Storm van 's Gravesande attempted to establish on the Cuyuni about 1754. The result of this attempt has already been shown.†

When the Dutch Governor heard of the way in which the Spaniards had destroyed the post, and made prisoners of the Dutch servants there stationed, he addressed a forcible protest to the Spanish Commandant in Guiana,‡ and likewise made a report to the West India Company,§ with the result that the States General presented a formal remonstrance to the Court of Spain.‖ Gravesande's letter having been referred by the Spanish Commandant to the Provisional Governor of Cumaná, the latter replied thereto, stating that the destroyed post was on the territory of his King, and refusing to restore the prisoners.¶ Gravesande caused a second letter to be sent to the Spanish Commandant demanding anew the restitution of the prisoners, as also compensation for the insult offered to the territory of his sovereigns.** That letter was returned to him unopened;†† and the remonstrance of the States General to the Spanish Court was never honored by a reply.

Continuation of same acts by Spaniards.

The only answer the Spanish Commandant gave to these remonstrances was a continuation of the very acts which brought them forth. The Spaniards captured all

* Appendix to Case, ii, 106.

† *Supra*, p. 122.

‡ Appendix to Case, ii, 122-125.

§ Appendix to Case, ii, 125.

‖ Appendix to Case, ii, 133-135.

¶ Appendix to Case, ii, 324.

** Appendix to Case, ii, 128-129.

†† Appendix to Case, ii, 130.

the Dutch boats they found fishing in the Orinoco * and the Waini; † they crowded the Dutch in all directions upon the land; ‡ they established further missions in the Cuyuni; § they drove the Caribs from that region; ‖ and the Dutch post-holder at Moruca in terror sought safety in the bush.¶ Renewed complaints by Gravesande were returned unopened, and his envoys driven away unheard. ** Sovereignty exercised by Spain.

The remonstrance of the States General to the Court of Spain was treated with the same contempt. †† Remonstrance treated with contempt.

By 1769 things had reached such a serious state that the Court of Policy and Director General of the Dutch Colony united in a memorial ‡‡ to the West India Company praying its most serious consideration of the great danger to the colony from Cuyuni above and the seacoast below. They called the attention of the Company to the continual pillage of its plantations, and to the absolute ruin of its fisheries. Thereupon it resulted that the States General in that year made another remonstrance to the Court of Spain. §§ That court did nothing but refer the matter to the Council of the Indies: ‖‖ meanwhile the acts complained of continued.¶¶ Remonstrance of 1769.

By 1775, though all the representations to the Spanish Court had remained fruitless, the States General nevertheless presented still another remonstrance to that government.*** Remonstrance of 1775.

* Appendix to Case, ii, 142, 143, 145.
† Appendix to Case, ii, 150.
‡ Appendix to Case, ii, 190.
§ Appendix to Case, ii, 157, 161.
‖ Appendix to Case, ii, 151.
¶ Appendix to Case, ii, 151.
** Appendix to Case, ii, 149, 163.
†† U. S. Commission, Report, I, 255.
‡‡ Appendix to Case, ii, 190.
§§ Appendix to Case, ii, 193, 198, 201.
‖‖ Appendix to Case, ii, 212.
¶¶ Appendix to Case, ii, 214, 215, 232.
*** Appendix to Case, ii, 225-227.

Remonstrance of 1775.

What this remonstrance left unsaid is quite as important as what it said. It referred mainly to the harboring of fugitive slaves; and it contained not a word regarding territory beyond the actual Dutch settlements. Its allusions to boundary were incidental merely; except that, referring to former complaints, it stated, *in effect*, that Spain had paid no attention to them, and that Holland now expected none.

The only reply was an acknowledgment of its receipt with the remark that "these acts of violence have caused the King much surprise, and that His Majesty has ordered the Ministry of the Indies to make the most minute inquiries into the fact, and to proceed to the condign punishment of the aggressors."*

Remonstrance ignored.

That is the last we ever hear of that remonstrance. At the time of its presentation, the remonstrance of 1759, except by further aggressions, had remained unanswered sixteen years, and that of 1769 six; this of 1775 was destined to share the fate of the others.

While special reference has thus been made to four different remonstrances, it must not be inferred that these were the only ones. Remonstrances by the Dutch were numerous and constant. All were ineffectual; and these four have been selected because they seem to have been the most formal.

Spanish proceedings on remonstrances of 1759 and 1769.

It is learned from Spanish sources that the Court of Spain having sent to Guayana the remonstrance of 1769 for a report, the papers were duly forwarded together with those of the former remonstrance of 1759. When they reached the Fiscal of the Council at Madrid, he found they were too voluminous to "consume uselessly" the time he needed for important affairs; and so, after he had kept them five years, he was inspired on one hot

* Blue Book 3, p. 189.

summer's day to refer them to a relator for examination and report.*

Spanish proceedings on remonstrances of 1759 and 1769.

They remained thus pigeon-holded for eleven years, and on May 27, 1785, the relator added his contribution. Whereupon the Fiscal, noting these facts, wrote:

> "Under this understanding it is observed by the exponent that to-day no resolution is required or any further step taken after the long lapse of over fifteen years, without any further mention of the subject by the Minister of Holland, leading to the belief that, after having been better informed, the Republic realizes the want of justice for the claim made, and has already desisted."†

The Council voted that the papers "show the want of foundation for the complaint of the vassals of Holland," and that it would take no further action in the matter.‡

Results of this remonstrance.

Twenty-six years had elapsed. The Council declined even to read the papers, for the Dutch claim of title was reported and seemed to them frivolous; Holland did not press it. If diplomacy could emphasize the expulsion by adding contempt, it had done so.

* Appendix to Case, ii, 429.

† Appendix to Case, ii, 441.

‡ Appendix to Case, ii, 441.

Purpose and effect of Schomburgk survey.

Venezuela might properly rest at this point, without entering further upon the history of the present century.

This boundary controversy had its rise in a survey suggested and undertaken in 1840 by one Schomburgk, a young German naturalist, who offered to the British Government to locate the boundary which he alleged to have been that claimed by the Dutch during their pos-

Purpose and effect of Schomburgk survey.

session of the colony. It was this alleged boundary of the Dutch, thus to be identified by him, which by order of the British Government was to be mapped and transmitted to the interested governments as a statement of the British claim. Thus did the British Government expressly disavow any other than a Dutch title to its Guiana possessions.

There is no pretence that any new title has been acquired by Great Britain since 1840; and the definition of the present boundary must, therefore, depend upon the extent of Dutch and Spanish rights in 1803.

This fact has very properly been recognized in the present treaty. It is thus affirmed in Article III, which reads as follows:

> "The tribunal shall investigate and ascertain the extent of the territories belonging to or that might lawfully be claimed by the United Netherlands or by the Kingdom of Spain, respectively, at the time of the acquisition by Great Britain of the Colony of British Guiana—and shall determine the boundary line between the Colony of British Guiana and the United States of Venezuela."

This being so, the story of the present century would seem to be unnecessary. However, a perusal of that story, particularly as regards the British colony, will serve to emphasize the fact that the Essequibo settlement was always, until very recent years, confined to the mouth of that river; and that Great Britain's present pretensions to territory west of that stream have not, in fact, as they could not have in law, anything in the history of the present century to support them.

XIII.—HISTORY OF BRITISH OCCUPATION. 1803–1850.

The British military occupation in Essequibo continued from 1803 to 1814. In the latter year, on August 13, the Dutch, by the Treaty of London, formally ceded to Great Britain "the establishments of Demerara, Essequibo and Berbice."*

Cession of "Demerara, Essequibo and Berbice to Great Britain.

On July 21, 1831, these three rivers were united into a single colony under the name of British Guiana.†

Union of the three.

In the meantime, Venezuela on July 5, 1811, declared its independence from Spain. In 1819 it became merged with New Granada, under the name of "Republic of Colombia." In 1830 it assumed a separate existence under the name of "Republic of Venezuela;" and finally, on March 30, 1845, its independence was formally recognized by Spain.‡

Venezuelan independence.

* His Britannic Majesty engages to restore to the Prince Sovereign of the United Provinces of the Netherlands, within the time which shall be specified herebelow, the colonies, factories and establishments of which Holland was in possession at the beginning of the late war, that is to say, on the 1st of January 1803, in the seas and continents of America, Africa and Asia, with the exception of the Cape of Good Hope and of the establishments of Demerara, Essequibo and Berbice, which the High Contracting Parties reserve the right to dispose of by a supplementary convention which shall be adjusted at once in conformity with the mutual interests of both parties. [Appendix to Case, iii, 44.]

† Appendix to Case, iii, 315; also Rodway (J.) History of British Guiana. 8°, Georgetown, 1893. ii, 284.

‡ "ARTICLE I. H. C. Majesty, making use of the power vested in her by decree of the Cortes Generales of the Kingdom, of 4th of December, 1836, renounces for herself, her heirs and successors the sovereignty, rights and action which she has upon the American territory known under the old name of Captaincy General of Venezuela, now Republic of Venezuela.

"ARTICLE II. In consequence of this renunciation and cession H. M. recognizes the Republic of Venezuela as a free, sovereign and independent nation, composed of the provinces and territories mentioned in her Con-

British and Venezuelan titles.

The British thus became vested with the rights of the Dutch; and Venezuela came to represent the title of Spain.

The year 1850 marks the date of the first important gold discoveries. It will be convenient, therefore, to consider by itself the period from 1803 to 1850.

For this period the facts pertinent to the present controversy may be grouped under two heads; 1st, Those which evidence the *extent* of British occupation; 2d, Those which relate to the *general condition of* the Essequibo settlement.

1st.—EXTENT OF BRITISH OCCUPATION.

Under this general head, it will be further convenient to consider: 1st, the occupation of the coast region; and 2d, the occupation of the interior.

1ST. AS TO THE COAST.

Lt. Gov. Myers, 1804.

On September 30, 1804, Lieutenant-Governor Myers wrote to Earl Camden, enclosing a memorandum which he said was the "result of information obtained from several persons in those Colonies best entitled to give them." This memorandum contains the following statement:

> *Extent.*—The distance from the Abari Creek on the east to the most distant military post at Morucco on the west is 123 miles.
>
> *Division.*—It is intersected by the rivers Demerary, Esequibo, and Pourmaron, and by several navigable creeks and canals.
>
> *Cultivation.*—From the Abari Creek to the River Demerary the plantations are in cotton. In the River Demerary, and from it to the east side of Esequibo River, they are in coffee and sugar.
>
> In the islands of the Esequibo they are in sugar.

stitution and other posterior laws, to wit: Margarita, Guayana, Cumana, Barcelona, Caracas, Carabobo, Barquisimeto, Barinas, Apure, Merida, Trujillo, Coro and Maracaibo and any other territories or islands which may belong to her. [Appendix to Case, iii, 48-49.]

From the west side of Esequibo River to Cape Orange they are in coffee, sugar, and cotton; and from Cape Orange, alongst the Araibish or Tiger coast, as far as there are Settlements towards the post at Morucco, they are in cotton.*

Lieut.-Gov. Myers, 1804.

Lieutenant-Governor Codd, in a letter to Major-General Murray, dated November 9, 1813, bears witness to the fact that, between the Arabian Coast and the Pomeroon, the region contained no settlers or plantations. He says:

Lieut.-Gov. Codd, 1813.

"I have also ordered the Post-holder Linau, at Moroco, to come up with selected Indians, and I intend making him scour the woods between the Arabian coast and the Pomeroon, with a view to dislodge any runaway negroes who may have established themselves there."† . . .

Certain regulations of the Court of Policy of June 5, 1817, regarding the militia of the colony, serve to define the actual limit of settlement at that time. These regulations assign two battalions to Essequibo; and make the following designation of territories from which those battalions were to be drawn:

Military regulations of 1817.

"In Essequibo, the first battalion shall consist of all the inhabitants from Borasira Creek upwards, as far as inhabited on the east side of the river, including the islands of Wakenaam, Leguan, Varken or Hog Island, Troolie Island, and all other islands in the river, except Tiger Island, and commencing on the west side of Schonhoven Creek, and upwards, as far as inhabited; the second battalion to consist of all the inhabitants from Schonhoven, including Tiger Island, with all the west seacoast, including Pomeroon River."‡

It will be noticed that on the coast the Pomeroon is the westernmost point named; and that up the Essequibo on the west side, everything is included under the description, from "Schonhoven Creek, and upwards, as

* Blue Book, 1, 156.
† Blue Book, 1, 160.
‡ Appendix to Case, iii, 63.

Military regulations of 1817.

far as inhabited." Schonhoven Creek is a small stream flowing into the very mouth of the Essequibo, opposite Hog Island.

Lieut.-Gov. D'Urban, 1827.

In a despatch from Lieutenant-Governor Sir B. D'Urban to Viscount Goderich, dated October 18, 1827, the Lieutenant-Governor transmits "An account of the extent and situation of the Crown lands" in the United Colony of Demerary and Essequebo; and, in the despatch states that, "the country possessed by individuals is a narrow border of the alluvial soil along the coasts and rivers' banks."*

Division into parishes, 1832.

Schomburgk, in his *Description of British Guiana*, published in 1840 (pp. 62–63), gives the division of Demerara and Essequibo into eleven parishes. Of these, only two, viz., St. John and Trinity, were on the west side of the Essequibo; the southernmost, St. John, extending as far south only as the Supinaam Creek. These two parishes, in the year 1832, contained only forty-seven plantations, all of them along the Arabian coast.†

Colonel St. Clair, 1834.

Colonel St. Clair, having spent some months in Guiana in the year 1834, published a work entitled *A Residence in the West Indies and America, with a Narrative of the Expedition to the Island of Walcheren.* In chapter vii. of this work he thus speaks of the Colony of Essequibo:

> "The Colony of Essequibo adjoins to Demerara, being under the same governor, and is our most leeward possession in this country. The creek or river called Morocco is the boundary line between this colony and the Spanish main, which is not far from the Pomeroon creek."‡

Whatever other value this statement may have, it is

---

* Blue Book, I, 167.

† Appendix to Case, iii, 313–314; atlas, map 86.

‡ St. Clair (Lt. Col. J. S.) Residence in the West Indies, etc., 2 vols. London, 1834, chapter vii.

at least good evidence as to the limits of actual occupation at the time. Colonel St. Clair, 1834.

For the year 1838 we have a number of authorities: they are; (*a*) Sir Henry Light, the Governor; (*b*) Mr. J. Hadfield, Crown Surveyor; and (*c*) Mr. William Crichton, Superintendent of Rivers and Creeks.

(*a*) Governor Light, in a despatch dated September 1, 1838, wrote: Governor Light, 1838.

> "The Pomaroon river, at the western extremity of Essequibo, may be taken as a limit to the country, though there is a mission supported by the colony on the Maracca river or creek, a short distance westward, where 500 Spanish Indians are collected in a settlement under a Roman-catholic priest, recommended from Trinidad for that purpose; he is reported to be effecting good."*

Further on, speaking of the region "between the Pomeroon and Orinoco," he says of it that it is a "coast of 100 miles . . . unoccupied by any person or under any authority."†

(*b*) Mr. Hadfield's testimony is recorded in the shape of a map dated August 1, 1838,‡ intended to show the "Parochial divisions, as well as the present extent of Cultivation of the Staple Productions, & the tracts of such that have been abandoned within the last 30 Y[rs]." Hadfield, 1838.

According to this map, the settlements on the west of the Essequibo were, at that time, limited to the Arabian coast between Supenaam creek and the mouth of the Pomeroon.

(*c*) Mr. Wm. Crichton, having explored the coast region west of the Pomeroon, made a report in which, referring to the rivers Waini, Barima, etc., he says: Crichton, 1838.

> "Your reporter had communication with the Indian Captains of the various nations inhabiting that portion of the country,

---

* Parliamentary Papers, 1839, Vol. 35, p. 278.

† Blue Book, 1, 285.

‡ Appendix to Case, atlas, map 79.

Crichton, 1838. who all concurred in declaring that there were no persons except Indians resident in either of these rivers or any of the creeks their tributaries, and as he found no deviation in their statements, he feels perfectly convinced of their truth. . . . The district in question contains a numerous population of Indians, viz., Warrows, Accaways, Caribesce, and Arrawaks, the former the most numerous, and, in the humble opinion of your reporter, it would be good policy to secure the absolute possession of it to this colony." *

Schomburgk, 1839. According to Schomburgk (*Description of British Guiana, p. 63*), there were on the west bank of the Essequibo, along the Arabian coast, in 1839, only forty-nine plantations.†

Schomburgk, 1840. A map of British Guiana by Schomburgk, published in Parliamentary Papers, 1840, Vol. 34, shows the extent of cultivation on the west side of the Essequibo in that year.‡ For that year there is also the "Local Guide" of British Guiana, published at Demerara. From that book (p. ii) the following statements are taken:

Local Guide, 1840.

"The inhabited part of the coast extends from the mouth of the Pomeroon in 7½° N. Latitude, 59° W. Longitude, to the mouth of the Corentyn, in 6° N. Latitude, 57° W. Longitude, a distance, following the indentations of the coast, of about 200 miles. The large islands in the mouth of the Essequibo are cultivated to a greater or less extent, particularly the two fine and fertile islands, Leguan and Wakenaam, each about fourteen miles long and three wide. The banks of the Essequibo are inhabited only by a few scattered wood cutters."

No extension of British occupation. There is no evidence of any extension of British settlements or occupation along the coast between this last date and the year 1850.

* Blue Book, 1, 186.

† Appendix to Case, iii, 315.

‡ Appendix to Case, atlas, map 82.

2D.—As to the Interior.

During the period under consideration, British occupation in the interior was limited to a single post at the junction of the Essequibo, Cuyuni and Mazaruni. At no time was there a pretence of anything beyond this. Above the falls of these three rivers the interior was practically unknown to the British. British occupation in the interior.

Mr. Rodway, speaking apparently of the time of the earliest British conquest in 1796, says that for the three rivers, Essequibo, Mazaruni and Cuyuni, there was only one post which was "always near the junction of the three rivers." Rodway, 1796.

He states that it was not, "however, quite settled; at one time, the site of the present Penal Settlement was chosen; then it was at Ampa, and at another time at Bartica;" and he adds that, "all of these places are near the junction of the three rivers."

In explanation of the fact that only one post was kept up in the interior, Mr. Rodway adds that "neither the King's nor Colony Chest could afford to keep up more than one," and, therefore, "that single post must be in a convenient place." *

Further light is thrown upon the location of this post by a report of H. W. Knollman, styled Protector of Indians in the Essequibo, made in 1808. Speaking of the postholder (evidently of this same Essequibo post), he says: Knollman, 1808

"The Postholder, Wahl, wishes to change the Post and bring the same to a certain hill, from whence he can oversee the three mouths of the rivers Essequibo, Cajoeny, and Massaroeny, and from whence he can communicate by signals with his Assistant at Bartica."†

---

* Appendix to Case, iii, 357.

† Same, p. 357.

Knoelman, 1808. This removal was allowed by the Court of Policy on April 29, 1808.*

Schomburgk, 1835. In a letter of September 25, 1835, existing at the Government office at Demerara, and published by Mr. Rodway, Schomburgk speaks of this post as the post "at Cuyuni." In a letter of October 1, 1835, he calls it "post Essequibo." He also calls it the "post on the Cuyuni." Later Schomburgk writes that on his return in 1836 he found that the post had been removed to Ampa. Ampa is a village on the right or eastern bank of the Essequibo, below the Cuyuni.

Hilhouse, 1830–31. In 1830 Mr. William Hilhouse made his first exploration of the Mazaruni. The following year he continued his work of exploration. His account throws light upon the location of the former extreme Dutch establishment in this quarter, shown also by Schomburgk on his map and erroneously called "a post" by Hilhouse. He says:

> "We halted the first night, to increase our stock of bread, at Caria island, about three hours above the post. * * * * * Caria was once a Dutch post; and several plantations were formerly on the adjacent banks of the river, but the only traces of them now left are a few cocoa trees on the east shore. Above Caria, on a small island, is a Caribisce settlement of one family, which is the only one of that nation now left on the Massaroony. Here begin the rapids, the fourth of which, Warimambo, is the most remarkable in this day's progress." †

Schomburgk, 1835. Referring to his movements in the last week of September, 1835, Schomburgk writes that, having gone up the Essequibo to the confluence,

> "We here left the main stream and sailed five miles up the Cuyuni to the post or station of the postholder, which stands in a beautiful situation on a mass of granite full 50 feet above the water, commanding a view of the three rivers—the Essequibo, the Cuyuni and Mazeruni, over which it is his duty to watch." ‡

* Appendix to Case, iii, 358.

† Royal Geogr. Soc. Journ., London, 1834, vol. 4, pp. 27–28.

‡ Royal Geogr. Soc. Journ., London, 1836, vol. 6, p. 225.

In Colonel St. Clair's work, above cited, speaking of Berbice, he writes as follows regarding the interior of the country in 1834: Colonel St. Clair, 1834.

"As I have before stated, the northerly boundary of this colony is the sea. The southerly, as in the rest of our settlements in Guiana, is undetermined, which, however, at this period is immaterial, as the Europeans in this country seem to be afraid of leaving the seashore, apparently anxious not to expose themselves to the fury of the native Indians, or to the vengeance of their black slaves, and therefore keeping within sight of their shipping."*

Codazzi's Atlas, published in 1840, contains a special map of the region in dispute,† and gives the site of the former Dutch fort as on the Cuyuni and at the mouth of the Tupuru, a short distance above the confluence of the Cuyuni and Mazaruni. It gives nothing, either Dutch or British, beyond that point. Codazzi, 1840.

Schomburgk's official report of August, 1841, contains the following statement, clearly indicating that, at that time, there was no occupation above the lowest falls of the Cuyuni: Schomburgk, 1841.

"But the difficulties which the Cuyuni presents to navigation, and those tremendous falls which impede the river in the first day's ascent, will, I fear, prove a great obstacle to making the fertility of its banks available to the colony."‡

The present penal settlement at the junction of the three rivers was established in pursuance of an Ordinance passed April 9, 1842. The wording of this Ordinance is confirmatory of what has already been stated with regard to the location of the prior "Cuyuni" or "Essequibo" post. It is as follows: Ordinance of April 9, 1842.

"Whereas it has been deemed expedient to erect and establish

---

* St. Clair (T. S.) Residence in the West Indies and America, etc., London, 1834, vol. —, chap. 10.

† Appendix to Case, atlas, map 80.

‡ Appendix to Case, iii, 119-120.

Ordinance of April 9, 1842.

a penal settlement at the old Post, near the junction of the Massaroony River with the River Essequibo, etc."*

Local Guide, 1843.

The "Local Guide" for 1843, after speaking of the few scattered woodcutters inhabiting the banks of the Essequibo, continues as follows:

"Above the rapids, which occur about 50 miles from its (Essequibo's) mouth, there are no inhabitants except Indians. The same is the case with the two great tributaries of the Essequibo, the Cayuni and the Mazaruni, which come from the west and the southwest. These rivers unite about eight miles from the Essequibo, and their united stream joins that river about forty miles from its mouth. A short distance above their junction these rivers become impeded by rapids, above which they are frequented only by a few wandering Indians. At their point of union with the Essequibo, called Bartica, is an Indian Missionary settlement; and three or four miles up their united stream, on the left bank, is the Colonial Penal Settlement, where the Colonial convicts, sentenced to hard labor, are employed in working a fine quarry of granite."†

No extension of British occupation.

There is no evidence of any extension of British settlement or occupation into the interior between this last date and the year 1850.

The above evidence, gathered from the statements of British officials and British documents, makes it clear that, at least as late as 1850, that is to say, less than 50 years ago, British occupation of the Essequibo, so far as its western bank was concerned, differed from Dutch occupation of the same river in 1648 only because of a few plantations along the Arabian or Arabisi coast. Actual settlement along the coast did not extend as far west as the Pomeroon; and, in the interior, except for a penal settlement, and a mission at or near the former site of fort Kykoveral, there was no settlement or occupation whatever.

* Local Guide of British Guiana, Demerara, 1843, p. 27.

† Local Guide of British Guiana, Demerara, 1843, p. ii.

2d.—CONDITION OF ESSEQUIBO COLONY.

A glance at the general condition of the colony itself during the first half of this century will disclose the fact that, like its predecessor of two hundred years before, it was generally on the brink of ruin; and that its continued existence, at least west of the Essequibo, was at times very doubtful.

Precarious condition of colony.

A brief reference will be made to but a few of the facts upon which this statement is based.

To begin with, during the opening years of the century, the Spaniards seem to have had as little regard for British rights west of the Essequibo, as they had formerly had for Dutch rights in the same region. The planters of the Arabian coast—the only planters west of the Essequibo—suffered constant attacks from the Spaniards; and in November, 1807, petitioned the Court of Policy for protection.*

Spanish attacks on Arabian coast.

But it was not from the Spaniards alone that the planters suffered damage. This same year of 1807 saw the abolition of the African slave trade, the first of those steps which in 1838 resulted in the total abolition of slavery from the Colony. †

Abolition of African slave trade, 1807.

However much applause the abolition of this inhuman trade may merit, it certainly came as a severe blow to the struggling planters whose dependence upon their slaves was complete. The blow itself came at a most inopportune moment. It came when the colony was already in a moribund condition.

It was a blow to the Colony.

---

* Appendix to Case, iii, 324.

† Slave catching by the Caribs had ceased by this time. This once powerful tribe had gradually dwindled in numbers, and a little later had become so reduced that Schomburgk, in 1840, wrote that there remained but few in British Guiana. He adds: "The Caribs inhabit the lower Mazaruni and Cuyuni; about 100 are located at the Corentyn, 80 at the Rupununi, 30 at the Guidaru, and their whole number (once the lords of the soil) does not at present surpass 300." [Schomburgk (R. H.), Description of British Guiana, London, 1840, p. 50; see *also* Appendix to Case, iii, 325.]

Condition of colony, 1806.

For some years before, the seat of government had been losing importance, even the residence of the Commandeur rapidly going to ruin. "At the meeting of the Court of January 28th, 1806, it was reported that the house of the Commandeur was uninhabitable." *

With the colony in the condition which this single fact sufficiently attests, the check to the slave trade threatened the very existence of the colony.

Alarming condition in 1811.

Year by year matters grew worse. On November 30, 1811, a meeting of the sugar planters was held to consider the alarming state of affairs, and the ruin that stared them in the face.†

End of Essequibo as a Spanish colony.

The colony itself had gradually shrunk; its importance becoming so impaired that the year 1812 witnessed its end as a separate entity. On April 1 of that year it ceased to exist as a distinct colony, and became merged with Demerara. Its archives were removed to Georgetown: its Commandeur and other officials lost their positions; and the old colony passed away. ‡

A few years later the coast plantations began to be abandoned or given up to the grazing of cattle. §

Compulsory manumission in 1831.

So things continued, between life and death, until 1831, when a second blow was struck at the slave trade. Compulsory manumission was then provided for;‖ and two years later, on August 24, 1833, the Emancipation Act was passed: this provided that after 1840 all slaves should be free.¶

Emancipation act, Aug. 24, 1833.

The effect of this final emancipation was almost the

* Appendix to Case, iii, 324.

† Appendix to Case, iii, 324-325.

‡ Appendix to Case, iii, 325.

§ Appendix to Case, iii, 325.

‖ Rodway (J.) History of British Guiana, Georgetown, 1893, vol. ii, p. 281.

¶ Rodway (J.) Historyof British Guiana, Georgetown, 1893, vol. iii, p. 11.

ruin of the colony. Speaking of the condition of affairs in 1842 and 1843, Rodway says: Effect of emancipation.

"Now began a general cry of 'ruin.' There had been plenty of croakers all along and they were quite ready with their 'I told you so' when things began to look black and lowering. In April [1842] the *Guiana Times* showed up the state of affairs from the pessimists' point of view. Pln. *Enfield* in Berbice, worth in 1829, £29,000, had been lately sold at Execution for £2,000 and *Port Morant* for $35,000 when it had been valued before the apprenticeship at as many pounds. *Industry* had stopped work—*Schoon-Ord* formerly worth over £36,000 could be had for £20,000—*Rome* and *Houston* now made only 600 instead of 700 hogsheads—*Vrow Anna* was insolvent—and *Nonpariel* had been bought the year before for £30,000 and the owner now wanted to sell it at a sacrifice. Such were the facts, but nothing was said about the compensation money for the slaves which must be taken into account in all these comparisons. A plantation with two hundred slaves was worth between thirty and forty thousands more than one without any, and here we see the great difference explained. It is undoubtedly true that emancipation meant a serious reduction of the estimated capital and, as a natural consequence, of all the advantages of its possession. Only about a third of the value of the slaves was received, so that every owner was mulcted in the amount of the other two-thirds, leaving him in so much the worse position as a borrower. From all that can be gleaned, the human property on an estate was always of more importance than the acreage in cultivation, and was therefore its prop and mainstay in all financial difficulties.

The few coffee plantations deteriorated in value to even a greater extent than those of sugar. In October 1843 two estates in No. 1 Canal, *Vreed-en-Vriendschap* and *Jacoba Constantia* were offered for sale, but nothing beyond two hundred dollars was bid for them. The price of coffee was very low at this time and that, with the scarcity of labour, led to an almost general abandonment of this cultivation as well as that of cotton." *

An official dispatch of June 18, 1849, from Lieutenant- Conditions in 1849.

* Appendix to Case, iii, 326-327, being pp. 64-65 of vol. iii of Rodway's History of British Guiana.

Conditions in 1849. Governor Walker to Earl Grey describes the conditions existing in that year. It is as follows:

"It is most melancholy to learn, that while the difficulties of the planters have continued since the abolition of slavery to become more and more severe, until now their ruin appears to be almost complete, and the depreciation of property once of such great value, has reached a point which has involved in the deepest distress great numbers of persons both in this country and the colony; at the same time the negroes, instead of having made a great advance in civilization as might have been hoped during the fifteen years which have elapsed since their emancipation, have on the contrary, retrograded rather than improved, and that they are now as a body less amenable than they were when that great change took place, to the restraints of religion and of law, less docile and tractable, and almost as ignorant and as much subject as ever to the degrading superstition which their forefathers brought with them from Africa."*

Commission of 1850 In January, 1850, a Commission was appointed to inquire into the state and prospects of the colony. Rodway thus speaks of its report:

"This report is most exhaustive, proving beyond doubt that the colony in general was virtually ruined. The Commissioners stated that they had examined the principal estate proprietors and attornies, as well as the leading merchants, and observed with deep concern the alarming picture of ruin and distress in which all classes with startling unanimity concurred in representing the then state of the once flourishing colony. Whole districts were fast relapsing into bush, and occasionally patches of provisions around huts of villagers were all that remained of what had formerly been most prosperous estates. In many places the road communication was difficult and would soon become utterly impracticable.

"Reviewing the whole coast line and commencing with Demerara, they said that the former estates in the Abary district, once blooming with fields of cotton, were nothing but a series of pestilent swamps, breeders of malignant fevers. From Mahaicony to Mahaica the only estate in cultivation was Pln. *Farm;* the others

* Appendix to Case, iii, 327.

were either given over to a few cattle, or abandoned, except a few patches of reef-land in provisions. On the upper west bank of the Mahaica creek the roads and bridges were in such a bad condition that the few remaining estates were entirely cut off except in the dry season.*

Commission of 1850.

"If Demerara were bad, Essequebo was worse. Unless a speedy supply of labour was obtained to cultivate the deserted fields of this once flourishing district, there was reason to fear it would relapse into utter abandonment. Leguan, for many years termed the garden of the colony, once contained twenty-three sugar and three coffee and plantain estates; these had been reduced to eight in sugar and but three of these were in full cultivation. From the termination of the Apprenticeship want of labour was severely felt. As soon as the people were at liberty, they left the island and went to Demerara to be near town. Then commenced the establishment of villages on the land itself, which quickly absorbed a number of the working people, for whom hunting and fishing had greater attractions than field work. Mr. MacKenzie, of Pln. *Amsterdam*, told them that it was no overdrawn description when he asserted that the cultivation was then limited to a third of the former number of estates, and these were but struggling desperately to avoid the doom which seemed inevitable. Forest trees were rapidly taking over the once smiling canefields, and the few remaining were scarcely discernible amid a savage bush.

"Wakenaam was not in quite such a deplorable condition. None of the estates were actually abandoned, but many were only nominally in cultivation, and the previous year's crop was less by six million pounds than that of 1829. In this island and Leguan over two thousand people lived in villages, for whom the abandoned cane-pieces afforded excellent hunting grounds and the surrounding waters good fishing. On Hog Island the cultivation had dwindled from 858 acres to 308, and the crop of sugar from nine hundred to two hundred hogsheads. It was kept up then by means of coolies whose service would soon expire, and unless a fresh supply could be obtained the cultivation would probably be abandoned. On Tiger Island the area had been reduced from 856 to 328 acres, and instead of a working population of 561 the number had been reduced to 125 creoles and 189 immigrants, the latter carrying on most of the cultivation.

---

* Appendix to Case, iii, 328.

Commission of 1850.

"Between the Supenaam and Iteribisce Creeks the coast was in a most deplorable condition. Of seven fine sugar estates, four nominally survived with greatly diminished cultivation. Three villages in this district contained nearly seven hundred creoles, a fourth of whom worked at times on the estates, but the remainder 'sit down, and hunt and steal both from the planters and each other. Unable to obtain labour, the proprietors seem to be keeping up a hopeless struggle against approaching ruin, and unless immigration recommenced their estates would have to be abandoned.' Between Iteribisce Creek and Capoey Creek three coffee and ten sugar plantations formerly existed; these had been reduced to eight in sugar and the produce to less than half. In 1829 the population was 2,764; it was then only 954. The villagers, however, numbered over 4,000, but so little work was performed by them that they could hardly be considered as a part of the labour supply. The Arabian coast, so long the boast of the colony, had become a mournful picture of departed prosperity. Here were formerly some of the finest estates in the colony and a large body of resident proprietors who freely expended their incomes on the spot. From Capoey Creek to *Better Success* there had been twenty-three plantations; three of these were virtually abandoned and the remainder in a languishing condition. The sugar crop here was also less than half, caused by the same want of labour. The district swarmed with villages, but no dependence could be placed on the people, and the estates were mostly worked by coolies. As the end of their engagements was approaching they were leaving to claim back passages, and the creoles were also leaving. From *Devonshire Castle* to the Pomeroon, where formerly there had been seven estates worth £176,000, the country was almost desolate." *

Such was the condition and extent of the British colony on the Essequibo River at the middle of the present century, only forty-seven years prior to the signing of the present treaty of arbitration.

* Appendix to Case, iii, 329-330.

XIV.—HISTORY OF BRITISH OCCUPATION. 1850–1896.

In view of the fifty year rule [Art. IV, Rule (a)] adopted by the present treaty, the expansion of British occupation subsequent to *1847* can have no effect upon the determination of the boundary line. Rule (c), however, is as follows: Fifty year clause

"(c) In determining the boundary-line, if territory of one Party be found by the Tribunal to have been at the date of this Treaty in the occupation of the subjects or citizens of the other Party, such effect shall be given to such occupation as reason, justice, the principles of international law, and the equities of the case shall, in the opinion of the Tribunal, require."

In order that the tribunal may be able to apply this rule, it becomes necessary to place it in possession of the facts connected with the recent occupation of a part of the disputed territory, by Great Britain. The beginning of that occupation dates, on the coast, only from 1884 (twelve years prior to the signing of the treaty), and, in the interior, only from 1880, or later, (not more than sixteen years prior to the present treaty). Beginning of British occupation, 1880 and 1884.

Prior to those dates, British settlement was still what it had been in 1850. Since those dates, all persons who have ventured into the disputed territory have gone there in the face of distinct warnings from both governments. They have, with open eyes, assumed all the risks involved; and, so far as the Venezuelan Government is concerned, it does not consider that they are entitled to any consideration. Recent settlements made in face of warnings.

The history of recent British occupation is so intimately connected with the history of the gold industry, Gold industry.

Gold industry.

that it will be best understood if a brief review of this be first given.

Caratal discovered, 1850.

In 1850 the rich gold fields of the Caratal were discovered on the banks of the Yuruari, where the Venezuelans already had extensive settlements.*

This was at once advertised in Georgetown, but the location of the mines was so far away that no attempt was made to visit them until the following year.†

In 1851 four tradesmen from Demarara went to the mines by way of the Orinoco, and returned later by the same route.‡

Excitement of 1857

In 1857 fresh reports of the Yuruari mines reached British Guiana; and a newspaper of Georgetown published a statement to the effect that the diggings "appeared to be in British territory."§ Immediately the public mind was fired. Proposals were made to build a road so that direct communication might be had with the mines. The Home Government at the same time was urged to bring about a settlement of the boundary question.‖

In August, 1857, the *Gazette* stated that many parties were anxious to try their fortunes at the diggings but were prudently waiting until a direct route could be opened.¶ Soon after a party started by way of the Moruca and the Waini, going thence across to the Cuyuni and on to the Yuruari.**

Others followed, but the route was always by the coast rivers, or else by sea to the Orinoco.††

Finally, in August (1859) a party made its way to

* Appendix to Case, iii, 333.
† Appendix to Case, iii, 333.
‡ Appendix to Case, iii, 334.
§ Appendix to Case, iii, 334.
‖ Appendix to Case, iii, 335.
¶ Appendix to Case, iii, 335.
** Appendix to Case, iii, 335.
†† Appendix to Case, iii, 335.

the mines by way of Cuyuni, but the return trip was wisely made by way of the Orinoco.* — Excitement of 1857.

After this the Venezuelan authorities prohibited further communication through the interior, with the result that no further expeditions were undertaken by that route.† — Venezuela forbad communication through interior.

Partly as a result of this prohibition, and partly because of the hardships which had to be endured by those who were bold enough to venture so far from home, the gold fever subsided, and for some years the Venezuelans continued in undisputed and exclusive possession of the Cuyuni-Mazaruni basin.‡

Referring to this gold excitement, im Thurn says of it: — im Thurn's statement.

> "Certain English expeditions were, indeed, sent to Tupuquen, but their sole result was a tardy acknowledgment from the English that the mines of that place were not in British territory."§

In 1863 the dormant gold fever again showed signs of its presence.‖ — First British attempt to occupy land in Cuyuni basin, 1863.

This brings us to the first attempt on the part of the British to actually occupy land in the Cuyuni basin. Their predecessors, the Dutch, had been expelled from there by the Spaniards in 1772: since that time only a few explorers had penetrated beyond the lowest falls of the Cuyuni and Mazaruni rivers.

In 1863 a number of gentlemen applied to Governor Hincks for a right to occupy a tract of land on the Cuyuni. The answer of the Governor was that he was precluded from granting them a license, and that he could only regard them as a community of British ad-

* Appendix to Case, iii, 337.

† Appendix to Case, iii, 338.

‡ Appendix to Case, iii, 338.

§ Appendix to Case, iii, 151.

‖ Appendix to Case, iii, 339.

First British attempt to occupy land in Cuyuni basin, 1863.

venturers acting on their own responsibility and at their own peril.*

Notwithstanding this rebuff, these "British adventurers" were bold enough to take the matter into their own hands, and to go into the Cuyuni, twenty miles beyond the Penal Settlement.†

Money was spent without any adequate return; and the company finding itself embarrassed sent a representative to London to sell its property.‡

Warning by Great Britain against settling in disputed territory, 1867.

When this became known, the British Government caused a notice to be published, January 30, 1867, declaring that it could not undertake to afford protection to British subjects encroaching upon the territory in dispute, "but must only recognize them as a community of British adventurers acting on their own responsibility, and at their own peril and cost." §

Attempt at mining abandoned.

The result of this was the failure of the Company, and the abandonment of its property. ‖

Speaking of this ineffectual effort of the British to mine in the Cuyuni, Mr. im Thurn says:

"In or about 1863 certain gold mines on the Cuyuni River, at a distance of about two days' journey from its mouth, were worked by an English company formed in Georgetown. No serious attempts to wash for gold were made higher up the Cuyuni by any English subjects. These English mines are very far from those of Tupuquen, which are at a distance, roughly speaking, of, at the very least, twenty or thirty days' journey from the mouth of the Cuyuni. Tupuquen undoubtedly lies very far on the Venezuelan side of the boundary as claimed by the English and as laid down by Sir Robert Schomburgk. Had we, therefore, claimed the mines at that place, it would have been most unwise and unwarrantable. But we made no such claim, and Mármol's attempt to

---

* Appendix to Case, iii, 339.

† Appendix to Case, iii, 339.

‡ Appendix to Case, iii, 340.

§ Appendix to Case, iii, 340.

‖ Appendix to Case, iii, 340.

quote such a claim as an act of aggression on our part must be based on a mistake. But he makes the statement in such apparent good faith as to suggest the idea that possibly not only his statement but the action of the Venezuelan Government was founded on a mistake which has never yet been rectified [not *ratified*, as erroneously printed]. It is just possible that the Venezuelan Government, hearing some rumor that the English were working gold on the Cuyuni, hastily adopted the conclusion that this was in the neighbourhood of Tupuquen and within their territory. However this may have been, they appealed to the British Government to stop the alleged invasion of their territory, and the British Government, having given notice to the gold mining company that they must work only as adventurers and not claim British protection, the works were abandoned." * Attempt at mining abandoned.

This occurred in 1867.

After the failure of the British Mining Company in 1867, nothing more was heard of gold mining in the disputed territory until about the year 1880. It then began to be rumored that some Frenchmen from Cayenne had discovered gold in the Puruni river, a branch of the Mazaruni. This led to other explorations in the same direction and gold mining at last obtained a start in the Cuyuni-Mazaruni basin. † No more heard of mining in Cuyuni until 1880.

The search for gold gradually extended to the coast region. In 1887 it was discovered in the Barima: a new impetus was thereby given to the gold industry; and a new rush into the disputed territory took place. This brought forth a new warning from the British Government in June, 1887, whereby all persons were cautioned that, in going into the disputed territory, they were doing so at their own risk.‡ Gold in the coast region. 1887. New warning by Great Britain in 1887.

* Appendix to Case, iii, 151.

† Appendix to Case, iii, 323.

‡ The following is from the *Royal Gazette*, Georgetown, of Wednesday, June 8, 1887:"A meeting of the Court of Policy was held yesterday, at which there were present: His Excellency the Lieutenant Governor (Chas. Bruce, Esq., C. M. G.); the Honourables F. J. Villiers, C. M. G. (Acting Government Secretary); A. Kingdon (Acting Attorney-General); G. Melville (Acting Auditor-General); A. H. Alexander (Immigration Agent-General) of the

New warning by Great Britain in 1887.

The warning deterred some: others ventured in, thus deliberately assuming the risks involved.

---

official section; Honorables F. Mulligan, W. Craigen, C. L. Bascour, B. H. Jones and J. J. Dare, of the elective section. The Court was constituted at 11.35 A. M., and sat with closed doors until 11.45, when the public were admitted.

"The Gold Industry and the Boundary Question.

"Threatened Collapse of the Gold Industry.

"His Excellency said: Hon. Gentlemen of the Court of Policy,—Before we proceed to the Order of the Day, I am anxious to make a statement with reference to the question of the boundary between this Colony and the Republic of Venezuela. Among the applications which have been received for mining licenses and concessions under the Mining Regulations passed under Ordinance 16 of 1880, 16 of 1886, and 4 of 1887, there are many which apply to lands which are within the territory in dispute between Her Majesty's Government and the Venezuela Republic. I have received instructions of the Secretary of State to caution expressly all persons interested in such licenses, or concessions, or otherwise acquiring an interest in the disputed territory, that all licenses, concessions or grants, applying to any portion of such disputed territory will be issued and must be accepted, subject to the possibility that, in the event of a settlement of the present disputed line, the land to which such licenses, concessions or grants applies may become a part of the Venezuelan territory; in which case, no claim to compensation from the Colony, or from Her Majesty's Government can be recognized; but Her Majesty's Government would, of course, do whatever may be right and practicable to secure from the Government of Venezuela a recognition and confirmation of licenses, etc., now issued. In making this statement I am aware that I shall disappoint the sanguine expectation of those who may have hoped that the proclamation of November 6, 1886, represented the final settlement of the boundary question. All, however, who have followed the course of public opinion in England must have seen that the question is not yet settled. The interpretation which I place on the instructions I have received is, that Her Majesty's Government desire to have their hands free to come to an early and permanent settlement of this long dispute. I am confident, and I ask you to share my confidence, that such a settlement will be based on the justice of our claims and the preservation of the integrity of this province.

"Mr. Mulligan was sure that what His Excellency had just stated and the despatch he had just quoted, would cause considerable annoyance outside, especially among those who had placed a great amount of capital in the gold venture on the faith of the proclamation which was recently published. It would have been very much better, and would not have reflected as much on the Imperial Government, had they taken no action whatever, but to allow matters to stand as they had been for many years disputed. People would then have known what they were about and would have been fully cognizant of all the risks they ran in venturing on the disputed territory, but after the appearance of the proclamation so recently issued, it was but natural that British subjects, assured of protection as such, should invest money in speculations such as had taken place. Very considerable amount of capital had been so invested, and it seemed now rather late in the day to be told that they were squatters and adventurers, and were simply working on their own lines. He expressed his sincere regret that this had taken place, but could not say that he was surprised, for when the proclam-

In 1888, the result of the gold discoveries in Barima was as yet problematical; and it was not until 1889

Results of gold mining still problematical in 1888.

---

ation was brought up in November, 1886, he said in this Court he thought it would do more harm than good, and that people would be induced by it to go digging gold in the disputed district with the result which he very much feared His Excellency's words foreshadowed.

"However, it was entirely in keeping with the miserable backward policy of the Imperial Government, and which they exhibited all over the world. Stanley's letter, for instance, recently addressed to a Geographical Society, on the condition of British influence at Zanzibar, and other parts of Africa, showed that the same backward policy of which we had here an example was being exhibited there. He thought it was cruel, and more than cruel, to reduce to such straits British subjects who had invested capital in this gold venture;—in fact, he knew there were some who had put their all in the venture. Those people were now told that in case of a settlement of this boundary question and a decision that the disputed territory on which they were now digging, belonged to Venezuela, they would have nothing to hope and nothing to claim from this colony or the Imperial Government. He hoped the elective members of the Court of Policy would at any rate protest against the action and draw the attention of the Imperial Government to the proclamation, and to the words then spoken by the Attorney-General in this Court when it was decided to issue that proclamation.

"Mr. Jones thoroughly indorsed all that had fallen from the senior elective member of the Court with reference to the despatch just quoted by His Excellency. The announcement which had been made would create an immense amount of heart-burning amongst those who had capital invested in what was considered to be an undertaking secured to them by proclamation from home. When the despatch of last November was received the feeling outside was that the British Government had taken up a position which they intended to stand by, but it seemed now that they had drifted back from their former opinion, and would no longer give any support to the operations which had been undertaken by private parties in the disputed territory. His own feeling regarding the boundary question had for many years past been that the only right solution of the boundary question would be by the appointment of a Royal Commission to meet a Commission from Venezuela, and that the commissioners should go over the whole grounds of the subject, and visit the whole of the boundary was as done recently with reference to Afghanistan. The boundary dispute here might not be such an important point as that of Afghanistan was to British rule in India, but it was certainly of great importance to us in this colony to have it settled, and it was of as great importance to the Government here to have that done as it was to the Government of India to have the boundary of Afghanistan settled. If such commission were appointed, he felt sure that there would not be those heart-burnings and feelings of distrust which the present and past policy of the British Government had created in the minds of the colonists, who looked on and saw the sort of game being played by British rule, or he might say, misrule.

"His Excellency said: I shall lose no time in conveying to the Secretary of State the vital importance to this Colony of an early settlement of this question (Mr. Mulligan: Hear, hear), and the rising importance of the gold industry. And I shall, of course, avail myself of the opportunity to represent to the Secretary of State what has been expressed in this Court, and what, I have no doubt, represent the general feelings of the community."

First important gold discoveries were in 1889.

(only seven years before the present treaty) that it assumed any considerable proportions.*

The foregoing account of the gold discoveries and of the gold industry in the disputed territory will suffice to show how recent both are: it will also throw light on the cause and present character of British occupation.

Cause and recent date of British occupation.

As to the interior, this occupation is fully explained by the gold discoveries: except for these the Cuyuni-Mazaruni basin would probably be to-day as free from British as it had been free from both Dutch and British for more than a century before. As to the coast, the gold discoveries furnish but half the explanation. The other half will appear later in the diplomatic history of the question. Suffice it here to say that, prior to the discovery of gold, and as early as 1884,

British occupation of Barima Point.

Mr. McTurk, a British official, acting under British authority, took forcible possession of the mouth of the Orinoco; and that, in 1885, the region along the coast, as far west as Barima point and the Amacura river, was organized into a separate "district" under the jurisdiction of a Special Commissioner.†

It has been stated that, except for the gold discoveries in the Mazaruni in 1880, except for the gold discoveries along the coast subsequent to that date, and except for the formal taking of possession of the mouth of the

[See also Rodway (J.) History of British Guiana, Georgetown, 1894, iii, 225.]

* "The change, great as it is, has been effected in the last three or four years, being in part due to the discovery by small cultivators of the extraordinary richness of the soil, but has occurred, I might almost say, chiefly within the year 1889, being due to the discovery of a rich and easily accessible gold area in the Barima.

"Writing in December, 1888, I could only describe the chance of the discovery of gold in the district as problematical. Only two or three months later gold had been discovered in considerable quantity, and within a year a very large part of the gold industry of the colony had been directed to these parts." [Im Thurn (E. F.) Report; published in 1890.]

† British Guiana and its Resources, London, 1895, pp. 76–77.

Orinoco in 1884 by Mr. McTurk, the British never had settlements of any kind, nor occupation of any nature, above the lowest falls of the Essequibo, Cuyuni and Mazaruni in the interior, nor beyond the plantations along the Arabian coast on the seaboard.

British occupation of Barima Point.

As witnesses to this, the following writers may be cited:

1. AS TO THE COAST.

The story of this region is best told by Mr. im Thurn in a paper read before the Royal Geographical Society in London on July 4, 1892, and published in the "Proceedings" of that Society for October, 1892, Vol. 14, pp. 665-687. The following extracts are taken from the article referred to:

Story of the coast region by im Thurn.

"During my nine years' work I have been actively engaged, first, in ascertaining the nature of the country, and then in transforming this from its state of desolate and unbroken swamp, smothered in densest tropical vegetation, and inhabited but by a few red men, into an integral part of the colony." (p. 665.)

* * * * * * * * * * *

"Though through fear of privateers, these at first went up the rivers, yet as soon as this fear was removed they cast longing eyes on the splendidly rich submerged land of the seacoast, and, with an experience and skill gained in their Low-Country homes, dammed back the sea along the southern coasts of the colonies, and reclaimed for cultivation a narrow strip of alluvial soil, extending along the sea and river edge, but hardly anywhere more than three or four miles in width. But their work ended northwest at the Pomeroun river. The whole interior of the country, and even the seacoast north of the Pomeroun—that is, the northwestern part of the colony—they left as Nature made it. Since the beginning of this century, when the country passed from the hands of the Dutch to those of the English, the latter have rather reduced than extended the area of cultivation; and though they have fairly maintained the quality, the land beyond the narrow belt of cultivation has remained as Nature made it and the Dutch left it. (p. 668.)

* * * * * * * * * * *

Story of the coast region by im Thurn.

"Though the settlements in the Pomerun were, as has been said, among the earliest, if not indeed the earliest, in what is now British Guiana, and though they have never been at any time completely abandoned, yet at no time have they attained the privilege of independent government, as was the case with the settlements on the Essequibo, Demerara, and Berbice Rivers. During the early part of this century there were flourishing settlements and substantial houses for some distance along the right bank, and also at intervals higher up, on both banks of the Pomerun; but of these hardly any record exists. About 1840, at the time of the visit of the brothers Schomburgk, the houses and the cultivation, though still partly existing, were already in decay, and for some time after that date the river remained practically abandoned to Redmen and to squatters. About twenty years ago there was a revival of agricultural industry by the settlement in those parts of a few Portuguese, and the development in this direction has since then been continuous. The Government of the colony was represented there up to 1872, by an official with somewhat vague powers, handed down from Dutch times, called a Post-holder. With the revival of industry by the Portuguese, this official was modernized into a magistrate. It was to this post that I was appointed in 1882. My jurisdiction extended nominally to the Orinoco; but hardly anyone capable of giving an intelligent account of the country had been beyond the Pomerun, or the small creek, the Moruka—a branch of the Pomerun—on which two missions, one Protestant, the other Roman Catholic, had been established about 1840.

"My station on the Pomerun then was the outpost in a northwesterly direction of the civilized part of the colony, and it immediately became my desire to explore the unknown part of the district under my charge. (pp. 669–670.)

* * * * * * * * * * *

"Even from the Redmen and the black squatters on the Pomerun I found it very difficult to get any information as to the great region beyond; but at last, in January, 1883, though unsuccessful in getting a guide, I started to see for myself what lay within my district beyond the known parts. (p. 670.)

* * * * * * * * * * *

"On the other hand, the higher part of the new district is (1892) being fast overrun by very successful gold diggers. But these agricultural and mining enterprises date, the former, only some half dozen years, the latter only some three years back." (p. 685.)

Story of the coast region, by im Thurn.

The same official, in his report for 1889, says:

"Remembering the desolate, uninhabited, unused, indeed unknown, condition of this latter sub-district when I first visited it in February, 1883, and now seeing its present condition at the close of the year 1889, I find it hard to realize that these are but two aspects of the same place. Then, as I passed down the Barima River, through about 120 miles of its lower course, I saw no house or sign of habitation, no human being, until we came to the sand bank at the sea, on which two or three men from the neighboring Amakooroo River were temporarily camped, for the purpose of fishing. In the Amakooroo itself, on the English side, there was not a house to be seen, though there were two or three cultivated plots, the owners of which reside on the opposite shore. In the sub-district the entire number of settlements, if we restrict the term only to such cultivated plots as had sufficient drainage, and on which the farmers lived, amounted therefore to but four. Moreover, at that time no travellers moved on the rivers, if we except the half dozen of settlers, and two or three hucksters trading with Indians."*

im Thurn supported by others.

Mr. im Thurn is confirmed in these statements by a number of other writers.

Brown, 1875.

Mr. C. Barrington Brown, the government geologist, describing his geological survey, wrote in 1875:

"The civilized and cultivated portion of the colony lies only along a narrow strip of sea-coast. * * * This portion, between the rear of the sugar estates and the confines of the colony, is known as the "Interior;" and, with the exception of a few settlements on the banks of the lower Berbice, Demerara and Essequibo rivers, it remains to-day in the same state as in the time of Raleigh."†

Rodway, 1893.

In his *Handbook*, published in 1893, Mr. Rodway says that:

"The settled portion of the colony extends along the sea-

* British Guiana. Administrative Reports for the year 1889, fol. Georgetown, Demerara, 1890, p. 17.

† Brown (C. Barrington). Canoe and Camp Life, etc., 8°, London, 1876, p. 1.

Rodway, 1893. coast from the west bank of the river Essequebo to the east bank of the Corentyne."*

2. AS TO THE INTERIOR.

Witnesses as to interior. Our witnesses as to these regions are again Mr. im Thurn, Mr. Brown and Mr. Rodway, and in addition to these Sir Clements R. Markham, President of the Royal. Geographical Society.

im Thurn, 1879. The following is the description which, in 1879, Mr. im Thurn gave of the territory in dispute:

"The territory in dispute commences on the western bank of the Essequebo River and extends to an undefined distance toward the Orinoco. Along and near the banks of the Essequebo, at least during the lower part of its course, is a fairly dense population of British subjects, and along and near the banks of the Orinoco is a fairly thick population of Venezuelans. But the intermediate space is inhabited only by some scattered Indians, and is visited only at long intervals by a few travelers, traders, adventurers or explorers."†

im Thurn, 1892. In 1892, in a passage already quoted in full, he says that "the whole interior of the country . . . . they (the Dutch) left as Nature made it."‡

Rodway, 1889. Mr. Rodway, writing in *Timehri* in 1889, said:

Up to the time of Robert Schomburgk's explorations, the interior of this country was almost unknown. The great lake of Parima was still retained on most of the maps of South America, but the best geographers had already expressed doubts as to the existence of any very large body of water in Guiana. Hillhouse had made some journeys up the Massaruni and also partial explorations of the country between the Essequebo and the Orinoco, but the upper districts of our great rivers were less known than they had been a century before, when the Dutch postholders must have had a good knowledge of the country. Humboldt's researches had left Guiana unexplored; he says, "With respect

---

* Rodway (J.). Hand-Book of British Guiana, 12°, Georgetown, Br. Guiana, 1893, p. 16.

† Appendix to Case, iii, 150.

‡ Royal Geog. Soc. Proc., London, 1892, Oct., xiv, 668.

to the continuation of the system of the mountains of Parime, southeast of the meridian of the Essequebo, the materials are entirely wanting for tracing it with precision. The whole interior of Dutch, French and Portuguese Guiana is a *terra incognita*, and the astronomical geography of those countries has scarcely made any progress during the space of thirty years.* Rodway, 1889.

The same author in his *Hand-Book for the Chicago Exhibition, 1892*, said: Rodway, 1892.

"*The Forest Region.*—Commencing at the sand-reefs, the flatness of the coast region gives place to an undulating country, which gradually rises to hills and then mountains. The greater portion of this vast territory is covered with primeval forest—a portion of that wilderness of vegetation which extends with only a few breaks over a great portion of South America. A few descendants of old settlers or their slaves live on the banks of the Demerara, Essequibo, and Berbice rivers, and here and there a woodcutter or gold seeker; these comprise, with the remnants of scattered tribes of Indians, the inhabitants of this region. Sometimes not a single human being can be found within a hundred miles, even the Indians having gone away for some unexplained reasons." †

Mr. Brown's testimony regarding this interior has already been quoted: he states that the "Interior . . . remains to-day (1875) in the same state as in the time of Raleigh." ‡ Brown, 1875.

Sir Clements R. Markham, in a review published in April, 1876, says: Markham, 1876.

"Both the colonies of British Guiana and Natal have recently published maps of the territories subject to their sway. . . .

"From a note placed under the title we learn that the boundaries laid down upon the map are those adopted by Sir Robert Schomburgk. . . .

"At present there are no settlements on the territories in dis-

---

* *Timehri*, being Jour. of Roy. Agl. & Com'l. Soc., Demerara, 1889, June. iii, 1.

† Rodway (J.) Hand-Book of British Guiana. Georgetown, Br. Guiana, 1892, p. 11.

‡ See p. 180 of this volume.

Markham, 1876. pute, or at most, unimportant ones, and an amicable settlement of these boundary questions could easily be arrived at."*

No British occupation until a dozen years ago.

From what has been above set forth, it must be apparent that, according to the evidence of British officials and British writers especially qualified to speak on the subject, the entire territory west of the Essequibo, excepting only a few plantations along the Arabian coast at the mouth of that river, had never been occupied by the British until within a dozen years past; and that the present occupation has been effected in the face of repeated warnings from both the Venezuelan and the British governments. A brief examination of the published census of the British colony may tend to emphasize the first of these statements. Such an examination will also serve to show that a statement made by Lord Salisbury, first in 1880, and again in 1895, was based upon erroneous information. The statement referred to was that, to admit Venezuela's claims to the territory in dispute,

Census of British Colony.

Lord Salisbury's statement.

"would involve the surrender of a province now inhabitated by 40,000 British subjects, and which has been in the uninterrupted possession of Holland and Great Britain successively for two centuries."†

Census of 1831.

The first census of the colony of which there is any record is that of 1831.‡

At that time the entire Essequibo colony on *both* sides of the river numbered 25,079 persons, of whom all but 1,526 were slaves; the whites numbering only 614.§

Census of 1851

In 1851 the total population had fallen to 24,925, and of these only 14,398 were on the west side of the Essequibo along the Arabian coast; of these again only 1,106

* Royal Geog. Soc. Journal, London, 1876, April, p. 103.

† Appendix to Case, iii, 218.

‡ Appendix to Case iii, 319.

§ Appendix to Case, iii, 320.

were Europeans.* There were no settlers west of the Pomeroon, and only a few scattered woodcutters above Hog Island in the Essequibo river. Census of 1851.

The last census of the colony, that for the year 1891, gives the following: Census of 1891.

Total population of Essequibo county	53,254
Of this total there were only 388 Europeans other than Portuguese, the balance being mainly East Indians, of which there were	22,502
And Blacks, of which there were	19,926
The population on the Upper Pomeroon was	952
" " Lower " "	1,673
" " Moruca was	1,349
" " Northwest District	942
Above first rapids of the Essequibo, including Potaro and the upper Essequibo gold fields	3,908
On the Mazaruni	312
On the Cuyuni	144

It does not appear how many of those credited to Mazaruni and Cuyuni were *above* the lowest falls of those streams; but, assuming that they were *all* settled there, the figures given show, that a line drawn from the mouth of the Moruca to the lowest falls of the Mazaruni and Cuyuni, and thence south along the Essequibo, would leave to the west only the following: Population in Cuyuni - Mazaruni basin.

Northwest District (between Moruca and Orinoco)	942
Cuyuni	144
Mazaruni	312
Total	1,398

None of these were in these regions in 1880 when Lord Salisbury first wrote of the "40,000 British subjects" inhabiting a province which had been "in the uninterrupted possession of Holland and Great Britain respectively for two centuries." None there in 1880.

* Appendix to Case, iii, 169.

Population in 1895.

There may have been a few more there in 1895 when this assertion was repeated; but it will be apparent, from the official census of the colony, that such population as was to be found there in 1895, or such as exists there to-day, is in any event small, and that it consisted and consists of persons who, after repeated warnings from both the British and Venezuelan Governments, have gone into that region during the last dozen years.

Character of present British "settlement."

In order that the Tribunal may be further able to judge of the equities to which present occupants may be entitled under the treaty, it is advisable that it be informed as to the *character* of the present British "settlement" in the disputed territory.

In this connection Mr. im Thurn may once more be quoted. Speaking of the class of people in the Barima region, he says:

"Agriculture in the district, probably because of the superior attractions of the gold industry, still makes very slow progress."

"Lastly, as concerns the gold industry, I think it right to put on record my sense of the growing necessity for better protection of the rights of persons and property at the gold fields. There is gathered together a large and varying body of men, the greater part of them taken from the most lawless and undisciplined classes of the colony; and there is not among them, nor within many days' journey of them, one single representative of the law." *

The following extract is taken from the annual report of E. P. Wood, Commissioner of the Department of Mines, dated July 23, 1895.

"So far the scratching that has been is nothing. It proves nothing. There is not a shaft or a 'borehole' down to two hundred feet in the Country, so that actually speculators have not much to guide them. The reason for this is that there is no

* British Guiana. Report of the Government agent of the North Western District of British Guiana for 1894–5. fol. Georgetown, Demerara, 1896, p. 1.

Character of present British "settlement."

mining population here, everything has to be taught.' . . . . The alluvial mining is rich, and although the work is not systematic, yet I consider that any party of five men, if they choose to be careful, can make good wages all the year round by working for themselves. . . . One of the greatest drawbacks has been the necessity of coming down [to the settlements] to pass gold [through the Government Royalty Office] and obtain provisions."

"Speaking generally, I think the industry is in about the same state as this time last year. But I think with the advent of English capital, management and workmen, that a better state of things will have commenced by this time next year, only commenced, though, as in my opinion it will take another five years before the Gold Fields of British Guiana will make any appreciable difference to the world's gold output. Without skilled labor from the outside nothing will ever be done. The natives in time will do, but they have to be taught, and without having capable men to direct and superintend their work, very little improvement can be expected." *

The following is from *Notes on British Guiana and its Gold Industry*, dated January 8, 1895, prepared by Mr. H. I. Perkins, Government Surveyor:

"There was no extensive mining done until 1884, which is the first year for which any record of Colonial gold has been obtained."

"The high rate of wages offered (64 cents per day with food and sleeping accommodations) induced the laboring population, chiefly black, to leave their homes in the Villages on the Coast to engage themselves to work in the bush for three or four months at a time."

"The really good men are very few and the majority are habitual malingerers." †

In the same publication (p. 11), Mr. Perkins thus describes the gold diggers' "habitations:"

"The architecture of a bush-house is neither elaborate nor expensive; the corner posts and cross beams are usually of round

---

* British Guiana. Administration Reports for 1894-5, fol. Georgetown, Demerara, 1896, p. 505.

† Perkins (H. I.), Notes on British Guiana and its Gold Industry, fol. Georgetown, 1895, p. 7.

Character of present British "settlement."

wood barked, and the rafters of round poles, also barked; on these is placed the roof, made of peculiar tough paper imported from the United States and called 'Neponsett,' or else palm leaves, which make a much cooler covering, are used; but, as leaves are not always to be obtained, paper is substituted."

In an anonymous work, of which the author is said to be Robert Tennant, published in London in 1895, and entitled *British Guiana and its Resources*, the author say:

"There are, it is estimated, upwards of 200 placers now in actual work, the returns from which vary from a few oz. to 1,000 oz. gold per month, or an average of about 50 oz. each; the aggregate capital invested in these workings does not, it is stated, amount to more than the value of a year's production." *

Mr. Rodway in 1892 wrote:

"In the upper Demerara [which is not within the disputed territory] quartz-mining is being commenced, but elsewhere only placer-washing is at present (1892) carried on." †

Mr. Perkins in 1894 wrote:

"During the year 1891 about 20,000 laborers were registered for the several districts, these serving on an average for about three months each, so that there were always four or five thousand diggerr in the bush."‡

It seems unnecessary to comment upon these facts: they speak for themselves.

---

* Appendix to Case, iii, 356.

† Handbook of British Guiana, Georgetown, 1893, p. 52.

‡ Perkins (H. I.) Notes on *British Guiana, and its Gold Industry* fol., Georgetown, January 8, 1895, p. 11.

XV.—REGARDING SPANISH AND VENEZUELAN OCCUPATION DURING THE 19TH CENTURY.

The extent and character of British occupation during the present century has been thus set forth because, according to the view of the question taken by the United States of Venezuela, the territorial rights of Great Britain can, in no case, exceed the limits which that occupation had reached fifty years ago.

Reasons for having set forth extent of British occupation.

This statement is not intended as an admission that Great Britain has a right to any territory west of the Essequibo, even though she may have been in unchallenged possession of it fifty years ago—a fact which Venezuela denies—it is merely intended to make clear from the start, that the limits of the Essequibo colony have depended upon the question of *actual* possession; and that all territory not lawfully occupied by the Dutch, or by their successors the British, belonged to Spain and belongs now to Venezuela, as a matter of course, and quite independently of whether, during the 18th and 19th centuries, such territory was or was not occupied by, or whether it was or was not under the exclusive political control of Spain or Venezuela.

It may further be added, that the proof already, though unnecessarily, adduced, showing the exclusive political control by Spain during the 18th century of the coast region and of the entire Cuyuni-Mazaruni basin, gives added strength, under the rules adopted by the present treaty, to Venezuela's title to the entire region; and that that title having been once proven, it is unnecessary, in the absence of any evidence of British title to the same territory, and until such evidence shall

Proof of Spain's control strenghtens Venezuela's title.

Unnecessary to prove continued possession by Venezuela.

be forthcoming, to present proof of *continued* possession or control by Venezuela of that region.* As a matter of fact, Spain, first, and then Venezuela, did continue in exclusive possession and control of the disputed territory until 1850, when under an agreement (hereafter to be more fully explained) with Great Britain, Venezuela withdrew for a time.

Burden of proof on Great British.

For the present, however, for the reasons above set forth, Venezuela considers that she is not called upon to support this allegation by proof. The burden is upon Great Britain to establish how far encroachments upon territory, originally Spanish, can, under the stipulation of the Treaty of Munster and under the rules adopted by the present treaty, confer title upon herself. In the meantime, and until such proof shall be forthcoming, Venezuela considers it unnecessary to set forth at length the history of Spanish and Venezuelan occupation and control during the present century.

While relying upon the correctness of the principle thus stated, Venezuela considers that there are two facts, whose importance and significance must excuse their present mention.

Pilot station at Barima, 1802.

The first of these is that, according to the testimony of Major McCreagh, an English officer, the Spaniards, already as early as 1802, were maintaining a regular pilot station at the Barima mouth of the Orinoco.† This station has continued to be maintained from or before that time to the present day; and its existence has been repeatedly recognized by the British Government.‡

---

* As a matter of fact the Appendices hereto do contain proof of this fact, but the documents which attest it have, in the main, been submitted with a view rather to show the restricted limits of British occupation than the extent or exclusiveness of Spanish and Venezuelan settlement and control.

† Appendix to Case, iii, 57.

‡ Appendix to Case, iii, 189-192.

Barima under Venezuela jurisdiction in 1836.

The second fact is that, in the year 1836, the British Consul at Angostura and the British Minister at Caracas both bore testimony to the fact, that Barima point was, at that time, under Venezuela's exclusive jurisdiction. The latter, on behalf of his government, went so far as to make a formal request of Venezuela to erect a light-house at Barima point.*

*Appendix to Case, iii, 189-190, 209.

XVI.—DIPLOMATIC CORRESPONDENCE.

Schomburgk's appointment as Commissioner.

The diplomatic history between Great Britain and Venezuela, relative to the boundary question, began in 1841, and was occasioned by the appointment of Mr. Schomburgk* as Commissioner to mark out the boundary.

By instruction of November 28, 1840, Sir Robert Ker Porter, the British Minister at Caracas, received instructions from his government "to inform the Venezue-

---

* Robert Hermann Schomburgk was born in Freiburg, Saxony, June 5, 1804, and died in Berlin, Germany, March 11, 1865. Between 1825 and 1830 he was in the United States, first at Boston and later at Richmond, Va., where he was in the tobacco business. Failing in this, he went to the West Indies in 1830, where he surveyed the island Anegada. His report and published observations on the cultivated plants of the West Indies brought him to the notice of the Royal Geographical Society, which, on November 19, 1834, engaged him to explore in Guiana. He reached Georgetown for the first time on August 5, 1835. His work in Guiana is comprised in the nine years between this date and May 20, 1844, when he took his final departure. On May 31, 1844, the instruments with which his boundary survey was made were presented by the governor to the "new Astronomical and Meteorological Society" of British Guiana.

In all six trips, or expeditions, for surveying and making collections, were made by Schomburgk, the first three under the auspices of the Royal Geographical Society, the last three under the auspices of the government.

First Expedition—September 21, 1835, to March 18, 1836.

Second Expedition—September 2, 1836, to March 30, 1837.

This was followed by a severe attack of yellow fever.

Third Expedition—September 12, 1837, to June 17, 1839.

In October, 1839, he went to England. Early in 1840, he published his little book entitled "Description of British Guiana." On May 25, 1840, he received one of the gold medals of the Royal Geographical Society. The King of Prussia decorated him with the Order of the Red Eagle. His engagement as Commissary for surveying the boundaries of British Guiana was read in the Court of Policy in Georgetown, October 29, 1840.

Fourth Expedition—April 19, 1841, to July 27, 1841.

Fifth Expedition—December, 1841, to January, 1843.

Sixth Expedition—February 14, 1843, to October 13, 1843.

On May 20, 1844, he left British Guiana and remained for some time at Barbados and wrote a history of that island, which was published in 1847. In 1848 he was made British Consul at St. Domingo. In 1857 he was sent to Siam as Her Majesty's Consul-General. In declining health, he returned to England in 1864, and retired on a pension. He died in Berlin, March 11, 1865.

Schomburgk's appointment as Commissioner.

lan Minister of Foreign Affairs that Her Majesty has issued a Commission to Mr. R. H. Schomburgk, authorizing him to survey and mark out the boundary between British Guiana and Venezuela." *

Venezuela, in 1841, proposed treaty to define boundary.

This information was conveyed to the Venezuelan Government on January 13, 1841; † and on the 28th of the same month the Venezuelan Minister of Foreign Affairs replied by proposing a treaty for the purpose of defining the boundary in question. ‡ The Minister also suggested that the appointment of Commissioners to mark out the boundary be deferred until after such a treaty had been concluded.§

Answer of British Government.

The answer of the British Minister, on the 30th of the same month, was that Mr. Schomburgk had already been commissioned by his government, and that he was probably already at work on the ground. ‖ He stated, however, that he would lay the matter before his government.¶

Survey and erection of posts by Schomburgk.

In the meantime, and without any further notice, Mr. Schomburgk actually began the survey, and erected posts at various points to mark the line by him laid out.

He made his first report on June 22, 1841; ** and followed it by a second report in August of the same year.††

Report that British flag had been hoisted in the Amacura.

On August 17, 1841, the Venezuelan Minister of Foreign Affairs, Mr. Aranda, wrote to Mr. O'Leary, the British representative at Caracas, asking information with

---

* Appendix to Case, iii, 193.

† Appendix to Case, iii, 193.

‡ Appendix to Case, iii, 194.

§ Appendix to Case, iii, 194.

‖ Appendix to Case, iii, 194.

¶ Appendix to Case, iii, 194.

** Appendix to Case, iii, 77.

†† Appendix to Case, iii, 97.

regard to a report received by him to the effect that a British flag had been hoisted at the mouth of the Amacura.*

Report that British flag had been hoisted in the Amacura.

Protest by Venezuela.

Mr. O'Leary, under date of August 21, 1841, denied any knowledge of the occurrence.† The Venezuelan Government thereupon appointed Commissioners to proceed to British Guiana "for the purpose of investigating the origin and design wherewith the British flag and other marks as of possession were planted at Barima and Amacura * * * * and also to make suitable reclamations and protests."‡

On October 5, 1841, Señor Fortique, the Venezuelan Minister in London, addressed a note to the Earl of Aberdeen, asking for an explanation of Schomburgk's conduct and urging, at the same time, "the necessity of proceeding to the negotiation of a treaty of boundaries as a preliminary step to the operation of demarcation."§

Instructions to Señor Fortique regarding negotiations.

The instructions sent at this time to Señor Fortique by his Government, relative to the proposed negotiations, were in part as follows:

"Although Venezuela's rights in Guayana extended to the banks of the Essequibo, as you should show, this Government being anxious to remove all obstacles to a speedy adjustment, is not disposed to insist upon its rights to that extent, it being manifest that England will not agree to surrender her establishments on the Pumaron and Moroco rivers. You may, therefore, direct the course of your negotiations accordingly, making gradual concessions until an agreement can be had on the following line of boundary between Venezuela and British Guiana, viz.: The Moroco from its mouth to its headwaters in the Imataca mountains; thence southward along the highest ridge of these mountains to Tupuro creek; thence along the waters of said creek to the Cuyuni river; thence along the northern side of the Cuyuni

* Appendix to Case, iii, 105–106.
† Appendix to Case, iii, 195.
‡ Appendix to Case, iii, 196.
§ Appendix to Case, iii, 197.

Instructions to Señor Fortique regarding negotiations.

to its confluence with the Essequibo; and thence southward along the left bank of the Essequibo to its confluence with the Rupuruni as a terminus."*

Lord Aberdeen's statement regarding Schomburgk's proceedings.

To Señor Fortique's note of October 5, the Earl of Aberdeen replied on October 21, 1841, stating, with reference to Mr. Schomburgk's proceedings, that the demarcation so made was merely a preliminary measure open to future discussion between the Governments of Great Britain and Venezuela, and that Mr. Schomburgk had left behind him no "guard-house, sentry box or other building bearing the British flag."†

Governor Light's statement on same subject.

In line with these declarations of Lord Aberdeen, Governor Light, on October 20, 1841, wrote to Señor Aranda and stated that,

"Mr. Schomburgk's mission was one purely of survey, with instructions from the Secretary of State for Foreign Affairs, Lord Palmerston, to 'erect landmarks on the ground in order to mark out by permanent erections the line of boundary so claimed by Great Britain; it would then rest with each of the three Governments, namely, Brazil, Venezuela, and the Netherlands, to make any objections which they might have to bring forward against these boundaries, and to state the reasons upon which such objections might be founded, and Her Britannic Majesty's Government would then give such answers thereto as might appear proper and just.'"‡

Governor Light added:

"I trust this explanation will be satisfactory to your Excellency; neither the Government of Venezuela nor of Great Britain having hitherto occupied the Barima, and that point marking the boundary claimed by the British Government, it will be prudent not to attempt an occupation which would complicate negotiation, and might lead to unpleasant discussion." §

Protest by Venezuela.

The Venezuelan Commissioners to British Guiana

---

* U. S. Commission, Report, vii, 6.

† Appendix to Case, iii, 198–199.

‡ Appendix to Case, iii, 197–198.

§ Appendix to Case, iii, 198.

failed in their mission, so far as negotiations for a boundary treaty were concerned, but they recorded their protest against the encroachments of the British; and, in a letter to Governor Light, dated October 26, 1841, they set forth the relations of Venezuela to the Orinoco delta in the following words:

Protest by Venezuela.

> "And to this plain and extended right to this territory must be added the necessary exclusive and constant use which Venezuela has always particularly enjoyed of the great mouth of the Orinoco called 'Boca de Navio,' including the two Rivers Amacura and Barima, which empty themselves into the said great mouth.
>
> All nations with whom we trade will bear witness to the ancient establishment and daily service of our 'pilot boats' between the Island Pagayos, in the River Orinoco, and Barima Point, which is the main point of entrance and exit by the great mouth of the Orinoco; which is for Venezuela, by right and necessity, what the mouths of the Thames and the Seine are to their respective nations.
>
> And besides the pilotage service, Venezuela has exercised its right of police and prevention of smuggling over all the southern bank of 'La Boca de Navios,' and at both sides, and at both mouths, of its two tributaries, the Barima and Amacura. Nor can Venezuela ever deprive herself of this use and right without considering it an offence, which she can never fear from her great and just friend Great Britain."*

Relations of Venezuela to Orinoco delta.

On October 23, 1841, in answer to inquiries by Governor Light, of British Guiana, Mr. Schomburgk made a special report setting forth the grounds upon which he based the British claim to Barima and Amacura.† This was an official report intended for the eyes of the public. On the same date he wrote to Governor Light a *confidential* letter, pointing out the importance to Great Britain

Schomburgk's *official* report of Oct. 23, 1841.

* Appendix to Case, iii, 199–200.

† Appendix to Case, iii, 121–125.

Schomburgk's *confidential* letter of Oct. 23, 1841.

of the possession of Point Barima as a point commanding the entrance to the Orinoco River.* In this letter he dwelt at length upon the fact that the occupation of Barima meant the commercial and the military control of the entire Orinoco region.

Venezuela's demand for removal of Schomburgk posts.

The Government of Venezuela, becoming better apprised as to the acts of Mr. Schomburgk, made a renewed and stronger protest against such acts, and demanded the removal of the posts which had been erected. This was in a note from Señor Fortique to the Earl of Aberdeen, dated November 18, 1841. In that note Señor Fortique made the following statement:

> "The Undersigned has subsequently been directed to assure Her Majesty's Government that Commissioner Schomburgk, overstepping, no doubt, the terms of his authorization, has at a point of the mouth of the Orinoco fixed several posts with Her Majesty's initials—has hoisted the British flag in that locality, solemnly attended by an armed force—and has proceeded to other acts of dominion and empire."†

Venezuela again urges a boundary treaty.

In a separate note of the same date Señor Fortique again urged upon the British Government the desirability of a treaty, and his readiness to negotiate it.‡

Schomburgk's memorial of Nov. 30, 1841.

On November 30, 1841, Mr. Schomburgk submitted a further letter, a memorial, and two maps to Governor Light. §

Venezuela again demands removal of Schomburgk posts.

Not receiving any reply to his notes of November 18, excepting a mere formal acknowledgment of their receipt, Señor Fortique again addressed himself to Lord Aberdeen on December 8, 1841. In his note of that date he again, and in stronger terms, requested the immediate removal of the posts erected

* Appendix to Case, iii, 125-127.

† Appendix to Case, iii, 200.

‡ Appendix to Case, iii, 202.

§ Appendix to Case, iii, 127-128.

by Schomburgk, and once more expressed his readiness to negotiate a boundary treaty.*

Venezuela again demands removal of Schomburgk posts.

In answer to this Lord Aberdeen replied, on December 11, 1841, stating that the erection of the posts was merely a preliminary measure, that they were not intended "as indications of dominion and empire on the part of Great Britain," and "that the British authorities have not occupied Point Barima." †

Lord Aberdeen's answer.

The Venezuelan Government, however, determined to remove every semblance of British authority within Venezuelan territory; and in a note of January 10, 1842, repeated its demand for the removal of the posts.‡ In reply to this Lord Aberdeen, on January 31, 1842, wrote stating that the British Government would order the removal of the posts.§

Venezuela repeats her demand.

Removal ordered by Great Britain.

The matter of the posts having been thus disposed of, on May 23, 1843, Señor Fortique once more urged upon Lord Aberdeen the necessity of determining by treaty the boundary between the two countries.‖ Negotiations were finally begun on January 31, 1844, when Señor Fortique submitted in writing the claims of Venezuela to all territory west of the Essequibo.** Lord Aberdeen answered the note last referred to in detail, entering into a discussion of Venezuela's claims as set forth by Señor Fortique, and presenting the claims of Great Britain.††

Negotiations for boundary treaty.

The views of the two governments were so far apart, however, that it at once became evident that nothing could be arrived at, if there were not mutual concessions. In proposing a compromise line which should give to

Importance of Orinoco mouth.

* Appendix to Case, iii, 202–204.
† Appendix to Case, iii, 204–205.
‡ Appendix to Case, iii, 205–207.
§ Appendix to Case, iii, 207–208.
‖ Appendix to Case, iii, 208.
** Blue Book 3, 248–251.
†† Blue Book 3, 251–254.

Importance of Orinoco mouth.

Venezuela the control of the Orinoco mouth, Lord Aberdeen in the following words recognized the importance to Venezuela of the command of that river:

"Believing, then, that the undivided possession of the Orinoco is the object most important for the interests of Venezuela, Her Majesty's Government are prepared to cede to the Republic a portion of the coast amply sufficient to insure Venezuela against the mouth of this her principal river being at the command of any foreign Power. With this view, and regarding it as a most valuable concession to Venezuela, Her Majesty's Government are willing to waive their claim to the Amacura as the western boundary of the British territory, and to consider the mouth of the Moroco River as the limit of Her Majesty's possessions on the sea-coast.

They will, moreover, consent that the inland boundary shall be marked by a line drawn directly from the mouth of the Moroco to the junction of the River Barama with the River Waini, thence up the River Barama to the Annama, and up the Annama to the point at which that stream approaches nearest to the Acarabisi, and thence down the Acarabisi to its confluence with the Cuyuni, from which point it will follow the bank of the Cuyuni upwards until it reaches the high-lands in the neighbourhood of Mount Roraima which divide the waters flowing into the Essequibo from those which flow into the Rio Branco.

All the territory lying between a line such as is here described, on the one side, and the River Amacura and the chain of hills from which the Amacura rises, on the other, Great Britain is willing to cede to Venezuela, upon the condition that the Venezuelan Government enter into an engagement that no portion of it shall be alienated at any time to a foreign Power, and that the Indian tribes now residing within it shall be protected against all injury and oppression."*

Lord Aberdeen's proposals rejected by Venezuela.

The line proposed by Lord Aberdeen was not acceptable to Venezuela, and the conditions attached in its acceptance were so at variance with the rights and dignity of that country that, for the time being, negotiations were suspended.

In 1850 there was a rumor that Great Britain had

* Appendix to Case, iii, 210-211.

taken possession of Barima Point on the coast, and of "Fuerto Viejo" on the Cuyuni. The excitement in Venezuela consequent upon this was so great that it was deemed prudent on the part of Great Britain to deny the truth of the report,* and at the same time to make a formal declaration that it had "no intention of occupying or encroaching upon the disputed territory."†

Rumor regarding "Fuerto Viejo."

"Agreement of 1850."

While making this declaration to Venezuela, the British Minister requested Venezuela to make a similar formal declaration to Great Britain.‡ This was done under date of December 20, 1850.§ This arrangement is what has come to be known as "The Agreement of 1850."

Negotiations resumed in 1876.

Negotiations for a boundary treaty were again taken up in 1876 by Señor Calcaño, then Minister of Foreign Affairs of Venezuela, and by the Earl of Derby. These were continued in London by Señor de Rojas, who, on February 13, 1877, wrote Lord Derby urging a settlement of the question, and suggesting that a mixed commission be appointed to survey the territory in dispute.‖

After waiting for more than two years without receiving any other reply than a mere formal acknowledgment of the receipt of his note and a promise of its consideration, Señor de Rojas, on May 19, 1879, once more addressed the British Government in a note of that date to the Marquess of Salisbury.¶

Great Britain's extreme claim stated.

On January 10, 1880, Lord Salisbury answered Señor de Rojas' note, and stated Great Britain's extreme claim, expressing at the same time the willingness of Her Majesty's Government to adopt a compromise line,

* Appendix to Case, iii, 211, 212.
† Appendix to Case, iii, 212.
‡ Appendix to Case, iii, 212.
§ Appendix to Case, iii, 213–214.
‖ Appendix to Case, iii, 214–215.
¶ Appendix to Case, iii, 215–217.

Great Britain's extreme claim stated.

and requesting Señor de Rojas to submit a proposition with that end in view.*

In answer to this, Señor Fortique, on April 12, 1880, wrote to Lord Salisbury, stating that Venezuela was disposed to make concessions from what she regarded as her strict right, and to agree to a compromise line. He then requested to know whether the British Government would be disposed to conduct negotiations for that purpose on the basis of the line proposed by Lord Aberdeen in 1844.† Señor de Rojas receiving no answer to this note (beyond the formal acknowledgment of its receipt), on September 27, 1880, addressed himself to Earl Granville requesting a reply. On February 12, 1881, Lord Granville wrote to Señor de Rojas stating that, "Her Majesty's Government are unable to accept the mouth of the Moroco as the boundary on the coast"; that it would consider a line commencing at a more northerly point on the coast, and would be glad to be favored with a general communication of the views of the Venezuelan Government.‡

Lord Granville's refusal to negotiate on basis of Lord Aberdeen's Line.

Señor de Rojas' proposal.

Señor de Rojas answered this note on February 21, 1881. He referred to the fact that Lord Aberdeen had himself proposed the Amacura mouth as a point of departure on the coast; but, in order to meet the views of Lord Granville, he proposed a line beginning one mile north of the mouth of the Amacura, and suggested that, if this were not satisfactory to the British Government, his own government was disposed to submit the matter to arbitration.§

Lord Granville's proposal.

This proposition was, on September 15, 1881, met by a counter-proposition on the part of Lord Granville,

* Appendix to Case, iii, 217–218.

† Appendix to Case, iii, 218–219.

‡ Appendix to Case, iii, 219–220.

§ Appendix to Case, iii, 220–222

a proposition which gave the starting point on the coast at a point distant "twenty-nine miles of longitude due east from the right bank of the river Barima," and which, in the following language, recognized the importance to Venezuela of the Orinoco mouth:

Lord Granville's proposal.

"This boundary will surrender to Venezuela what has been called the Dardanelles of the Orinoco. It will give to Venezuela the entire command of the mouth of that river, and it yields about one-half of the disputed territory, while it secures to British Guiana a well-defined natural boundary along almost its whole course, except for about the first 50 miles inland from the sea, where it is necessary to lay down an arbitrary boundary in order to secure to Venezuela the undisturbed possession of the mouths of the Orinoco; but even here advantage has been taken of well-defined natural landmarks. The Barima, connected as before mentioned by its tributaries with the center of the country of Essequibo, is also connected with the Waini by a channel through which the tide flows and ebbs."*

Lord Granville's proposals rejected by Venezuela.

The proposition of Earl Granville was referred, by Señor de Rojas, to the Venezuelan Government, and after careful consideration was rejected, for the reason, among others, that the Constitution forbade the alienation of territory belonging to the Republic.

Dr. Seijas urges arbitration.

In his note of November 15, 1883, to Colonel Mansfield, Dr. Seijas, the Venezuelan Minister of Foreign Affairs, reaffirmed the right of Venezuela to all territory west of the Essequibo, and again proposed to submit the question to arbitration.†

Great Britain's refusal.

To this proposition the British Government answered on March 29, 1884, refusing to submit the question to arbitration.‡ On April 2, 1884, Dr. Seijas again urged arbitration upon the British Minister at Caracas, and asked him in default thereof, to make a suggestion as

* Appendix to Case, iii, 156.

† Appendix to Case, iii, 223–224.

‡ U. S. Commission, Report, vii, 71.

Great Britain's refusal.

to an "acceptable course for attaining the solution of this difficulty." *

At various times the proposition to arbitrate was repeated by Venezuela, and as often refused on the part of Great Britain.

Toward the latter part of 1884 General Guzman Blanco, having been appointed Envoy Extraordinary and Minister Plenipotentiary to represent Venezuela in London, arrived in that city. The special purpose of his mission was to bring about a settlement of the boundary question.

There were at that time pending between the two countries two other questions, viz., the differential duties upon imports from British Colonies into Venezuela, and certain claims of British creditors against the Republic.

New negotiations begun by Gen. Guzman Blanco.

General Guzman Blanco, in a memorandum communicated to Sir Julian Pauncefote on December 13, 1884, proposed that these questions be settled simultaneously.† Negotiations were conducted on this basis, and on April 6, 1885, a *Project of Treaty* was submitted by General Guzman Blanco to Earl Granville. This Project contained a general clause agreeing to submit "any difference which cannot be adjusted by the usual means of friendly negotiation" to the arbitration of a third power.‡

Draft Treaty submitted by Lord Granville.

Negotiations proceeding satisfactorily, on June 8, 1885, General Guzman Blanco submitted to Earl Granville a formal *Draft Treaty* in which was retained the arbitration clause above referred to.§

On June 18 Lord Granville sent to General Guzman Blanco copies of the proposed treaty in print, and asked his approval of certain conditions proposed by the

* Appendix to Case, iii, 224–226.

† Appendix to Case, iii, 226–227.

‡ Appendix to Case, iii, 227, 228.

§ Appendix to Case, iii, 229.

British Government.* These were in the main acceptable to Venezuela, but, before the treaty could be concluded, Earl Granville was succeeded by the Marquess of Salisbury, who, under date of July 27, 1885, wrote to General Guzman Blanco objecting to certain words which had been the subject of discussion between Earl Granville and General Guzman Blanco, and then added:

Draft Treaty acceptable to Venezuela, but withdrawn by Lord Salisbury.

"Her Majesty's Government are unable to concur in the assent given by their predecessors in office to the general arbitration Article proposed by Venezuela, and they are unable to agree to the inclusion in it of matter other than those arising out of the interpretation or alleged violation of this particular Treaty." †

General Guzman Blanco's reply to Lord Salisbury, dated August 5, 1885, was in the nature of a protest against the refusal of the British Government to respect the engagements of the previous government which had already given formal assent to the arbitration article.‡ After some ineffectual attempts on the part of General Guzman Blanco to continue negotiations they were suspended.

Protest by Venezuela.

British interests requiring that the boundary question should no longer remain in suspense, on June 7, 1886, the Earl of Rosebery instructed Mr. F. R. St. John, the British Minister at Caracas, to inform the Venezuelan Government that the British Government intended "to proceed at once to define the boundary of the British possessions in Guiana," and that the line which they intended to trace would run as follows:

Lord Rosebery's instructions to define the boundary.

"The initial point to be fixed at a spot on the sea shore 29 miles of longitude due east from the right bank of the River Barima, and to be carried thence south over the mountain or hill called on Schomburgk's original map the Yarikita Hill, to the 8th parallel

* Appendix to Case, iii, 229–230.

† Appendix to Case, iii, 231.

‡ Appendix to Case, iii, 231-232.

Lord Rosebery's instructions to define the boundary.

of north latitude; thence west along the same parallel of latitude until it cuts the boundary line proposed by Schomburgk, and laid down on the map before mentioned; thence to follow such boundary along its course to the Accarabisi, following the Accarabisi to its junction with the Cuyuni; thence along the left bank of the River Cuyuni to its source, and from thence in a south-easterly direction to the line as proposed by Schomburgk to the Essequibo and Corentyne."*

Lord Rosebery added:

You will add that instructions have been sent to the Governor of British Guiana authorizing him to grant licenses forthwith for gold-mining within the territory, which will be at once marked as British territory, and without requiring him to withhold the issue of such licenses until the completion of the line of demarcation."†

Negotiations once more renewed.

After the sending of these instructions, the presence of General Guzman Blanco presented an opportunity to once more enter into negotiations; and after some preliminary correspondence, Lord Rosebery, on July 20, 1886, submitted to General Guzman Blanco the following basis of negotiation:

Lord Rosebery's proposal.

"*Boundaries.*—It is proposed that the two Governments should agree to consider the territory lying between the boundary-lines respectively proposed in the 8th paragraph of Señor Rojas' note of the 21st February, 1881, and in Lord Granville's note of the 15th September, 1881, as the territory in dispute between the two countries, and that a boundary-line should be traced within the limits of this territory, either by an Arbitrator or by a Joint Commission, on the basis of an equal division of this territory, due regard being paid to natural boundaries. Her Majesty's Government attach special importance to the possession by British Guiana of the mouth of the River Waini, and they desire, therefore, to stipulate that the line should start from the sea-coast westwards of that point, due compensation being found in some other portion of the disputed territory for this departure from the basis of an equal division. The question of the cession

* Appendix to Case, iii, 160.

† Appendix to Case, iii, 160.

to Venezuela of the Island of Patos will be considered in connection with the boundary negotiations. The River Orinoco to be entirely free to commerce and navigation.*

Lord Rosebery's proposal.

Gen. Guzman Blanco's answer.

General Guzman Blanco made no immediate reply to this proposition, but on July 28, 1886, addressed a strong note to the Earl of Rosebery, rehearsing the diplomatic history of the preceding forty years, reminding Lord Rosebery especially of the agreement of 1850 whereby both countries had declared that they would not occupy nor encroach upon the disputed territory, calling attention to recent flagrant violations of this agreement by British officials, and demanding reparation therefor and the re-establishment of the *status quo ante*.†

On the following day, July 29, 1886, General Guzman Blanco addressed a second note to Lord Rosebery, in answer to the latter's note of July 20. In this second note General Guzman Blanco declined the proposition of the British Government to draw a conventional boundary somewhere between the line proposed by Señor de Rojas on February 21, 1881, and that proposed by Lord Granville on September 15, 1881. He reiterated the statement, made so many times by him and by his predecessor, that the Venezuelan Constitution forbade the alienation of territory; and he once more spoke of arbitration as the only way out of the difficulty.‡

Negotiations interrupted.

General Guzman Blanco's departure for Venezuela interrupted negotiations.

Meanwhile, on October 21, 1886, the British Government caused the following notice to be published in the *London Gazette:*

---

* Appendix to Case, iii, 54.

† Appendix to Case, iii, 234-246.

‡ Appendix to Case, iii, 247-252.

Notice published by Great Britain.

COLONIAL OFFICE, Downing Street, October 21, 1886.

THE COLONY OF BRITISH GUIANA.

WHEREAS the boundary-line between Her Majesty's Colony of British Guiana and the Republic of Venezuela is in dispute between Her Majesty's Government and the Government of Venezuela:

And whereas it has come to the knowledge of Her Majesty's Government that grants of land within the territory claimed by Her Majesty's Government as part of the said Colony have been made, or purport to have been made, by or in the name of the Government of Venezuela.

Notice is hereby given, that no title to land, or to any right in, or over, or affecting any land within the territory claimed by Her Majesty's Government as forming part of the Colony of British Guiana, purporting to be derived from or through the Government of Venezuela or any officer or person authorized by that Government, will be admitted or recognized by Her Majesty or by the Government of British Guiana; and that any person taking possession of, or exercising any right over, any such land under colour of any such title, or pretended title, will be liable to be treated as a trespasser under the laws of the said Colony.

A map showing the boundary between British Guiana and Venezuela, claimed by Her Majesty's Government, can be seen in the Library of the Colonial Office, Downing Street, or at the Office of the Government Secretary, Georgetown, British Guiana.*

Rural Constable Commissioned for the Amacura in 1885; and post erected in 1886.

On March 1, 1885, more than a year prior to General Guzman Blanco's departure from London, the British Minister commissioned a Rural Constable for the Amacura River.† In August, 1886, a British Post was erected on that river.†

Venezuela's protest.

These facts coming to the knowledge of the Venezuelan Government, and that government despairing of any settlement of the boundary question with Great Britain, proceeded to erect a light-house at Point Barima, and sent Commissioners to the Amacura, the Barima, the

* Appendix to Case, iii, 161.
† Appendix to Case, iii, 253.
† Appendix to Case, iii, 163.

Waini, and to Georgetown, to protest against the encroachments of Great Britain, and to warn British settlers that they were on Venezuelan soil.*

Venezuela's protest.

Upon its return to Caracas, the Commission reported to the Venezuelan Government that two British Commissioners were on the right bank of the Amacura, acting there as Rural Constables under the authority of the British Government.† Thereupon, on January 26, 1887, the Venezuelan Minister of Foreign Affairs addressed a note to Mr. F. R. St. John, the British Minister at Caracas, informing him of the above facts, protesting against such acts, demanding the immediate evacuation of the territory between the Orinoco and Pomaroon Rivers, and stating that, in case of either no reply or of a refusal, diplomatic relations would be broken off. ‡

Diplomatic relations suspended.

After some further fruitless interchange of notes diplomatic relations were, on February 20, 1887, suspended by Venezuela. §

Negotiations for renewal of diplomatic relations.

In 1890, the Venezuelan Government received an intimation from Sir Andrew Clarke and Captain Lowther that Great Britain was disposed "to evacuate the invaded territory, and to submit the case to the arbitration of a friendly Power, provided Venezuela would declare diplomatic relations to be re-established between the two countries." In consequence of this, on January 10, 1890, Señor Urbaneja, Venezuelan Minister at Paris, addressed a note to the Marquess of Salisbury, stating that Venezuela was desirous of renewing diplomatic relations, and had empowered him to negotiate and sign a treaty for that purpose. ‖ In the reply of the British

* Appendix to Case, iii, pp. 162-163, 183-185, 252, 253.

† Appendix to Case, iii, 255.

‡ Appendix to Case, iii, 255-260.

§ Appendix to Case, iii, 272.

‖ Appendix to Case, iii, 273-274.

Negotiations for renewal of diplomatic relations.

Foreign Office the following condition was laid down:

As regards the frontier between Venezuela and the Colony of British Guiana, Her Majesty's Government could not accept as satisfactory any arrangement which did not admit the British title to the territory comprised within the line laid down by Sir R. Schomburgk in 1841. They would be ready to refer to arbitration the claim of Great Britain to certain territories to the west of that line.*

Señor Urbaneja's proposal.

Señor Urbaneja, in reply (February 13, 1890), referred to the statement which had been made to his government by Sir Andrew Clarke and Captain Lowther, and stated that, it had been upon the faith of those representations that Venezuela had "thought fit to appoint a Confidential Agent to conclude a Preliminary Agreement for the re-establishment of diplomatic relations with the Government of Her BritannicMajesty."† Señor Urbaneja then proceeded to discuss the conditions laid down by Lord Salisbury, and concluded by proposing "an arbitration which shall include all the territory from the Essequibo, and the evacuation of the invaded territory from the Pomeroon onward in the direction of the Orinoco." ‡

Great Britain's reply.

Replying to this note, on March 19, 1890, Sir T. H. Sanderson repeated that "Her Majesty's Government . . . cannot admit any question as to their title to territory within the line surveyed by Sir R. Schomburgk in 1841." §

Negotiations suspended.

This attempt on the part of Venezuela to re-establish diplomatic relations thus proved abortive.

In June of 1890, Señor Pulido, appointed Plenipotentiary *ad hoc* of Venezuela, arrived in London, and through him Venezuela again made an effort to bring

* Appendix to Case, iii, 274.
† Appendix to Case, iii, 276.
‡ Appendix to Case, iii, 275.
§ Appendix to Case, iii, 278.

about a re-establishment of diplomatic relations. On the 24th of that month Señor Pulido submitted to the Foreign Office a *memorandum* in answer to the last communication of the Foreign office to Señor Urbaneja. In this *memorandum* Señor Pulido proposed a preliminary joint survey of the region in dispute, and its subsequent submission to arbitration in case of disagreement as to a proper boundary line.* Great Britain, on July 27, 1890, rejected this proposal.

Renewed efforts by Venezuela.

In May of 1893, a third attempt at re-establishing diplomatic relations with Great Britain was made by Venezuela. In that month Señor Michelena arrived in London, having been appointed "Confidential Agent" of Venezuela.

Another effort to re-establish Diplomatic relations.

On May 26, 1893,† he submitted to the Earl of Rosebery a *pro-memoria* of the bases for the re-establishment of diplomatic relations. The *pro-memoria* submitted contemplated the appointment of delegates to conclude a frontier treaty, and a submission of doubtful points to arbitration.‡

On July 3, 1893, the advances of Venezuela were once more rejected by Great Britain,§ and Señor Michelena left London without anything having been accomplished.

Great Britain's refusal.

In the meantime, and as early as 1886, the Government of the United States of America had manifested its interest in the question, by offering its good offices in the matter to the British Government. These were declined at the time, and also on various subsequent occasions when they were renewed in different forms. Finally, however, in the month of February, 1896, the

Interest of the United States.

* Appendix to Case, iii, 279–281.

†Appendix to Case, iii, 285–286.

‡ Appendix to Case, iii, 286–287.

§ Appendix to Case, iii, 287–288.

Successful negotiations initiated by the United States in 1896.

negotiations which resulted in the present treaty were initiated. In those negotiations the United States, with the consent of the two interested governments, took an active part.

The objections of the British Government to submit to arbitration the entire territory in dispute had been stated by Lord Salisbury in his instructions to Sir Julian Pauncefote, dated November 26, 1895, to be that British settlements had gradually spread over the country and that Her Majesty's Government could not, in justice to the inhabitants, offer to surrender such settlements to foreign rule.

The question of British settlements having thus been recognized, from the first, as the sole stumbling block, the discussion in the subsequent negotiations was directed to that point.

Present treaty of arbitration.

The Treaty of Washington of February 2, 1897, is the result.

XVII.—CONCLUSION.

The United States of Venezuela, upon the evidence herewith submitted, and upon that referred to, claim that the following propositions of fact have been fully established: Propositions of fact.

1. Spain was the first nation to discover South America, to explore it, and to take formal possession of it.

2. Spain was the first nation to discover and explore Guiana.

3. Spain was the first nation to establish settlements on the Orinoco and Essequibo rivers, and in the eastern parts of Guiana; and the first and only nation to take formal possession of, and to occupy, Guiana *as a whole.*

4. For more than a century after discovering Guiana, Spain maintained exclusive possession of the entire region between the Orinoco and the Amazon; held it; and exercised exclusive political control over it: she expelled and excluded other nations from it; and otherwise asserted her sovereignty over it.

5. Apart from this general control of Guiana *as a whole,* Spain, from early in the 16th century, and before any other nation had attempted to gain a foothold therein, exercised a special and exclusive control over the Orinoco and Essequibo rivers, and over all the territory adjacent thereto; and, as late at least as 1615, was maintaining a colony on the Essequibo river.

6. The Dutch were subjects of the King of Spain, and in 1581 revolted against him.

Propositions of fact.

7. The earliest relations of the Dutch, with Guiana in general, and with the Essequibo in particular, were limited to trade and to hostile operations against the Spaniards. They began to trade to the Essequibo not earlier than 1625; and not long after, during the temporary absence of the Spaniards, established a trading post in that river, at or near the site previously fortified by the Spaniards—a site still, at that time, belonging to Spain.

8. At the date of the Treaty of Munster, January 30, 1648, the holdings and possessions of the Dutch in the Essequibo were limited to the island subsequently known as Kykoveral.

9. At that date the Dutch did not hold and were not in possession of any part of the territory now in dispute.

10. The *Cuyuni-Mazaruni Basin*, being the region bounded on the north by the Imataca mountains; on the east by the Blue mountains, by the lowest falls of the Cuyuni and Mazaruni rivers, and by the Ayangcanna mountains; on the south by the Ayangcanna and Pacaraima mountains; and on the west by the divide separating the waters of the Caroni and Orinoco rivers from the waters of the Cuyuni and Mazaruni rivers, is a geographical and political unit, the material occupation of a part of which, by the nation first discovering and exploring it, is in law attributive and constructive possession of the whole.

11. This *Cuyuni-Mazaruni Basin* is a tract of land geographically separate from and independent of the Essequibo river; and no part of said basin was held, possessed or controlled by the Dutch at the date of the Treaty of Munster.

Propositions of fact.

12. By the Treaty of Munster the Dutch engaged to neither sail to nor trade in any places held and possessed by the King of Spain.

13. By the same treaty the Dutch engaged to respect the sovereignty of Spain over all lordships, towns, castles, fortresses, commerce and countries at that time held or possessed by Spain, and to do nothing which might be an infraction of the treaty.

14. Twice during the latter part of the 17th century, the Dutch, in violation of the Treaty of Munster, attempted to plant settlements west of the Essequibo river, on the banks of the Pomeroon. These attempts were ineffectual, the proposed settlements being in each case attacked, and the Dutch driven therefrom. The first of said settlements lasted less than eight years; and the second less than three years.

15. Except for these attempts at settlement by the Dutch on the Pomeroon, Spain, during the whole of the 17th century exercised exclusive political control of the entire territory west of the Essequibo river.

16. Twice during the 18th century the Dutch, in violation of the Treaty of Munster, attempted to establish slave and trading posts on the Cuyuni river. These attempts were ineffectual: one of these posts was attacked and destroyed by the Spaniards: the second was abandoned by the Dutch, because of fear of the Spaniards.

17. During the whole of the 18th century Spain exercised exclusive political control of the *Cuyuni-Mazaruni Basin*, down to the lowest falls of the Cuyuni and Mazaruni rivers.

18. During a part of the 18th century the Dutch, with the permission of Spain, and together with other

Propositions of fact.

nations, traded to the main mouth of the Orinoco river, and to other parts of the Orinoco delta.

19. At various times during the 18th century, the Dutch, in violation of the Treaty of Munster, attempted to establish, and in some cases for brief periods maintained, slave trading stations near the mouths of the Pomeroon and Moruca rivers.

20. Except for these attempts to establish stations near the mouths of the Pomeroon and Moruca rivers, Spain, during the whole of the 18th century exercised exclusive political control of the coast region between the Moruca and the mouth of the Essequibo. During the entire century she exercised exclusive political control of the Orinoco river, of its entire delta, and of all the coast region between the main mouth of the Orinoco and the Moruca.

21. The entire coast region from Barima point southeast as far as the divide separating the waters of the Moruca from the waters of the Waini, is an integral part of the Orinoco delta.

22. The region bounded on the north and northeast by the Gulf of Paria and the Atlantic Ocean; on the east by the Atlantic Ocean, and by the divide separating the waters of the Moruca from the waters of the Waini; on the south by the Imataca mountains; and extending thence westward, is a geographical and political unit, the material occupation of a part of which, by the nation first discovering and exploring it, is in law attributive and constructive possession of the whole

23. From the date of her original settlement of the Orinoco in the 16th century, until her title to the region in dispute became vested in Venezuela, Spain had material occupation of a large part of the Orinoco

region last above described; and held, possessed and exercised exclusive political control over the whole of it.

Propositions of fact.

24. At no time, either before or after the date of the Treaty of Munster, did the Dutch, for a period of fifty consecutive years, exercise exclusive political control or lawfully occupy any part of the territory lying between the Essequibo and Orinoco rivers.

25. Except as hereinbefore stated, Spain, during the entire period of Dutch occupation of the Essequibo, continuously exercised exclusive political control of every part of the territory lying between the Essequibo and Orinoco rivers.

26. By the Treaty of London of August 13, 1814, the Netherlands ceded to Great Britain the Settlements of Demerara, Essequibo and Berbice.

27. Venezuela revolted from Spain April 19, 1810. On March 30, 1845, Spain recognized Venezuela's independence and formally renounced in her favor all the sovereignty, rights and claims previously her own in the territory formerly known as the Captaincy-General of Venezuela. Said territory comprised the region now in dispute.

28. During a portion of the present century, in violation of the Treaty of Munster, Great Britain has occupied a strip of land along the coast between the Essequibo and the Pomeroon rivers, known as the *Arabian* or *Arabisi Coast:* Venezuela has repeatedly protested against such occupation, and has, in every way possible, short of war, asserted her rights to the territory so occupied.

29. Except for said occupation of said *Arabian Coast*,

Propositions of fact.

Great Britain has at no time, for a consecutive period of 50 years, held any part of the territory now in dispute or exercised control of any kind thereover.

30. From the time of the acquisition by Great Britain of the colony now known as British Guiana, until Spain's title to the territory in dispute became vested in Venezuela, Spain, except for said occupation of said *Arabian Coast* by Great Britain, continuously held, possessed and exercised exclusive political control of the entire region between the Orinoco and Essequibo rivers.

31. From the date when Spain's title to the territory in dispute became vested in Venezuela, until the year 1850, Venezuela, except for said occupation of said *Arabian Coast* by Great Britain, continuously held, possessed and exercised exclusive political control of the entire region between the Orinoco and Essequibo rivers.

32. In the year 1850 Venezuela and Great Britain agreed that, pending the settlement of the boundary question, neither would occupy or encroach upon the territory then in dispute.

33. Thereafter, and subsequent to the year 1880, Great Britain, in violation of the said agreement of 1850, and of the Treaty of Munster, forcibly entered upon and took possession of the territory lying between the Essequibo river and the line first published in 1886, since claimed by Great Britain to be the *Schomburgk Line*. Said territory included not only the entire region which was in dispute in 1850, but also territory belonging to Venezuela, the title to which had never been questioned prior to 1886.

34. Venezuela has repeatedly protested against such

occupation; and has in every way possible, short of war, asserted her rights to the territory so occupied.

Propositions of fact.

35. The occupation, by British subjects or by persons under British protection, of the territory above described, dates from subsequent to 1880 in the *Cuyuni-Mazaruni Basin*, and from subsequent to 1884 in the *Orinoco Delta Region*. It was undertaken after due warning from the Venezuelan Government that titles thus sought to be acquired would not be recognized, and after due notice from the British Government that persons so entering into said territory must do so at their own peril.

Propositions of law.

To the foregoing propositions of fact, Venezuela will claim that the following propositions of law are applicable:

1. Discovery gives the discovering nation, if not an absolute, at least an inchoate title, sufficient to protect it during a reasonable time pending the actual reduction of the territory to possession.

2. Discovery, when accompanied by public claim of sovereignty, and followed by reduction to possession, confers a complete title.

3. The material occupation of a part of a tract of land in the name of the whole, by the nation which first discovered and explored said tract, is constructively an occupation of the whole.

4. When a nation, claiming title to a whole tract by material occupation of a part, reaches out and actually controls adjacent territory inhabited only by savages, and excludes all other nations therefrom, it thereby exercises physical acts of sovereignty over it, and is in actual political occupation of it.

Propositions of law.

5. A nation having made a settlement on unoccupied land has a right to exclude other nations therefrom.

6. All nations must refrain from disturbing a nation which has settled a country that was vacant at the time of settlement; and an entry by any other nation or people upon territory so previously settled is an act of trespass.

7. A state continues to possess everything it has subjected to its power with a view to its use; and it is not the exercise of usage but the faculty of usage that is the necessary element of possession.

8. Non-user is not abandonment: neither will abandonment be presumed against nations. Before it can be accepted as a fact an actual desertion must be proven with an intention to renounce title.

9. When land is vacant one may enter upon part in name of the whole; but he who comes after enters adversely, and his possession extends *in law* only so far as it does *in fact*. When the original possessor is thus disseized, though his possession of the whole was only by occupation of a part, yet the first is deemed to be disseized only to the extent of the land physically occupied by the second.

10. Ownership of the mouth of a river does not, of itself, give title to the watershed.

11. A nation owning the watershed and the firm banks of a river, by virtue of such ownership, owns and possesses the delta islands and shores below, though uninhabited or uninhabitable. They are not "vacant" lands.

12. If a natural barrier exist between the coast region

and the interior, that barrier will be the boundary between the two. Propositions of law.

13. A nation is bound to faithfully observe its treaty engagements; and no acts committed by it in violation of such engagements can be made the basis of title, especially as against the nation with whom such treaty was concluded.

14. Rule (a) under Article IV of the present treaty is:

"Adverse holding or prescription during a period of fifty years shall make a good title. The Arbitrators may deem exclusive political control of a district, as well as actual settlement thereof, sufficient to constitute adverse holding or to make title by prescription."

Venezuela has accepted this rule, but she submits and will claim that *time* is but one of many elements essential to create title by prescription. Prescription to be effective against nations, as against individuals, must be bona-fide, public, notorious, adverse, exclusive, peaceful, continuous, uncontested, and maintained under a claim of right. Rule (a) fixes 50 years as the *period* of prescription, but leaves its other elements unimpaired.

In conclusion, Venezuela invokes the judgment of this high Tribunal to the following effect: Judgment invoked.

1. Spain's discovery of America gave her the right to reduce to possession the countries discovered; and pending the exercise of that right, during a reasonable period, no other nation had a right, without the consent of Spain, to acquire such countries.

2. Spain having discovered Guiana, and having, within a reasonable time thereafter, under a claim of sovereignty, and earlier than any other nation or people, occupied said province as a whole by the establishment

Judgment invoked. of colonies and settlements on the Orinoco and Essequibo rivers and in other parts of Guiana, thereby reduced it as a whole to possession, and became vested with a complete title thereto.

3. Spain having, for more than a century after her discovery of Guiana, had exclusive possession thereof as a whole; and having, from early in the 16th century, and before any other nation had attempted to gain a foothold in Guiana, exercised a special and exclusive control over the Orinoco and Essequibo rivers and over the territory adjacent thereto; and having, until at least as late as 1625, excluded all other nations and peoples from said rivers and adjacent territory; exercised thereby physical acts of sovereignty thereover, and was in actual and exclusive political occupation and control thereof in 1625.

4. The region between the Orinoco and Essequibo rivers, and all the territory appurtenant to those rivers, having been in the continuous occupation and under the continuous exclusive political control of Spain from early in the 16th century until at least as late as 1625; and the Dutch having, between the date last mentioned and January 30, 1648, established a trading post on the Essequibo; and the possessions of the Dutch in the said Essequibo river on January 30, 1643, having been limited to the said trading post located upon the island of Kykoveral; Spain was, on said January 30, 1648, in possession and exclusive political control of all territory lying west of the Essequibo river, between that river and the Orinoco.

5. Neither the early relations of the Dutch with Guiana prior to 1648, nor the establishment by them, prior to said date, of a trading post in the Essequibo

river, gave them a right to the soil, nor sovereignty over the territory occupied. Judgment invoked

6. The Dutch not having come as occupants of *terra nullius*, but as mere trespassers on territory belonging to Spain, no valid title to the land occupied by them in the Essequibo river vested in them until, by the Treaty of Munster, Spain released and confirmed to them the possession of such land.

7. The Dutch having come to the Essequibo as disseizors, and the Treaty of Munster having released and confirmed to them only such places as they then actually held and possessed, the territory thus released and confirmed was limited to such land only as was in fact then physically occupied by them.

8. The places actually occupied by the Dutch in the river Essequibo at the date of the Treaty of Munster having been limited to the island subsequently known as Kykoveral, the Treaty of Munster released and confirmed to them the title to that island only and the right of free ingress thereto and egress therefrom by way of the Essequibo river itself.

9. The region bounded on the north by the Imataca mountains; on the east by the Blue mountains, by the lowest falls of the Cuyuni and Mazaruni rivers, and by the Ayangcanna mountains; on the south by the Ayangcanna and Pacaraima mountains; and on the west by the divide separating the waters of the Caroni and Orinoco rivers from the waters of the Cuyuni and Mazaruni rivers, being a geographical and political unit; and a part of said region having, during the latter part of the 16th century, during all of the 17th and 18th centuries, and during the 19th century up to the time when Venezuela became vested therewith, been physi-

Judgment invoked. cally occupied by Spain; and no other nation having, during said period, occupied or had exclusive political control of any portion thereof in a manner, or for a time sufficient to furnish the basis for a prescriptive title thereto, Spain thereby had, during the whole of said period, attributive and constructive possession of all and of every part of said region.

10. The region described in the paragraph last preceding, known as the *Cuyuni-Mazaruni Basin*, being a geographical and political unit; and a part of said region having, during the 19th century, from the time when Spain's title thereto became vested in Venezuela, been physically occupied by Venezuela; and no other nation having, during said period, occupied or had exclusive political control of any portion thereof in a manner or for a time sufficient to furnish the basis for a prescriptive title thereto, Venezuela has thereby had, during the whole of said period, attributive and constructive possession of all and of every part of said region.

11. Said *Cuyuni-Mazaruni Basin* being a tract of land geographically separate from and independent of the Essequibo river; and no part of said basin having been in the possession, occupation or control of the Dutch at the date of the Treaty of Munster, that treaty conferred upon the Dutch no right or title whatsoever thereto.

12. The efforts of the Dutch twice during the latter part of the 17th century to establish settlements on or near the Pomeroon, having been ineffectual as well as in violation of the Treaty of Munster, cannot be made the basis of title to that region.

13. The efforts of the Dutch twice during the 18th cen-

tury to establish slave and trading posts on the Cuyuni river, having been ineffectual as well as in violation of the Treaty of Munster, cannot be made the basis of title to that region.

Judgment invoked.

14. Spain having expelled and excluded the Dutch from the *Cuyuni-Mazaruni Basin* during the 18th century, and having during the whole of said century exercised exclusive political control over said basin, her original title thereto was thereby further strengthened and confirmed.

15. Spain having, during the whole of the 18th century, exercised exclusive political control of the Orinoco river, of its entire delta, and of all the coast region between the main mouth of the Orinoco and the mouth of the Essequibo, her original title thereto was thereby further strengthened and confirmed.

16. Spain, from the date of her original settlement of the Orinoco in the 16th century until her title to the region in dispute became vested in Venezuela, having held and possessed the entire interior Orinoco region, possessed also the mouth of the Orinoco.

17. The region bounded on the north and northeast by the Gulf of Paria and the Atlantic Ocean; on the east by the Atlantic Ocean, and by the divide separating the waters of the Moruca from the waters of the Waini; on the south by the Imataca mountains; and extending thence westward, being a geographical and political unit; and a part of said region having, during the 16th, 17th and 18th centuries and during the 19th century up to the time when Venezuela became vested therewith, been physically occupied by Spain; and no other nation having, during said period, occupied or had exclusive political control of any portion thereof; Spain

Judgment invoked.

thereby had, during the whole of said period, attributive and constructive possession of all and of every part of said region.

18. The region described in the paragraph last preceding being a geographical and political unit; and a part of said region having, during the 19th century from the time when Spain's title thereto became vested in Venezuela been physically occupied by Venezuela; and no other nation having, during said period, occupied or had exclusive political control of any portion thereof in a manner or for a period sufficient to furnish the basis for a prescriptive title thereto; Venezuela has thereby had during the whole of said period attributive and constructive possession of all and of every part of said region.

19. Spain having, during the entire period of Dutch occupation of the Essequibo, exercised exclusive political control of the entire region lying between the Orinoco and the Essequibo rivers, except that at various times during the latter part of the 17th century the Dutch ineffectually attempted to establish and maintain colonies on the Pomeroon river, and except that at various times during the 18th century the Dutch ineffectually attempted to establish and maintain slave trading posts in the Cuyuni river and near the mouths of the Moruca and Pomeroon rivers; and said attempts by the Dutch having been unlawful and in violation of the Treaty of Munster; the original title of Spain to the entire region was thereby further strengthened and confirmed.

20. At the time of the acquisition by Great Britain of the colony now known as British Guiana, the territories belonging to or that might lawfully be claimed by the

United Netherlands were all located east of the Essequibo river.

Judgment invoked.

21. At the time of the acquisition by Great Britain of the colony now known as British Guiana, the territories belonging to or that might lawfully be claimed by the Kingdom of Spain comprised the entire territory between the Orinoco and Essequibo rivers.

22. Spain having, from the time of the acquisition by Great Britain of the colony now known as British Guiana until Spain's title to the region in dispute became vested in Venezuela, continued to exercise exclusive political control of the entire region between the Orinoco and Essequibo rivers, except only of the strip of land known as the *Arabian Coast*, lying between the mouth of the Essequibo river and the mouth of the Pomeroon river; and the occupation of said strip of land by Great Britain during a portion of the present century having been unlawful and in violation of the Treaty of Munster; and Venezuela having continued thereafter until 1850 to exercise exclusive political control of the same territory, except only of said *Arabian Coast*, the original title to the entire region, formerly vested in Spain and now vested in Venezuela, has thereby been further strengthened and confirmed.

23. The present occupation by Great Britain of a portion of the territory now in dispute, being in violation of the Treaty of Munster and of the agreement of 1850, and having been effected subsequent to the year 1880, in the interior, and subsequent to 1884, on the coast, cannot be made the basis of title to that region.

24. The boundary line between the United States of Venezuela and the Colony of British Guiana, begins at

Judgment invoked.

the mouth of the Essequibo river; runs thence southward along the mid channel of said river to its junction with the Cuyuni and Mazaruni rivers; thence around the island of Kykoveral, leaving said island to the east; thence along the mid channel of said Essequibo river to the boundary line separating the territory of the United States of Venezuela from the territory of the United States of Brazil.

25. The present occupation by British subjects and persons under British protection having been effected subsequent to 1880 in the interior, and subsequent to 1884 on the coast, and having been undertaken after due warning from the Venezuelan Government that titles thus sought to be acquired would not be recognized by it, and after notice from the British Government that persons so entering into said territory must do so at their own peril, said subjects and persons may be regarded by Venezuela as mere trespassers, and Venezuela is under no obligation to recognize any British titles which such subjects or persons may have acquired to lands situate within said territory.

J. M. DE ROJAS,
Agent of Venezuela.

WASHINGTON, D. C., March 16, 1898.

Milton Keynes UK
Ingram Content Group UK Ltd.
UKHW050835231023
431156UK00004B/16

9 798891 849280